yptography

THE JAVA™ SERIES

Exploring Java™

Java™ Threads

Java™ Network Programming

Java™ Virtual Machine

Java™ AWT Reference

Java™ Language Reference

Java™ Fundamental Classes Reference

Database Programming with JDBC™ and Java™

Java™ Distributed Computing

Developing Java Beans™

Java™ Security

Java™ Cryptography

Also from O'Reilly

Java™ in a Nutshell

Java™ in a Nutshell, Deluxe Edition

Java™ Examples in a Nutshell

Netscape IFC in a Nutshell

Java™ Cryptography

Jonathan Knudsen

O'REILLY®

Beijing · Cambridge · Farnham · Köln · Paris · Sebastopol · Taipei · Tokyo

Java ™ Cryptography
by Jonathan Knudsen

Copyright © 1998 O'Reilly & Associates, Inc. All rights reserved.
Printed in the United States of America.
Cover photo by Kevin Thomas, © O'Reilly & Associates, Inc.

Published by O'Reilly & Associates, Inc., 101 Morris Street, Sebastopol, CA 95472.

Editor: Mike Loukides

Production Editor: Mary Anne Weeks Mayo

Editorial and Production Services: Benchmark Productions, Inc., Boston, MA

Printing History:

> May 1998:   First Edition

ISBN: 1-56592-402-9   [2/01]
[M]

For Luke and Daphne

Table of Contents

Preface

Who Are You?

This book is written for moderately experienced Java developers who are interested in cryptography. It describes cryptographic development in Java. If you know nothing about cryptography, don't worry—there's a whole chapter (Chapter 2) that describes the concepts. The main thrust of this book is to detail the classes and techniques that you need to add cryptographic functionality to your Java application.

This book stubbornly sticks to its subject, cryptographic development in Java. If you're curious about the mathematics or politics of cryptography, pick up a copy of Bruce Schneier's *Applied Cryptography* (Wiley). Although I will implement the ElGamal cipher and signature algorithms in Chapter 9, I'm demonstrating the Java programming, not the mathematics. And although I explain how the Java cryptography packages are divided by U.S. export law (Chapter 3), I won't try to explain the laws in detail or comment on them. A solid book on the mathematics of cryptography is the *Handbook of Applied Cryptography* by Alfred J. Menezes et al. (CRC Press). For a recent look at the politics of cryptography, see *Privacy on the Line: The Politics of Wiretapping and Encryption*, by Whitfield Diffie and Susan Landau (MIT Press).

If you need to get up to speed with Java development, I suggest these O'Reilly books:

- David Flanagan's *Java in a Nutshell* provides a speedy introduction to Java for the experienced developer.

- *Exploring Java*, by Pat Niemeyer and Joshua Peck, has a gentler learning curve for the less experienced developer.

For an overview of the entire Java Security API, try Scott Oaks' *Java Security*, also published by O'Reilly.

About This Book

This book is organized like a sandwich. The outer chapters (1, 2, and 12) provide context for the rest of the book. Chapters 3 through 11 (the meat) are a methodical and pragmatic description of cryptographic programming in Java, including numerous useful examples.

Chapter 1, *Introduction*, describes cryptography's role in secure systems development and introduces some short examples of cryptographic programming.

Chapter 2, *Concepts*, introduces the fundamental concepts of cryptography: ciphers, message digests, signatures, and random numbers.

Chapter 3, *Architecture*, presents a bird's-eye view of Java cryptographic software packages and introduces the Provider Architecture that underlies the Java Security API.

Chapter 4, *Random Numbers*, describes cryptographic random numbers in Java.

Chapter 5, *Key Management*, describes the key management classes that are included with the JDK.

Chapter 6, *Authentication*, shows how to use message digests, signatures, and certificates for authentication.

Chapter 7, *Encryption*, covers encryption: symmetric and asymmetric ciphers, cipher modes, and hybrid systems.

Chapter 8, *Signed Applets*, describes how to create signed applets.

Chapter 9, *Writing a Provider*, describes how to write a security provider. It includes classes that implement the ElGamal cipher and signature algorithms.

Chapter 10, *SafeTalk*, presents a completely functional application, a cryptographically enabled network talk application.

Chapter 11, *CipherMail*, includes another complete application, a cryptographically enabled email client.

Chapter 12, *Outside the Box*, talks about noncryptographic security issues you should know about.

Appendix A, *BigInteger*, discusses the `BigInteger` class, which is useful for implementing the mathematics of cryptographic algorithms.

Appendix B, *Base64*, presents classes for base64 conversion.

Appendix C, *JAR*, describes the `jar` archiving tool, which is used to bundle up Java applets and applications.

Appendix D, *Javakey*, includes a description of the JDK 1.1 `javakey` tool, which is used to manage a database of keys and certificates.

Appendix E, *Quick Reference*, contains a quick reference listing of the cryptographic classes covered in this book.

What's Not in This Book

This book does not discuss:

- `ClassLoaders`
- The bytecode verifier
- `SecurityManagers`
- Access control and permissions

For a thorough treatment of these subjects, see O'Reilly's *Java Security*.

About the Examples

Versions

The examples in this book run with the Java Developer's Kit (JDK) 1.2 and the Java Cryptography Extension (JCE) 1.2. The examples in the book were tested with JDK 1.2beta3 and JCE 1.2ea2. Some of the topics covered are applicable to JDK 1.1, especially the `Identity`-based key management discussed in Chapter 5 and the `MessageDigest` and `Signature` classes in Chapter 6. However, anything involving encryption requires the JCE. The only supported version of the JCE is 1.2, and it only runs with JDK 1.2. (Although the JCE had a 1.1 release, it never progressed beyond the early access stage. It is not supported by Sun and not available from their web site any longer.)

The signed applets in Chapter 8 work with HotJava 1.1, Netscape Navigator 4.0, and Internet Explorer 4.0.

File Naming

This book assumes you are comfortable programming in Java and familiar with the concepts of packages and `CLASSPATH`. The source code for examples in this book should be saved in files based on the class name. For example, consider the following code:

```
import java.applet.*;
import java.awt.*;
```

```
public class PrivilegedRenegade extends Applet {

   ...

}
```

This file describes the `PrivilegedRenegade` class; therefore, you should save it in a file named *PrivilegedRenegade.java*.

Other classes belong to particular packages. For example, here is the beginning of one of the classes from Chapter 9:

```
package oreilly.jonathan.security;

import java.math.BigInteger;
import java.security.*;

public class ElGamalKeyPairGenerator
     extends KeyPairGenerator {

   ...

}
```

This should be saved in *oreilly/jonathan/security/ElGamalKeyPairGenerator.java*.

Throughout the book, I define classes in the `oreilly.jonathan.*` package hierarchy. Some of them are used in other examples in the book. For these examples to work correctly, you'll need to make sure that the directory containing the *oreilly* directory is in your CLASSPATH. On my computer, for example, the *oreilly* directory lives in *c:\Jonathan\classes*. So my CLASSPATH contains *c:\Jonathan\classes*; this makes the classes in the `oreilly.jonathan.*` hierarchy accessible to all Java applications.

CLASSPATH

Several examples in this book consist of classes spread across multiple files. In these cases, I don't explicitly `import` files that are part of the same example. For these files to compile, then, you need to have the current directory as part of your classpath. My classpath, for example, includes the current directory and the Java Cryptography Extension (JCE—see Chapter 3). On my Windows 95 system, I set the CLASSPATH in *autoexec.bat* as follows:

```
set classpath=.
set classpath=%classpath%;c:\jdk1.2beta3\jce12-ea2-dom\jce12-ea2-dom.jar
```

Variable Naming

The examples in this book are presented in my own coding style, which is an amalgam of conventions from a grab bag of platforms.

I follow standard Java coding practices with respect to capitalization. All member variables of a class are prefixed with a small *m*, like so:

```
protected int mPlainBlockSize;
```

This makes it easy to distinguish between member variables and local variables. Static members are prefixed with a small *s*, like this:

```
protected static SecureRandom sRandom = null;
```

And final static member variables are prefixed with a small *k* (it stands for *constant*, believe it or not):

```
protected static final String kBanner = "SafeTalk v1.0";
```

Array types are always written with the square brackets immediately following the array type. This keeps all the type information for a variable in one place:

```
byte[] ciphertext;
```

Downloading

Most of the examples from this book can be downloaded from *ftp://ftp.oreilly .com/pub/examples/java/crypto/*. Some of the examples, however, cannot legally be posted online. The U.S. government considers some forms of encryption software to be weapons, and the export of such software or its source code is tightly controlled. Anything we put on our web server can be downloaded from any location in the world. Thus, we are unable to provide the source code for some of the examples online. The book itself, however, is protected under the first amendment to the U.S. Constitution and may be freely exported.

Font Conventions

A constant width font is used for:

- Class names and method names.
- Source code.
- Example command-line sessions. The input you type is shown in boldface.

Italic is used for:

- Paths and filenames.
- New terms where they are defined.
- Internet addresses, such as domain names and URLs.

Boldface is used for the names of interface buttons.

Request for Comments

If you find typos, inaccuracies, or bugs, please let us know.

O'Reilly & Associates, Inc.
101 Morris Street
Sebastopol, CA 95472
(800)998-9938 (in the United States or Canada)
(707)829-0515 (international or local)
(707)829-0104 (fax)
bookquestions@oreilly.com

Acknowledgments

My wife, Kristen, now knows more about cryptography than anyone else I know. I'd like to thank her for her encouragement and enthusiasm throughout this project, and for proofreading. My gratitude also goes to Mike Loukides, who suggested this book to me in the first place, and patiently guided me through its creation. I'll always be grateful to Mike and to Frank Willison, who believed me when I told them I knew how to write and that I really did want to work from my home. I'm also grateful to Tim O'Reilly, who somehow has created a successful company based on quality and integrity.

This book has benefitted from the thorough scrutiny of its technical reviewers. I owe many thanks to Li Gong, Jim Farley, Gary Luckenbaugh, Michael Norman, and David Hopwood for using their time and expertise to suggest improvements to the manuscript. Chapter 8 would not exist but for the kindness of friends and family. When I had ungodly trouble with Authenticode, Matt Diamond pointed me in the right direction. When I somehow broke my machine so it would not sign code, my father allowed me to use his computer. Thanks for helping me through a difficult chapter. And thanks go to Michael Norman for helping me test SafeTalk, the application in Chapter 10. Thanks also to Jan Leuhe, Li Gong, and the rest of the security and cryptography teams at Sun for being so helpful and responsive.

O'Reilly's production group and Benchmark Productions put the finishing touches on this book. Mary Anne Weeks Mayo was the project manager. Nancy Kruse Hannigan served as copyeditor; Beth Roberts was the proofreader; quality was assured by Dmitri Nerubenko, Ellie Fountain Maden, and Sheryl Avruch. Andrew Williams and Greg deZarn-O'Hare managed production at Benchmark. Jennifer Coker created the index. Mike Sierra tweaked the Frame tools to finesse the interior design. Robert Romano prepared the crisp illustrations. The book's interior was designed by Nancy Priest. Hanna Dyer designed the cover, based on a series design by Edie Freedman.

1

Introduction

This book is about cryptographic programming in Java[TM]. This chapter presents the "big picture" of secure systems and quickly moves to the specifics of cryptography. I begin by describing secure systems design. Next I explain what cryptography is and describe its role in secure systems development. This chapter concludes with a pair of "teaser" examples: two short Java applications that will whet your appetite for the rest of the book.

Secure Systems

Computer applications enable people to do work. Applications are parts of a larger system (a business, usually) that also involves people, fax machines, white boards, credit cards, paper forms, and anything else that makes the whole system run. *Secure systems* make it hard for people to do things they are not supposed to do. For example, a bank is designed as a secure system. You shouldn't be able to withdraw money from someone else's account, whether you try at the teller window, or by using the bank machine, or by telephone. Of course, you could bribe the teller or disassemble the bank machine, but these things are usually not worth the cost.

Secure systems are designed so that the cost of breaking any component of the system outweighs the rewards. Cost is usually measured in money, time, and risk, both legal and personal. The benefits of breaking systems are generally control, money, or information that can be sold for money. The security of the system should be proportional to the resources it protects; it should be a lot harder to break into a brokerage than a magazine subscription list, for example.

The term "secure systems" is a little misleading; it implies that systems are either secure or insecure. In truth, there is no absolute security. Every system can be broken, given enough time and money. Let me say that again, *every system can be broken*. There are more secure and less secure systems, but no totally secure systems. When people talk about secure systems, they mean systems where security is a concern or was considered as part of the design.

The job of the application programmer is to make an application that costs as much to break as any other component in the system. Building a secure application usually involves a three-way balancing act. The cost of having your application broken must be balanced against both the application's cost and the application's ease of use. You could spend a million dollars to build a very secure application, but it wouldn't make sense if the cost of a break-in would be measured only in thousands. You might build a moderately secure application instead, but it won't do you any good if it's too hard to use.

The security of any application is determined by the security of the platform it runs on, as well as the security features designed into the application itself. I'll talk about platform security later in this chapter. Chapter 2, *Concepts*, explains the concepts of security that can be programmed into an application. The most important tool applications use for security is *cryptography*, a branch of mathematics that deals with secret writing.

This is serious stuff! Unfortunately, in application development, security is often relegated to the *we'll-add-that-later-if-we-have-time* list.* Security should be a part of your design from the beginning, not a neglected afterthought. The information that your application harbors is valuable. The application's users value this information; this implies that the users' competitors and any number of third parties might also find the information valuable. If the cost of stealing that information is small compared with its value, you are in trouble.

The meteoric growth of Internet applications is closely shadowed by the meteoric growth of computer crime opportunities. The Internet is not a safe place. Only applications that are strong and well guarded have a place there. Even on a closed company network, applications should be secure, to limit damage or loss from authorized users. Even on a single, nonnetworked computer, applications should be secure, to limit damage or loss from unauthorized users.

The field of computer security is fascinating and volatile. In it you can find fire-and-brimstone security professionals, preaching about the dangers of badly applied cryptography, paranoid propeller-heads who believe the government reads everybody's email, and a healthy dose of wide-eyed programmers who can't understand why Sun made their lives so difficult with that damned sandbox thing. Overshadowing the

---

* For a sobering assessment of secure system design, see Bruce Schneier's paper, "Why Cryptography Is Harder Than It Looks…" at *http://www.counterpane.com/whycrypto.html*. Mr. Schneier is the author of the legendary *Applied Cryptography* (Wiley), which is a must if you want to understand the mathematics behind cryptography.

whole field is the National Security Agency (NSA), an intimidating behemoth of unimaginable and unfathomed cryptanalytic power. The U.S. government, furthermore, categorizes some cryptographic software as weaponry and limits its export. All in all, it's a combination of a tent revival and *Star Wars*. The stories behind cryptographic algorithms are much more interesting than the math itself.

This book describes the cryptographic classes in the Java Security API. The Security API is fresh and exciting, but it will not make Java programs secure at the drop of a hat. Security is a tricky, evolving mind game. The purpose of this book is to describe how you can use cryptography to make your Java applications more secure.

Cryptography

Cryptography is the science of *secret writing*. It's a branch of mathematics, part of *cryptology*. Cryptology has one other child, *cryptanalysis*, which is the science of breaking (analyzing) cryptography.

The main security concerns of applications are addressed by cryptography. First, applications need assurance that users are who they say they are. Proving identity is called *authentication*. In the physical world, a driver's license is a kind of authentication. When you use a computer, you usually use a name and password to authenticate yourself. Cryptography provides stronger methods of authentication, called signatures and certificates. I'll talk about these in Chapter 6, *Authentication.*

Computer applications need to protect their data from unauthorized access. You don't want people snooping on your data (you want *confidentiality*), and you don't want someone changing data without your knowledge (you want to be assured of your data's *integrity*). Data stored on a disk, for example, may be vulnerable to being viewed or stolen. Data transmitted across a network is subject to all sorts of nefarious attacks. Again, cryptography provides solutions; I'll discuss them in detail in Chapter 6 and Chapter 7, *Encryption.*

So what can you do with cryptography? Plenty. Here are just a few examples:

Secure network communications
> Cryptography can protect your data from thieves and impostors. Most web browsers now support SSL, a cryptographic protocol that encrypts information before it is transmitted over the Internet. SSL allows you to buy things, using your credit card number, without worrying too much that the number will be stolen.

Secure hard disk
> You can encrypt the files on your hard disk so that even if your enemies gain physical access to your computer, they won't be able to access its data.

Secure email
> Email is notoriously easy to steal and easy to forge. Cryptography can make it hard to forge email and hard to read other people's messages.

Although cryptography is heavily mathematical, there isn't much math in this book. One of the really nice things about the Java Security API is that, like any good software library, it hides a lot of complexity. The Security API exposes concepts, like `Signature` and `Cipher`, and quietly deals with the underlying details. You can use cryptography effectively in a Java application without knowing too much about what's going on underneath the hood. Of course, this implies you need to trust Sun to write the Security API correctly. This book should tell you what you need to know to use cryptographic concepts properly in your Java applications.

Platform Security

One of the things that makes Java so interesting is the security features that are built in to the platform itself. Java was designed to enable small programs, *applets*, to be downloaded and run without danger. Applets are nifty, but without the right precautions they would be very dangerous. Java's bytecode verifier, `ClassLoader`, and `SecurityManager` work in tandem to safely execute downloaded classes.

The Java Development Kit (JDK™) 1.2 (in beta as this book goes to press) includes some interesting security enhancements, including the concepts of protection domains, permissions, and policies. I won't rehash Java's platform security features here. For a good summary, see *Exploring Java* by Pat Niemeyer and Joshua Peck (O'Reilly). For a more thorough treatment, including the new JDK 1.2 features, see *Java Security* by Scott Oaks (O'Reilly). The security that the Java platform provides comes "for free" to application developers. Application-level security, however, needs to be developed into the application. This book is about programming application-level security through the use of cryptography.

Application-level security can compensate for an insecure platform, in some cases. Internet Protocol (IP) networks, for example, are insecure. It's impossible to prevent packet snooping, Domain Name System (DNS) spoofing, or foul-ups like misdelivered email. A carefully crafted application, however, can compensate for an insecure platform like the IP network. If the body of your email is encrypted, for example, it won't do anyone any good to view a message.[*] If you encrypt all data that you send over the network, then a packet sniffer won't be able to pick up much useful information.

Astute Inequalities

At the 1997 JavaOne conference, the Java Security Architect, Li Gong, gave a presentation on Java security. One of his slides is particularly useful for understanding Java

---

[*] If you're especially careful, you might be interested in concealing the mere existence of the email. In this case, you'd need to take more elaborate precautions than simply encrypting the email.

security and cryptography. It contains a list of five inequalities, to which I've added explanations.*

Security != cryptography

Adding cryptography to an application will not make it secure. Security is determined by the overall design and implementation of a system; cryptography is a tool for building secure systems.

Correct security model != bug-free implementation

Even if you have a great design (model), bugs in your implementation can be exploited by attackers. With a correct design, however, you can focus on debugging the implementation. If your design is not secure, you have to go all the way back to the drawing board before you even think about debugging.

Testing != formal verification

Although testing is a great idea, it won't prove to anyone that a system is secure. In the real world, "formal verification" means extensive reviews of your system's design and implementation by knowledgeable security people. A cheap way to do this is to post your application's source code to the Internet and invite people to poke holes in it.

Component security != overall system security

System security is a chain, and any link can be broken. Even if the components of a system are secure, they may interact in insecure ways.

Java security != applet containment

A lot of the buzz about Java security has centered around the applet "sandbox" and the security of applets running in browsers. (Go look at *comp.lang.java.security*, for example, and you'll find it's mostly filled with applet sandbox questions.) In truth, this is only a small part of the Java security picture. Most of this book is about the rest of the picture.

Hello, zoT1wy1njA0=!

Let's jump right into Java cryptography with some examples. The first example can be run by anyone who has the Java Development Kit (JDK) 1.1 or later installed. The second example uses classes from the Java Cryptography Extension (JCE). To run it, you will need to download and install the JCE, which is available in the United States and Canada only at *http://java.sun.com/products/jdk/1.2/jce/*. Chapter 3, *Architecture*, discusses these pieces of software and how they fit together.

Don't worry if you don't understand everything in these programs. They are demonstrations of what you can do with cryptography in Java, and everything in them will be explained in more detail elsewhere in the book.

---

* To see the whole presentation, see *http://java.sun.com/javaone/sessions/slides/TT03/index.html*.

Masher

Our first example demonstrates how a *message digest* works. A message digest takes an arbitrary amount of input data and creates a short, digested version of the data, sometimes called a digital fingerprint, secure hash, or cryptographic hash. Chapters 2 and 6 contain more detail about message digests. This program creates a message digest from a file:

```java
import java.io.*;
import java.security.*;

import sun.misc.*;

public class Masher {
  public static void main(String[] args) throws Exception {
    // Check arguments.
    if (args.length != 1) {
      System.out.println("Usage: Masher filename");
      return;
    }

    // Obtain a message digest object.
    MessageDigest md = MessageDigest.getInstance("MD5");

    // Calculate the digest for the given file.
    FileInputStream in = new FileInputStream(args[0]);
    byte[] buffer = new byte[8192];
    int length;
    while ((length = in.read(buffer)) != -1)
      md.update(buffer, 0, length);
    byte[] raw = md.digest();

    // Print out the digest in base64.
    BASE64Encoder encoder = new BASE64Encoder();
    String base64 = encoder.encode(raw);
    System.out.println(base64);
  }
}
```

To use this program, just compile it and give it a file to digest. Here, I use the source code, *Masher.java*, as the file:

```
C:\ java Masher Masher.java
nfEOH/5M+yDLaxaJ+XpJ5Q==
```

Now try changing one character of your input file, and calculate the digest again. It looks completely different! Try to create a different file that produces the same message digest. Although it's not impossible, you probably have a better chance of winning the lottery. Likewise, given a message digest, it's very hard to figure out what input produced it. Just as a fingerprint identifies a human, a message digest identifies data but reveals little about it. Unlike fingerprints, message digests are not unique.

A message digest is sometimes called a *cryptographic hash*. It's an example of a *one-way function*, which means that although you can calculate a message digest, given some data, you can't figure out what data produced a given message digest. Let's say that your friend, Josephine, wants to send you a file. She's afraid that your mutual enemy, Edith, will modify the file before it gets to you. If Josephine sends the original file and the message digest, you can check the validity of the file by calculating your own message digest and comparing it to the one Josephine sent you. If Edith changes the file at all, your calculated message digest will be different and you'll know there's something awry. Of course, there's a way around this: Edith changes the file, calculates a new message digest for the changed file, and sends the whole thing to you. You have no way of knowing whether Edith has changed the file or not. Digital signatures extend message digests to solve this problem; I'll get to them in Chapter 6.

So how does this program work? It operates in four distinct steps, indicated by the source comments:

1. Check command-line arguments. `Masher` expects one argument, a filename.

2. Obtain the message digest object. We use a *factory method*, a special static method that returns an instance of `MessageDigest`. This factory method accepts the name of an algorithm. In this case, we use an algorithm called MD5.

   ```
   MessageDigest md = MessageDigest.getInstance("MD5");
   ```

   This type of factory method is used throughout the Security API.

3. Calculate the message digest. Here we open the file and read it in 8-kilobyte chunks. Each chunk is passed to the `MessageDigest` object's `update()` method. Finally, the message digest value is calculated with a call to `digest()`.

4. Make the result readable. The `digest()` method returns an array of bytes. To convert this to a screen-printable form, we use the `sun.misc.BASE64Encoder` class. This class converts an array of bytes to a `String`, which we print.

SecretWriting

The next example uses classes that are found only in the Java Cryptography Extension (JCE). The JCE contains cryptographic software whose export is limited by the U.S. government. If you live outside the United States or Canada, it is not legal to download this software. Within the United States and Canada, you can get the JCE from *http://java.sun.com/products/jdk/1.2/jce/*.

Base64

Base64 is a system for representing an array of bytes as ASCII characters. This is useful, for example, when you want to send raw byte data through a medium, like email, that may not support anything but 7-bit ASCII.

The base64 system is fully described in RFC 1521, in section 5.2. You can download this document from *ftp://ds.internic.net/rfc/rfc1521.txt*. It's another number system, just like octal or hexadecimal. Whereas octal uses three bits per digit and hexadecimal uses four, base64 uses six bits per digit.

Fortunately, there are two undocumented Java classes that take care of all the details. `sun.misc.BASE64Encoder` takes an array of bytes and generates a `String` containing the base64 digits. A corresponding class, `sun.misc` `.BASE64Decoder`, takes a `String` and produces the original byte array.

These classes are undocumented, so Sun has no obligation to support them or keep them around in future releases of Java. If you don't have the `sun.misc` classes available, Appendix B, *Base64*, has listings for base64 conversion classes that can be used for the examples in this chapter. Once you have entered and compiled the base64 classes, replace the `import sun.misc.*` statement with `import oreilly.jonathan.util.*` and the examples should work without further change.

Base64 is used in the examples in this chapter simply as a utility, to make byte arrays into easily displayable ASCII strings. The example in Chapter 11, *Cipher-Mail*, however, puts base64 to a much more practical use. That chapter includes a cryptographically enabled email application. Encrypted data is converted to base64 to be sent through the Internet, since many mailers only support ASCII.

The `SecretWriting` program encrypts and decrypts text. Here is a sample session:

```
C:\ java SecretWriting -e Hello, world!
Lc4WKHP/uCls8mFcyTw1pQ==


C:\ java SecretWriting -d Lc4WKHP/uCls8mFcyTw1pQ==
Hello, world!
```

The -e option encrypts data, and the -d option decrypts it. A *cipher* is used to do this work. The cipher uses a *key*. Different keys will produce different results. `SecretWriting` stores its key in a file called *SecretKey.ser*. The first time you run the program, `SecretWriting` generates a key and stores it in the file. Subsequently, the key is loaded from the file. If you remove the file, `SecretWriting` will create a new key. Note that you must use the same key to encrypt and decrypt data. This is a property of a *symmetric cipher*. We'll talk more about different flavors of ciphers in Chapter 7.

"Hello, world!" can be encrypted to many different values, depending on the key that you use. Here are a few sample ciphertexts:

```
Lc4WKHP/uCls8mFcyTw1pQ==
xyOoLnWOH0eqRwUu3rQHJw==
hevNJLNowIzrocxplKI7dQ==
```

The source code for this example is longer than the last one, but it's also a more capable program:

```java
import java.io.*;
import java.security.*;

import javax.crypto.*;

import sun.misc.*;

public class SecretWriting {
  public static void main(String[] args) throws Exception {
    // Check arguments.
    if (args.length < 2) {
      System.out.println("Usage: SecretWriting -e|-d text");
      return;
    }

    // Get or create key.
    Key key;
    try {
      ObjectInputStream in = new ObjectInputStream(
          new FileInputStream("SecretKey.ser"));
      key = (Key)in.readObject();
      in.close();
    }
    catch (FileNotFoundException fnfe) {
      KeyGenerator generator = KeyGenerator.getInstance("DES");
      generator.init(new SecureRandom());
      key = generator.generateKey();
      ObjectOutputStream out = new ObjectOutputStream(
          new FileOutputStream("SecretKey.ser"));
      out.writeObject(key);
      out.close();
    }

    // Get a cipher object.
    Cipher cipher = Cipher.getInstance("DES/ECB/PKCS5Padding");
```

```
// Encrypt or decrypt the input string.
if (args[0].indexOf("e") != -1) {
  cipher.init(Cipher.ENCRYPT_MODE, key);
  String amalgam = args[1];
  for (int i = 2; i < args.length; i++)
    amalgam += " " + args[i];
  byte[] stringBytes = amalgam.getBytes("UTF8");
  byte[] raw = cipher.doFinal(stringBytes);
  BASE64Encoder encoder = new BASE64Encoder();
  String base64 = encoder.encode(raw);
  System.out.println(base64);
}
else if (args[0].indexOf("d") != -1) {
  cipher.init(Cipher.DECRYPT_MODE, key);
  BASE64Decoder decoder = new BASE64Decoder();
  byte[] raw = decoder.decodeBuffer(args[1]);
  byte[] stringBytes = cipher.doFinal(raw);
  String result = new String(stringBytes, "UTF8");
  System.out.println(result);
}
}
}
```

SecretWriting has to generate a key the first time you use it. This can take a few
seconds, so be prepared to wait.

In the meantime, let's look at the steps in this program:

1. Check command-line arguments. We expect an option, either −e or −d, and a
   string.

2. Next we need a key to use the cipher. We first attempt to deserialize the key
   from a file named *SecretKey.ser*. If this fails, we need to create a new key. A
   KeyGenerator object creates keys. We obtain a KeyGenerator by using a
   factory method, in just the same way that we obtained a MessageDigest in
   the Masher example. In this case, we ask for a key for the DES (Data Encryption Standard) cipher algorithm:

   ```
   KeyGenerator generator = KeyGenerator.getInstance("DES");
   ```

   The key generator must be initialized with a random number to produce a
   random new key. It takes a few seconds to initialize the SecureRandom, so be
   patient.

   ```
   generator.init(new SecureRandom());
   ```

   This done, we are set to generate a key. We serialize the key to the *SecretKey.ser*
   file so that we can use the same key the next time we run the program.

3. Having obtained our key, we obtain a cipher in much the same way:

   ```
   Cipher cipher = Cipher.getInstance("DES/ECB/PKCS5Padding");
   ```

This specifies the DES algorithm and some other parameters the `Cipher` needs. We'll talk about these in detail in Chapter 7.

4. Finally, we encrypt or decrypt the input data. The `Cipher` is created in an uninitialized state; it must be initialized, with a key, to either encryption mode or decryption mode. This is accomplished by calling `init()`. When encrypting, we take all of the command-line arguments after the -e option and concatenate them into one string, `amalgam`.

Then we get a byte array from this string and encrypt it in the call to `Cipher`'s `doFinal()` method:

```
byte[] stringBytes = amalgam.getBytes("UTF8");
byte[] raw = cipher.doFinal(stringBytes);
```

Finally, as in the `Masher` example, we convert the raw encrypted bytes to base64 and display them.

Decrypting is the same process in reverse. We convert the command-line argument from base64 to an array of bytes. We then use our `Cipher` object to decrypt this:

```
byte[] stringBytes = cipher.doFinal(raw);
```

We create a new `String` from the resulting byte array and display it. Note that we specify an encoding for converting between a `String` and a byte array. If we just used the default encoding (by calling `getBytes()` with no argument), then the ciphertext produced by this program might not be portable from one machine to another. We use UTF8 as a standard encoding because it can express all Unicode characters. For more information on UTF8, see *http://www.stonehand.com/unicode/standard/wg2n1036.html*. You don't really have to understand how UTF8 works; just think of it as a standard way to convert from a string to a byte array and back.

This is only a demonstration program. Note that its key management is not secure. `SecretWriting` silently writes the secret key to a disk file. A secret key must be kept secret—writing it to a file without notifying the user is not wise. In a multiuser system, other users might be able to copy the key file, enabling them to decode your secret messages. A better approach would be to prompt the user for a safe place to put the key, either in a protected directory, in some sort of protected database, on a floppy disk, or on a smart card, perhaps. Another approach is to encrypt the key itself before writing it to disk. A good way to do this is using password-based encryption, which is covered in Chapter 7.

Although `SecretWriting` doesn't do a whole lot, you can see how it could be expanded to implement a cryptographically enabled email application. I'll develop such an application in Chapter 11.

2

Concepts

At the application programming level, there are many options for making a program secure. Cryptography is the biggest, baddest tool in the application programmer's arsenal. But it is important to realize that a cryptographically enabled program is not necessarily a secure one. Without a carefully planned and constantly scrutinized security strategy, cryptography won't do you much good.

Correctly used, cryptography provides these standard security features:

- *Confidentiality* assures you that data cannot be viewed by unauthorized people.

- *Integrity* assures you that data has not been changed without your knowledge.

- *Authentication* assures you that people you deal with are not imposters.

Random numbers are used in many cryptographic algorithms. I'll talk a little bit about computer-generated random numbers at the end of the chapter. I'll wrap up by discussing the cryptographic algorithms used in this book.

Confidentiality

Most of us don't want other people to read our mail, which is why we use letters instead of postcards. Almost all information on the Internet is transmitted on the equivalent of postcards. Even if nobody is deliberately spying on you, electronic mail is frequently misdelivered. If you mistype a recipient's address, your mail might get sent to a system administrator somewhere. It's surprisingly easy for information you thought was confidential to be available to hundreds of thousands of people on the Internet.

Even data on your computer's hard disk is surprisingly available to your coworkers, the people who clean your office, and anyone else who might have physical access to your computer. If you are considering leaving your current job, you probably wouldn't feel comfortable leaving a copy of your résumé on your office computer; someone might find it.

To protect your information from prying or curious eyes, you need to take extra precautions. A common way to protect information is to *encrypt* it at the sending end and *decrypt* it at the receiving end. Encryption is the process of taking data, called *plaintext*, and mathematically transforming it into an unreadable mess, called *ciphertext*. Decryption takes the ciphertext and transforms it back into plaintext. The mathematical algorithm that performs the transformations is called a *cipher*. Figure 2-1 shows how this works.

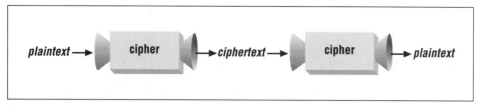

Figure 2-1: Operation of a cipher

To protect data on a hard disk, you would encrypt it before writing it on the disk. You could decrypt the ciphertext whenever you wanted to look at the information (or to print copies of your résumé).

A trivial cipher is *rot13*. The algorithm for rot13 simply rotates each character of a text message through 13 positions. One application of rot13 transforms plaintext to ciphertext, and a second application of rot13 transforms the ciphertext to plaintext. Rot13 was originally developed to render potentially offensive jokes unreadable in Internet newsgroups. Anyone who inadvertently stumbled upon one of these jokes would just see a jumble of rot13 ciphertext. Those who really wanted to see the jokes had to decrypt them first.

Rot13 is not very secure; anyone with the rot13 algorithm can decrypt rot13 ciphertext. Let's say that Maid Marian wants to send a secret message to Robin Hood, and she encrypts it with rot13. If the Sheriff of Nottingham can intercept the message, he can decrypt it, as shown in Figure 2-2.

The Sheriff doesn't even have to know that he's intercepting rot13 ciphertext. If he's an amateur cryptanalyst, he should be able to decrypt the ciphertext without knowing the algorithm used. The rot13 algorithm is a variation on the Caeser cipher, which, as its name implies, was hot stuff about 2000 years ago. Cryptograms are another variation on this type of cipher, where each letter in a message is replaced with another. Modern ciphers use much more complicated transformations than rot13.

Useful ciphers use *keys* to encrypt and decrypt data. A key is a secret value, like a password or a bank card code. It is not human-readable, the way a password is, and

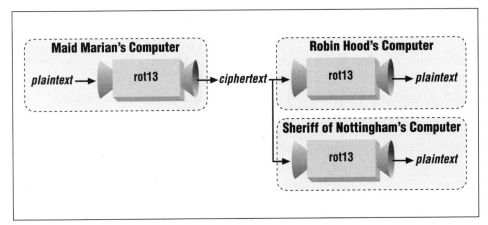

Figure 2-2: Intercepting a rot13 message

it is longer than a bank card code. You can think of it as a sequence of bytes. It can be stored in memory or on a disk drive. If you encrypt the same plaintext using different keys, you will get different ciphertexts. Similarly, ciphertext can only be decrypted to the original plaintext using the proper key.

Symmetric Ciphers

A *symmetric* cipher uses the same key at the sending and receiving end, as shown in Figure 2-3. Symmetric ciphers are also called *private key* or *secret key* ciphers.

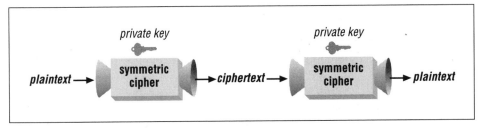

Figure 2-3: Operation of a symmetric cipher

Using a symmetric cipher can be awkward. You have to keep the key a secret, and you have to trust your recipient to keep the key a secret also. If someone else obtains the key, you and your recipient have to agree on a new key in a secure manner. For example, let's say Maid Marian and Robin Hood are using a symmetric cipher to exchange messages. If the Sheriff of Nottingham somehow obtains Robin Hood's copy of the private key, then Marian needs to generate a new private key. Then she has to figure out how to get a copy of the private key to Robin Hood without letting anyone else find out about it.

You could run into the same problem with the server and client parts of an application. If you want to keep people from snooping on the data that passes between the client and server, you could use a symmetric cipher. But both the client and the server need to know the private key. If the key is discovered, your entire system is suddenly insecure. To avoid this problem, you could program each client with a different private key, but this would quickly become a distribution headache.

Asymmetric Ciphers

The shortcomings of symmetric ciphers are addressed by *asymmetric* ciphers, also called *public key* ciphers. These ciphers actually involve a public key, which can be freely distributed, and a private key, which is secret. These keys are always generated in matching pairs. Public keys really are public; you can publish them in a newspaper or write them in the sky. No one can violate your privacy or impersonate you without your private key. The mechanism for distributing public keys, however, is a big challenge. I'll talk more about this in the section on certificates, later in this chapter.

Data encrypted using the public key can be decrypted using the private key. No other key will decrypt the data, and the private key will decrypt only data that was encrypted using the matching public key. In some cases, the reverse of the process also works; data encrypted with the private key can be decrypted with the public key. If Marian wants to send a message to Robin Hood, she can encrypt it using Robin Hood's public key. Only the matching private key, which should be known only to Robin Hood, can be used to decrypt the message. Figure 2-4 shows how this works.

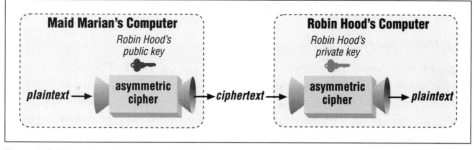

Figure 2-4: Operation of an asymmetric cipher

The Sheriff can intercept this message, but it doesn't do him any good because the message can be decrypted only with Robin Hood's private key. And as long as Robin Hood keeps his private key secret, he can give his public key to anyone who wants it, even the Sheriff. With the public key, the Sheriff can send Robin messages (if he wants), but can't decode anything that others send. In particular, he can't use the public key to compute Robin's private key, at least not without spending the entire Gross National Product of mediaeval England on state-of-the-art computers.

Asymmetric ciphers are much slower than symmetric ciphers, so they are not usually used to encrypt long messages. I'll talk more about this later.

So What Is a Key, Anyway?

It's easiest to think of keys in a conceptual way. First, visualize a cipher as a machine. To run the machine, you need to stick a key in it. You can stuff plaintext in one side and get ciphertext out the other side. You can run the cipher in reverse to convert ciphertext to plaintext.

In practice, the cipher is a mathematical formula. A key is just a special number, or a few special numbers, that are used in the formula. A public key for an ElGamal cipher, for example, consists of three numbers, called p, g, and y. When you use an ElGamal cipher to encrypt data, the p, g, and y values are used mathematically to transform the plaintext into ciphertext. (For more on ElGamal, see Chapter 9, *Writing a Provider*).

There are many ways to store keys. You could just write the key's values out to a file, or you might add a header with additional information about the key. In the `SecretWriting` example in Chapter 1, *Introduction*, we serialize a key to a file. If your filesystem isn't protected from intrusion, you'll have to be careful about writing private keys to files. One solution is to encrypt the keys themselves, perhaps with a passphrase, before writing them out. (See Chapter 7, *Encryption*, for more information on this.) Another solution for storing private keys is to put them on removable media, like floppy disks or smart cards.

Hybrid Systems

Hybrid systems combine symmetric and asymmetric ciphers. The beginning of a conversation involves some negotiation, carried out using an asymmetric cipher, where the participants agree on a private key, or *session key*. The session key is used with a symmetric cipher to encrypt the remainder of the conversation. The session key's life is over when the two participants finish their conversation. If they have a new conversation, they'll generate a new session key, which makes the cryptanalyst's job harder.

The terms used to describe cryptographic systems can be confusing. An asymmetric cipher uses a public and a private key. A symmetric cipher uses a private key too, but sometimes it's called a secret key or a session key. Finally, symmetric ciphers are sometimes called secret key ciphers.

Distributing Keys

How exactly would Marian get Robin Hood's public key? This could happen in several different ways. Robin Hood could post the key on a network server for Marian to pick up, email it to Marian, put it on a disk and hand the disk to Marian, or write the value of each byte on a piece of paper and send each piece to Marian by carrier pigeon. Because public keys are meant to be distributed, Robin Hood doesn't care if the Sheriff of Nottingham intercepts this communication. He does care, however, if the Sheriff gives Marian a bogus public key instead of Robin Hood's real public key. If the Sheriff is successful in this skullduggery, he can impersonate Robin Hood, causing him and Marian serious trouble. There is a solution to this problem, called *certificates*; I'll talk about them later in this chapter, in the section on authentication.

Key Agreement Protocols

A *key agreement protocol* or *key exchange protocol* is a system in which two parties can agree on a secret value. Even if someone is listening to everything the two parties say, they can still agree on a secret value without revealing it. This is useful in situations where the two parties would like to agree on a key that can be used to encrypt a subsequent conversation.

Integrity

When you download a file over the Internet, you'd like to be sure that the file you get is the one you wanted; you'd like to be assured of the file's *integrity*. Many people make the following assumptions, consciously or unconsciously, when they download a file from a server:

- The file is not a malicious program.

- The file has not been replaced, unbeknownst to the server's owners, by a malicious program.

- There is not another computer between you and the server, sending you a different file than the one you want or modifying the file that gets sent to you. This is the "man-in-the-middle" attack.

This is a hefty batch of assumptions, not stuff that gives you a warm fuzzy feeling. Although these assumptions are geared toward executable files, any type of download is at risk. You want to be sure that you get what you thought you were getting.

For example, Maid Marian runs an FTP server. One of the files she puts on it, for public consumption, is her schedule for the next couple of weeks. Journalists and paparazzi check this schedule regularly, as does Robin Hood. Robin Hood is always suspicious, so he'd like some assurance that the schedule file he downloads is not a counterfeit.

A *message digest* can be used to verify data integrity. A message digest is a special number calculated from a set of input data.[*] Figure 2-5 shows how this works.

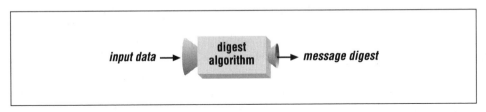

Figure 2-5: A message digest

Let's try to use the message digest in our previous example to ensure data integrity. It involves a few steps:

1. Marian calculates the message digest of her schedule file and places the digest value on the server.

2. Robin Hood downloads both the file and the message digest.

3. Robin Hood calculates the message digest of the file and compares it to the downloaded message digest value.

If the calculated message digest matches the downloaded message digest, then eveything is copacetic, right? Wrong. If the Sheriff of Nottingham is sneaky enough (he is), he could break into Marian's FTP server and post a different schedule with a matching message digest file. Another possible attack is the man-in-the-middle attack, where the Sheriff intercepts files traveling from Marian's server to Robin Hood and replaces them with his own files.

In this case, the use of the message digest has gained us little, except to make it a little harder for the Sheriff to forge a file. The message digest becomes useful when it's paired with other cryptographic techniques.

A Message Authentication Code (MAC), for example, is basically a message digest with an associated key. It produces a short value based on both its input data and the key. In theory, only someone with the same key can produce the same MAC from the same input data.

Another approach to authentication comes from the combination of a message digest and an asymmetric cipher. If Marian encrypts the message digest with her

---

[*] If you are familiar with hash functions, it will help you to know that a message digest is a lot like a hash value, except longer. Message digests are sometimes called secure hash functions or cryptographic hash functions.

private key, Robin Hood can download the encrypted message digest, decrypt it using Marian's public key, and compare the message digest to one that he computes from the downloaded file. If they match, then he can be sure that the file is correct.

The encrypted message digest is called a *signature*; Marian has *signed* the file. Figure 2-6 shows this process.[*]

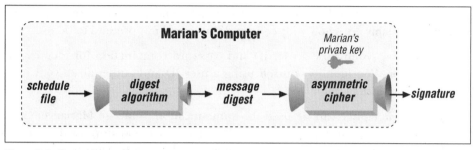

Figure 2-6: Generating a signature

Figure 2-7 shows how Robin Hood can *verify* the signature. First, Robin Hood decrypts the signature, using Marian's public key. This leaves him with a message digest value. Then he calculates the message digest of the schedule file himself. If the two message digest values match, Marian's signature is verified.

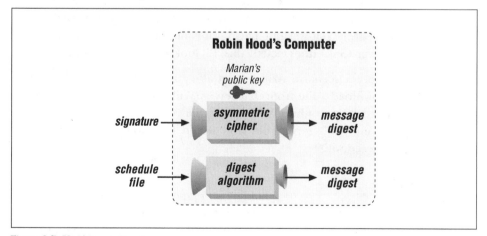

Figure 2-7: Verifying a signature

---

* Not all signature algorithms work this way. In some algorithms, the steps of digesting and encrypting are collapsed into a single signing step. ElGamal, presented in Chapter 9, is an example of a signature algorithm with a single signing step. Here, the steps of digesting and encrypting are shown separately, for clarity.

Authentication

At some fundamental level, you want to be sure that the people you deal with are really who they say they are. The process of proving identity is called *authentication.*

When you call someone on the telephone, you identify yourself by saying your name. The sound of your voice authenticates you to the person on the other end of the line. When you use an automated bank machine, your bank card identifies you and your secret code authenticates you. Someone else using your bank card would presumably not know your code and thus could not pretend to be you.

Most computer systems use a user ID and password combination for identity and authentication. You identify yourself using a user ID and authenticate your identity with a password.

An asymmetric cipher can be used for authentication. Suppose Marian encrypts her schedule file using her private key. When Robin Hood downloads Marian's schedule file, he decrypts it using her public key. He can be sure that the file is from Marian because only Marian's private key could have encrypted the file in the first place.

Asymmetric ciphers are *computationally expensive,* a nice computer science synonym for *slow.* Unfortunately, it's not practical to use an asymmetric cipher for entire conversations. Typically, an asymmetric cipher is used to authenticate the participants of a conversation; the conversation itself is encrypted with a symmetric cipher, using a special one-time key called a *session key.* Now the challenge is exchanging the session key without having anyone else find out about it. The Secure Sockets Layer (SSL) does exactly this; I'll look at it in detail in Chapter 7.

Let's consider another scenario. Will Scarlet also runs an FTP server, and Robin Hood wants to download a file from that server. Will has signed the file. Unfortunately, Robin Hood does not have Will's public key on hand. He could download the public key from Will's server, but how would he know that the public key hadn't been tampered with?

Certificates

If Marian already knows Will's public key, she can help Robin Hood, using something called a *certificate.* A certificate is a statement, issued by one person, that the public key of another person has a certain value. Essentially, a certificate is a signed public key. Marian creates the certificate by placing some information about her, some information about Will, and Will's public key value into a file. She then signs the file with her own private key, as shown in Figure 2-8. Robin Hood (or anyone else) can download this certificate and verify it using Marian's public key. Robin Hood trusts Marian, so he also now has a trustworthy copy of Will's public key, which he can use to verify files signed by Will.

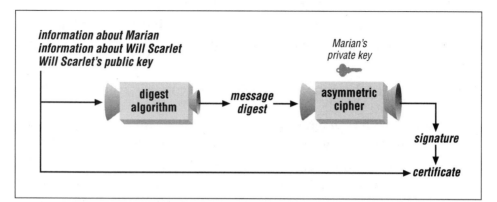

Figure 2-8: Creating a certificate: Marian is the signer, and Will Scarlet is the subject

As Figure 2-8 shows, the information about Marian and Will Scarlet, as well as Will Scarlet's public key, is placed directly in the certificate. This same information is signed by Marian. The resulting signature is placed in the certificate with the rest of the data. Anyone who downloads the certificate can verify its contents using the signer's (Marian's) public key. The verification process is as follows:

1. Calculate a message digest for the certificate contents (except the signature).

2. Decrypt the signature using the signer's (Marian's) public key. The result is a message digest.

3. Compare the decrypted message digest to the calculated message digest. If they match, the certificate is valid and you now know the value of Will's public key.

Certificate Chains

To verify a certificate, you need a public key. To verify a public key, you need a certificate. Essentially, one certificate can be verified by another, which is verified by another, and so forth. This is called *certificate chaining*. The chain can't be infinite, so where does it start? The certificate chain starts with a certificate whose issuer and subject are the same. Usually such a certificate is issued by a *Certificate Authority* (CA), an ostensibly dependable institution like VeriSign or the U.S. Postal Service.

As far as Robin Hood is concerned, Marian is completely trustworthy. She serves as a CA in certifying Will Scarlet's public key to Robin Hood.

How do certificate chains work? Let's say that Robin Hood want to verify the authenticity of a file that has been signed by Little John. Little John supplies Robin with a certificate chain consisting of two certificates:

- The first certificate contains Little John's public key. It was issued by Friar Tuck.

- The second certificate contains Friar Tuck's public key and was issued by Maid Marian.

Robin Hood already has a trustworthy, self-signed certificate from Marian. He uses Marian's public key to verify the signature on Friar Tuck's certificate. Then he uses Friar Tuck's public key to verify Little John's certificate. Now, finally, he can trust Little John's public key and use it to verify the integrity of the downloaded file.

Using certificates to prove authenticity, then, depends on a chain of certificates that ultimately terminates on a self-signed certificate issued by a CA. Self-signed certificates, though, aren't secure at all. Anyone can generate a self-signed certificate, claiming to be the Post Office or the Emperor of Tibet. Why would you ever trust a self-signed certificate? You can trust a self-signed certificate if you're able to verify it. One convenient way to verify certificates is to calculate a message digest of the entire certificate, commonly known as a *certificate fingerprint*. To verify a fingerprint, call the people who issued the certificate and have them read off the numbers of the fingerprint. Another option is for the CA to widely publish their self-signed certificate's fingerprint, perhaps in newspapers and magazines as well as online. If you obtain a fingerprint from several sources, and they all match the fingerprint on the self-signed certificate you possess, then the certificate is likely to be trustworthy.

Currently, most self-signed certificates are embedded into web browsers. When you download and run a browser, it can recognize certificates issued by a dozen or so popular CAs, using internal self-signed certificates from these CAs. How do you know that somebody tricky hasn't modified the self-signed certificates as you downloaded the browser? You don't. If you're worried about this attack, you should verify the self-signed certificate fingerprints in the browser before you accept any certificates issued by these CAs. Alternately, you should download the browser in a secure manner, perhaps using SSL (see Chapter 7).

Random Numbers

Random numbers are crucial in cryptography. They are used to create cryptographic keys and, in some cases, to encrypt or sign data. A random number is one whose value cannot be predicted. A *random number generator* (RNG) is a device that produces random numbers.

It's fairly easy for humans to generate random numbers. You can sit down with a pair of dice or a deck of cards, and generate as many random numbers as you

---

Certificate Authorities:
At Odds with the Internet?

Some people believe that hierarchical certificates are not a good way to authenticate users. The existence of many certificates chains, all leading back to a small group of CAs, is seen as a security weakness. It does focus a lot of attention on the CA's private key. Anyone possessing this key can issue all sorts of bogus certificates and have them trusted by a large group of users. According to the Meta Certificate Group (MCG, *http://mcg.org.br/*), the centralized architecture of traditional certificates won't work in the distributed environment of the Internet. They are hard at work on a better solution, called Meta Certificates, but the hierarchical certificate structure remains a de facto standard.

---

want. It's much harder to convince a computer to generate random numbers. Computers are designed to be methodical and deterministic. Some computers can use specialized hardware to generate random numbers, by measuring an unstable electronic circuit or radioactive decay or some other random process. Most of us, however, don't have this kind of hardware. Furthermore, such solutions tend to be very platform-specific, which is not good for Java programmers.

As with horseshoes and hand grenades, "close" has to be good enough. Computers, therefore, use a *pseudo-random number generator* (PRNG) as a source of "random" data. A PRNG uses an algorithm to generate an endless sequence of ostensibly random numbers. Usually a message digest function is used iteratively to make it difficult to determine the past or future output of the PRNG. The PRNG is initialized, or *seeded*, using a small set of truly random data.

That's the way it's supposed to work. Programmers who are not familiar with cryptography usually seed the PRNG with the current value of the system clock. Anyone with access to the same PRNG can use the same seed, which allows them to make good guesses of keys and other random data that has been generated. Let's say, for example, that Marian generates a key pair using a PRNG seeded with the system clock. The Sheriff of Nottingham, if he knows approximately when Marian generated the key pair, can easily guess the seed value for the PRNG. He can then generate the same key pair and cause Marian all sorts of trouble. Even if he doesn't know exactly when Marian generated the key pair, just knowing an approximate time makes his life a lot easier. He can write a program to try a whole range of seed values until he manages to generate the same key pair that Marian generated.

Good seeds come from really random processes, like radioactive decay or an unstable electronic circuit. Some computers use the input from a disconnected audio input as random data. Most good random data generating depends heavily on specific hardware. These types of solutions are hard to implement in platform-independent Java.

Algorithms

In this section, I'll briefly discuss the impact of key size on security. Then I'll introduce the algorithms that will be used in this book.

Size Does Matter

Key size affects the security of signatures and ciphers. In general, the longer the key, the harder it will be for an attacker to decrypt your ciphertext or forge a signature. Basically, longer keys have more possible values. If your attacker is trying every possible key to find the right one (a *brute-force* attack), a longer key gives the attacker more work. Keep in mind, however, that key size is only part of the story. A long key won't do you much good if the algorithm itself is weak.

Asymmetric ciphers and signatures have a variable key size. It's up to your application or users to choose an appropriate key length. Although longer keys are more secure, they are also slower. Picking the right key size is a trade-off between finding a comfortable level of security and having your application run too slowly.

Symmetric ciphers can either have a fixed or variable key length; it depends on the algorithm.

Names and Numbers

Table 2-1 summarizes the algorithms that I'll use in this book. We'll implement the ElGamal signature and cipher algorithms in Chapter 9. All the other algorithms have been implemented as part of software supplied by Sun™.

Table 2-1: Algorithms Used in This Book

Name	Type	Reference
MD5	Message digest	RFC 1321 *ftp://ds.internic.net/rfc/rfc1321.txt*
SHA-1	Message digest	NIST FIPS 180-1 *http://www.nist.gov/itl/div897/pubs/ fip180-1.htm*
HmacMD5	MAC	RFC 2104 *ftp://ds.internic.net/rfc/rfc2104.txt*
HmacSHA1	MAC	RFC 2104 *ftp://ds.internic.net/rfc/rfc2104.txt*
DSA	Signature	NIST FIPS 186 *http://www.nist.gov/itl/div897/pubs/ fip186.htm*

Table 2-1: Algorithms Used in This Book (continued)

Name	Type	Reference
ElGamal	Signature	*Applied Cryptography*, by Bruce Schneier (Wiley)
DES	Symmetric cipher	NIST FIPS 46-2 *http://www.nist.gov/itl/div897/pubs/fip46-2.htm*
DESede	Symmetric cipher	ANSI X9.17 or ISO 8732 *http://www.ansi.org/*
PBEWithMD5AndDES	Symmetric cipher	PKCS#5 *http://www.rsa.com/rsalabs/pubs/PKCS/html/pkcs-5.html*
ElGamal	Asymmetric cipher	*Applied Cryptography*, by Bruce Schneier (Wiley)
DH	Key exchange	PKCS#3 *http://www.rsa.com/rsalabs/pubs/PKCS/*

Choosing an algorithm is tricky business. You need to choose something that's secure enough for your application, while at the same time taking into account licensing issues, patent restrictions, and countries' import and export laws. Except for DSA, all the algorithms in Table 2-1 are free of licensing and patent restrictions.[*] With the exception of the cipher and key exchange algorithms, they can also be freely exported from the United States.

MD5

The MD5 message digest algorithm was developed by Ronald Rivest (the R in RSA Data Security, Inc.) in 1991. It's an updated version of MD4, an earlier algorithm. It produces a 128-bit message digest value. MD5 has recently been found to have some weaknesses in its collision resistance, which normally prevents an attacker from finding two messages with the same digest. For new applications, use SHA-1 (or something else) instead.

SHA-1

SHA-1 stands for Secure Hash Algorithm. It was developed by the NIST (National Institute of Standards and Technology) in conjunction with the NSA. Like MD5, SHA-1 is based on MD4. The changes made in SHA-1, however, are considerably different from the changes made in MD5. Also, SHA-1 produces a message digest value that is 160 bits long, which increases its resistance to attack. Note that this

---

[*] There is some controversy surrounding DSA, and it's not at all clear what the outcome will be. See *Applied Cryptography*, by Bruce Schneier, for more details. The consensus is that DSA is not patented. Sun, for example, supplies DSA without a license.

algorithm is often called SHA. There was a SHA-0, which is now obsolete. SHA and SHA-1 are now used to mean the same thing.

HmacMD5 and HmacSHA1

HmacMD5 and HmacSHA1 are two MAC algorithms based on the familiar message digest algorithms MD5 and SHA-1. The key used with these algorithms should be at least as long as the output of the message digest: use a 16-byte key for HmacMD5 and a 20-byte key for HmacSHA1.

DSA

DSA stands for Digital Signature Algorithm. It was developed by the NSA and released as a standard by the NIST. It is actually a combination of DSA and SHA-1. You can use any key size from 512 to 1024 bits, in 64-bit increments. The signature size depends on the key size.

ElGamal signatures

The ElGamal signature algorithm can use any key size. In Chapter 9, I'll show you how to implement the ElGamal signature algorithm. ElGamal became patent-free as I wrote this book. As with DSA, the size of the signature depends on the key size.

DES

DES stands for Data Encryption Standard. It's a symmetric cipher, first published in 1975 and based largely on research performed at IBM. The National Security Agency (NSA) also had a hand in the algorithm, although its involvement and motives are still a subject of debate. At any rate, DES has withstood more than 20 years of intense cryptanalytic scrutiny. Its weakest part is its 56-bit key size (stored in 8 bytes), which makes it vulnerable to key search attacks. The NSA is rumored to have machines that will break DES ciphertext in a matter of minutes, but, of course, nobody knows for sure except the NSA, and they're not talking.

DESede

DESede, also called triple DES, is a variant of the DES cipher algorithm. In fact, there are several variations on DESede itself. In the version I'll be using, blocks of plaintext are transformed into ciphertext using three DES keys and three applications of a normal DES cipher:

1. The plaintext is encrypted using the first key.

2. The result of step 1 is decrypted using the second key.

3. The result of step 2 is encrypted using the third key, producing ciphertext.

It is this process of encryption, decryption, and encryption that gives DESede its name. Decryption is the reverse of encryption:

1. Ciphertext is decrypted using the third key.

2. The result of step 1 is encrypted with the second key.

3. The result of step 2 is decrypted with the first key, producing plaintext.

DESede ciphertext is much harder to cryptanalyze than DES ciphertext. Effectively, you have increased your key length to 168 bits because DESede uses three 56-bit DES keys. Note that if all three keys are equal, DESede is identical to DES. A variation of DESede uses two keys instead of three. If you're trying to exchange ciphertext with another cryptographic application, make sure you understand which DESede variety you're using.

PBEWithMD5AndDES

PBE stands for *passphrase-based encryption*. This is a technique whereby a passphrase is used as the basis for a cipher key. For some applications, PBE is an attractive technique because it's easier to manage a passphrase than a cryptographic key. In this particular variant of PBE, an MD5 message digest is used to digest the passphrase. The digest value is then used as a DES key. One approach to this is described in PKCS#5, a document published by RSA Data Security, Inc.

ElGamal ciphers

ElGamal is a strong asymmetric cipher algorithm that became free of patent restrictions in 1997. Like ElGamal signatures, ElGamal ciphers can use key pairs of any length. The ElGamal cipher has the interesting property that it produces ciphertext that is about twice as large as the plaintext. Again, you'll see how to implement ElGamal in Chapter 9.

DH

DH stands for *Diffie-Hellman*, a system by which two parties can agree on a secret session key. The protocol is designed so that an eavesdropper will not know the value of the secret key, even if he or she is able to hear the entire exchange between the two parties. Diffie-Hellman was first published in 1976 and was the opening chapter in the story of public key cryptography. Like ElGamal, Diffie-Hellman's patent expired as I wrote this book.

3

Architecture

Java cryptography software comes in two pieces. One piece is the JDK itself, which includes cryptographic classes for authentication. The other piece, the Java Cryptography Extension (JCE), includes so-called "strong cryptography." In this chapter I'll talk about these two pieces of software and the architecture that houses them. In particular, I'll cover:

- The separation of cryptographic concepts and implementations (algorithms)

- The separation of the public methods of a concept class from its inner workings

- The use of factory methods in the cryptography classes

- The provider architecture

Alphabet Soup

The Java Security API is a set of packages that are used for writing secure programs in Java. In particular, the classes and interfaces in the following packages are part of the Security API:

- `java.security`

- `java.security.cert`

- `java.security.interfaces`

- `java.security.spec`

- `javax.crypto`

- `javax.crypto.interfaces`

- `javax.crypto.spec`

Here are the major pieces and their acronyms:

JCA

The overall design of the cryptography classes is governed by the Java Cryptography Architecture (JCA). The JCA specifies design patterns and an extensible architecture for defining cryptographic concepts and algorithms. The JCA is designed to separate cryptographic concepts from implementations. The concepts are encapsulated by classes in the `java.security` and `javax.crypto` packages. Implementations are supplied by *cryptographic providers*. (There's more on this later, in the section on the provider architecture.) The JDK 1.2 comes with a default provider, named SUN, that implements a few cryptographic algorithms.

JCE

The U.S. government considers certain types of cryptographic software to be weapons and limits their export. Sun, therefore, split its cryptography classes into two groups. The first group is included in the `java.security.*` packages that are part of JDK 1.2. These classes can be exported without restriction. The second group, the Java Cryptography Extension, is for U.S. and Canadian distribution only. The JCE is an extension of the JCA and includes another cryptographic provider, called SunJCE.

The JCE is a *standard extension library*, which means that although it is not a part of the core JDK, it is a package that works with the JDK. The current version of the JCE, 1.2, follows the naming convention for standard extension libraries by defining all its classes in the `javax.crypto.*` namespace.

Access control

A number of classes in `java.security` are concerned with access control, security policy, and permissions. These do not relate directly to cryptography; to find out more, read O'Reilly's *Java Security*.

Other players

At least two groups outside the United States have implemented the JCE, based on its specifications, and are distributing the result without being encumbered by U.S. export law. Like the JCE, these packages include extensions to the cryptographic concept classes as well as algorithm implementations. Unlike the JCE, these packages are not hampered by U.S. export controls.

Additionally, some software companies are offering cryptographic providers that plug in to the JCA.

Figure 3-1 shows the various groups of security software. As the picture shows, the JCA encompasses classes included in the JDK 1.2 core as well as extensions from the JCE.

Table 3-1 summarizes Java security software and where you can find it, as of this writing. It includes three JCE reimplementations developed outside the United States.

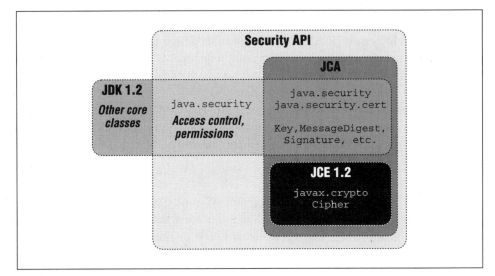

Figure 3-1: Java Security API software

Table 3-1: Java Security Download Locations

Package	Location
JCA	*http://java.sun.com/products/jdk/1.2/*
JCE	*http://java.sun.com/products/jdk/1.2/jce/*
Cryptix	*http://www.systemics.com/software/cryptix-java/*
IAIK	*http://wwwjce.iaik.tu-graz.ac.at/*
JCP	*http://www.jcp.co.uk/products/*

Concept Classes

The `java.security` and `javax.crypto` packages have classes and interfaces that represent the cryptographic concepts that were introduced in Chapter 2, *Concepts*. Table 3-2 summarizes the cryptographic concepts represented in the classes included in JDK 1.2 and JCE 1.2.

Table 3-2: Cryptographic Concept Classes

Class or Interface	Description
`java.security.cert.Certificate`	A cryptographic certificate
`javax.crypto.Cipher`	A cipher

`java.security.Key, java.security`
`.PrivateKey, java.security`
`.PublicKey, javax.crypto.SecretKey`
	A key, used for signing or encryption

`javax.crypto.KeyAgreement`	A secret key exchange protocol

Table 3-2: Cryptographic Concept Classes (continued)

Class or Interface	Description
`java.security.KeyFactory`	Translates public and private keys from one format to another
`javax.crypto.KeyGenerator`	Creates keys for symmetric ciphers
`java.security.KeyPairGenerator`	Creates pairs of public and private keys for signing or encryption
`javax.crypto.Mac`	A Message Authentication Code (MAC)
`java.security.MessageDigest`	A cryptographic hash function
`javax.crypto.SecretKeyFactory`	Translates secret keys from one format to another
`java.security.SecureRandom`	A cryptographically strong random number engine
`java.security.Signature`	A digital signature

API and SPI

The methods in the cryptographic concept classes are divided into two groups. The first group of methods is the Application Programming Interface, or API. It consists of all `public` methods that you can use to work with an instance of a concept class. The second group of methods is the Service Provider Interface, or SPI. This is the set of methods that subclasses must implement. By convention, SPI method names all begin with `engine`.

In JDK 1.1, the SPI and API methods were mixed together in the cryptographic concept classes. The `java.security.Signature` class, for example, contained API methods like `initSign()` and `verify()` as well as SPI methods like `engineInitSign()` and `engineVerify()`. To implement a signature algorithm, you would create a subclass of `Signature` and define all the SPI methods.

In JDK 1.2, API methods and SPI methods are split into separate classes. `Signature`, for example, now contains only API methods. A separate class, `java.security.SignatureSpi`, contains all the SPI methods. To implement a signature algorithm now, create a subclass of `SignatureSpi` and define the SPI methods. Whenever you implement a cryptographic algorithm, you'll need to follow a similar process. In Chapter 7, *Encryption*, and Chapter 9, *Writing a Provider*, we'll create implementations for `KeyPairGenerator`, `Signature`, and other concept classes by implementing the SPI of those classes.

Factory Methods

The JCA makes extensive use of factory methods to supply instances of its classes. The basic model is to ask a concept class for an instance that implements a particular algorithm. For example, the following code produces a `MessageDigest` instance that uses the MD5 algorithm:

```
MessageDigest md5;
md5 = MessageDigest.getInstance("MD5");
```

Like all the factory methods in the JCA, this one will throw a `NoSuchAlgorithm-Exception` if the requested algorithm is not available.

The instance that is returned to you from a factory method is some descendant of the class you asked for. But it doesn't really matter; this is one of the perks of object-oriented programming. The preceding code might return a `sun.security.provider.MD5`, but you can do everything you need to do by treating it as a `MessageDigest`.

The following concept classes have `getInstance()` methods:

- `javax.crypto.Cipher`
- `javax.crypto.KeyAgreement`
- `java.security.KeyFactory`
- `javax.crypto.KeyGenerator`
- `java.security.KeyPairGenerator`
- `javax.crypto.Mac`
- `java.security.MessageDigest`
- `javax.crypto.SecretKeyFactory`
- `java.security.Signature`

These classes also have an overloaded version of `getInstance()` that accepts an algorithm name and a provider name. I'll discuss this in detail a little later.

Right now, I suggest you bask in the simplicity of this style of programming. Changing algorithms is just as simple as changing the argument to `getInstance()`. You don't have to know a thing about the algorithms themselves because you have to deal with only the concept class—the `MessageDigest`, or `Signature`, or whatever else. If you want, you can create an application that allows the user to choose cryptographic algorithms from whatever cryptographic providers are available.

Standard Names

Asking for algorithms by name implies that there is a standard name for each cryptographic algorithm. Table 3-3 shows the standard algorithm names that are supported by the SUN provider (supplied with JDK 1.2) and the SunJCE provider (part of the JCE). For more information on the algorithms themselves, refer back to Chapter 2.

Table 3-3: Standard Algorithm Names

Concept class	Algorithms supported by Sun	Algorithms supported by SunJCE
Cipher		DES, DESede, PBEWithMD5AndDES
KeyAgreement		DH
KeyFactory	DSA	
KeyGenerator		DES, DESede
KeyPairGenerator	DSA	
Mac		HmacMD5, HmacSHA1
MessageDigest	MD5, SHA-1	
SecretKeyFactory		DES, DESede, PBEWithMD5AndDES
Signature	DSA	

The Provider Architecture

At the root of the JCA is the idea of security *providers*. A provider supplies algorithms for the cryptographic concept classes. In practice, a provider is a collection of algorithm classes headed up by a java.security.Provider object. This is confusing terminology; provider (small *p*) refers to the concept, while Provider refers to a specific class.

When you use a factory method to request a specific algorithm, it is the provider architecture, behind the scenes, that supplies the algorithm. The java.security.Security class manages security providers. When a program calls one of the factory methods to obtain a useful cryptographic object, the factory method asks the Security class to provide the object. The Security class, in turn, examines its providers to find a class that matches the requested cryptographic concept and algorithm.

The Security class keeps track of providers by keeping a list of their corresponding Provider objects. When it needs a particular algorithm, it asks each Provider, in turn, if it implements a particular algorithm. Each Provider knows about the other classes in the provider's repertoire and will return an appropriate instance if possible. The Provider is, in effect, the boss of the algorithm team.

JDK 1.2 comes with a default provider, called SUN. JCE 1.2 comes with an additional provider, SunJCE.

What Are Factory Methods?

You'll recall that classes can define both *class methods* and *instance methods*. The class methods are usually called static methods and are defined using the `static` keyword. The instance methods are just called methods. Static methods don't need an instance to run. `main()`, for example, is a famous static method. Regular instance methods are always run on a particular instance of a class and typically manipulate its data or call other instance methods.

A *factory method*, then, is a special kind of static method that returns an instance of a class. In JDK 1.0.2, factory methods were used indirectly in the `Socket` class (see `setSocketImplFactory()`). In JDK 1.1 and later, factory methods are much more prevalent. They are sprinkled throughout the `java.text` package as well as the `java.security` package. By convention, factory methods are named `getInstance()`.

A factory method is an example of a *design pattern*, a pattern of programming that turns up again and again in object-oriented programming. For a thorough and interesting treatment of design patterns, take a look at *Design Patterns: Elements of Reusable Object-Oriented Software* by Erich Gamma, Richard Helm, Ralph Johnson, and John Vlissides (Addison-Wesley, 1995).

As a dialogue, a call to `MessageDigest.getInstance("MD5")` looks like this:

- Your program to `MessageDigest`: "Please get me an instance that implements the MD5 algorithm."

- `MessageDigest` to `Security`: "Please give me a message digest object that implements MD5. I don't care which provider supplies it."

- `Security` to installed `Providers`: "Do any of you have an MD5 message digest class?"

- SUN provider to `Security`: "Yes, the class is `sun.security.provider.MD5`."

- `Security` to `MessageDigest`: "Yes, I found the class; here is an instance."

- `MessageDigest` to your program: "Here you go!"

It works the same way for the factory methods of other cryptographic constructs, like `Signature` or `KeyGenerator`. Even though there's a lot going on under the hood, it's very easy to obtain an object that implements a particular cryptographic algorithm.

The installed providers are ordered by preference. If you had more than one installed provider that supported MD5 message digests, the provider listed first would be used. If you want an algorithm from a specific provider, you can use an overloaded version of getInstance(). The following code requests a KeyPair-Generator for the ElGamal algorithm, as implemented by the Jonathan provider. (Construction of the Jonathan provider is explained in Chapter 9.)

```
KeyPairGenerator kpg = KeyPairGenerator("ElGamal", "Jonathan");
```

Providers can be configured in two ways. You can edit a properties file, which is called *static* provider configuration, or you can manage providers at runtime, which is *dynamic* provider configuration.

To configure providers statically, you'll need to edit the *java.security* file, which is found in the *lib/security* directory underneath your main JDK installation directory. Inside this file, each installed provider is represented by a line with the following format:

```
security.provider.n=providerclassname
```

The provider's class name should be fully specified; *n* is a number that determines the preference order of the providers. The first (default) provider is numbered 1. If you have not installed any additional providers, then your *java.security* file will have a single provider entry, like this:

```
security.provider.1=sun.security.provider.Sun
```

Adding a provider at runtime is simple once you've done all the provider programming. Just call Security.addProvider() or Security.insertProviderAt() with an instance of your provider class. When the Security class is first initialized, it reads the providers specified in the *java.security* file and installs them. Thereafter, programs are free to add and remove providers as they see fit.

The Security class has a suite of methods for managing Providers at runtime:

public static int addProvider(Provider provider)
> This method adds the given provider at the end of the provider preference list and returns the position of the provider (zero-based). You cannot add a provider class type more than once; if you try, this method returns –1.

public static Provider getProvider(String name)
> This method returns the named provider or null if it is not found.

public static Provider[] getProviders()
> This method returns an array of all the currently installed cryptography providers.

public static int insertProviderAt(Provider provider, int position)
> This method adds the given provider at the given one-based position in the provider preference list. If you try to add a provider that is already installed, this method returns –1. Otherwise, it returns the one-based position of the provider. Inserting a provider at position 1 puts it at the top of the list.

public static void removeProvider(String name)

This method removes the named provider.

In general, you don't ever need to worry about providers or the provider architecture. Using the factory methods, you simply ask for an algorithm from a cryptographic class, and it either succeeds or fails. In some cases, however, you may want to use a certain provider. Additional factory methods are defined for this purpose. There are actually two overloaded `getInstance()` methods, one of which allows you to specify a provider name. For example, `MessageDigest` includes the following methods:

```
public static MessageDigest getInstance(String algorithm)
public static MessageDigest getInstance(String algorithm, String provider)
```

The other cryptographic concept classes follow this pattern.

Installing the JCE

Currently, the JCE ships as a Java Archive (JAR) file. Once you've downloaded it, you should add this JAR to your CLASSPATH. To use the JCE algorithms, you'll have to install SunJCE as a provider, as described in this chapter. For example, I decided to add the SunJCE provider to my system statically. Therefore, I added a line for the SunJCE provider to my java.security file. The section on providers looks like this with the SunJCE provider installed:

```
security.provider.1=sun.security.provider.Sun
security.provider.2=com.sun.crypto.provider.SunJCE
```

Key Management

To exchange data securely, you'll need to keep track of your own private and public keys as well as the public keys of all the people with whom you wish to converse securely. What you need is something like an address book that correlates individuals to their keys and certificates. The JCA contains support for exactly this, based around the `Identity` and `KeyStore` classes. For more information about this, take a look at Chapter 5, *Key Management*.

Summary

The JCA is more a state of mind than a concrete set of classes. Most importantly, it separates cryptographic concepts from their implementations. The concepts are represented by the classes in the `java.security` and `javax.crypto` packages, while implementations are supplied by cryptographic providers. Using cryptography in a Java program is wonderfully simple. Because the API exposes concepts, rather than implementation details, it's easy to change the algorithms or providers that your program uses. Under the hood, there's a more complicated picture, but you won't have to worry about this unless you want to do something tricky, like develop your own provider.

4

Random Numbers

Random numbers are important for cryptography. As we discussed in Chapter 2, *Concepts*, computers are not very good at producing truly random data. Instead, they rely on a pseudo-random number generator (PRNG). A *cryptographically strong* PRNG, seeded with truly random values, is a PRNG that does a good job of spewing out unpredictable data. But if the PRNG is not cryptographically strong, or if the seed data is not random, the security of your application can be compromised.

In this chapter, I'll talk about a cryptographically strong PRNG that was introduced in JDK 1.1, `java.security.SecureRandom`. The rest of the chapter discusses how to produce random seed data from keyboard events.

SecureRandom

The JDK includes a class, `java.util.Random`, that implements a PRNG. Although it's fine for light-duty use, it has the following shortcomings:

- It uses an algorithm that produces a predictable sequence of numbers.

- If you don't give `Random` a seed value, it uses the value of the system clock. This is a predictable seed. Let's say that you create a random number in order to create a cryptographic key. If an attacker knows *when* you created the random number, even approximately, he or she can guess at likely values of the random number seed. With a relatively small amount of guessing, the attacker can guess which random number seed you've used. From this, the attacker can generate the same supposedly random cryptographic key that you just generated. Now the attacker can impersonate you or read your secret messages.

A stronger PRNG, `java.security.SecureRandom`, was introduced in JDK 1.1. This class is based around a message digest. SecureRandom uses the SHA-1 (Secure Hash Algorithm) message digest algorithm, which produces a 20-byte digest. Here's how it works:

- The SecureRandom is created using a seed. The seed value is digested, and the resulting value is stored as part of the SecureRandom's internal state. An internal counter is initialized to zero.

- Every time SecureRandom needs to create more pseudo-random numbers, the message digest is updated with the internal state and the counter, which is incremented. This data is digested and returned as the new pseudo-random data.

Because of the irreversible nature of the message digest, it's very hard to predict the past and future values of the PRNG even if you know its present output.

In practice, you don't have to worry about the details. Just create a SecureRandom instance and call its nextBytes() method to get pseudo-random data. In the example that follows, a SecureRandom is used to generate 100 bytes of pseudo-random data:

```
SecureRandom sr = new SecureRandom();
byte[] pseudoRandom = new byte[100];
sr.nextBytes(pseudoRandom);
```

SecureRandom provides two constructors:

public SecureRandom()

This constructor creates a new SecureRandom and initializes it with automatically generated seed data. This process is called self-seeding and is discussed in the next section.

public SecureRandom(byte[] seed)

This constructor takes the given seed data and uses it to initialize a new SecureRandom instance.

If your application collects truly random data, it can be used to update a SecureRandom's seed using setSeed().

public synchronized void setSeed(byte[] seed)

This method updates the internal state of the SecureRandom with a new set of random seed data. The new data does not replace the original seed, but supplements it.

When you need pseudo-random data, call nextBytes().

public synchronized void nextBytes(byte[] bytes)

This method fills the given byte array with pseudo-random data.

Self-Seeding

If you don't specify a seed value when you construct a SecureRandom, one will be generated for you. This is where it gets confusing. The SecureRandom class has a static member variable, also a SecureRandom, called the seed generator. It is used to generate seed values for new SecureRandom instances. Every time you create a SecureRandom using new SecureRandom(), the seed generator is used to seed your SecureRandom instance.

So how does the seed generator get seeded? SecureRandom uses an algorithm based on the timing of threads on the system to generate some supposedly random data. It uses this data to seed the seed generator itself.

Thus, real random seed generation occurs only once, the first time you construct a SecureRandom. It has two disadvantages:

* It takes a few seconds (5–10 seconds on my Pentium 90).

* The thread timing algorithm is not thoroughly tested. It may have weaknesses that cryptanalysts could exploit.

As Sun says in the SecureRandom documentation,

> This empty constructor automatically seeds the generator. We attempt to provide sufficient seed bytes to completely randomize the internal state of the generator (20 bytes). Note, however, that our seed generation algorithm has not been thoroughly studied or widely deployed. It relies on counting the number of times that the calling thread can yield while waiting for another thread to sleep for a specified interval.

> The first time this constructor is called in a given Virtual Machine, it may take several seconds of CPU time to seed the generator, depending on the underlying hardware. Successive calls run quickly because they rely on the same (internal) pseudo-random number generator for their seed bits.

Keyboard Timing

In this section, I'll develop an alternate method of seeding a SecureRandom. This method is based on measuring the timing of keyboard events, a method that has been used for years in PGP (Pretty Good Privacy, a popular cryptography application). The basic idea is to measure the time between successive keystrokes using a fast timer (a resolution of 1 millisecond or better is preferable). For each keystroke, one or two low-order bits of timing information will appear random. Take as many bits as you need to seed your PRNG. Even a very good, very consistent typist will probably not be able to type with millisecond precision, which means the seed bits are truly random.

This method does require that the user type data for a few seconds, which is not particularly user friendly. In contrast, the self-seeding algorithm in SecureRandom has no impact on your user interface, except that it will hang up your application for a few seconds the first time it is run. The method presented here, however, is under your control.

Seeder

The Seeder class listens to KeyEvents and builds up a seed value of a certain length. When the seed is completed, Seeder will fire off an ActionEvent. Seeder doesn't care where the keyboard events come from; it just implements the KeyListener interface. We'll make Seeder part of the oreilly.jonathan.util package, so that we can easily use it later.

```
package oreilly.jonathan.util;

import java.awt.AWTEventMulticaster;
import java.awt.event.*;

public class Seeder
    implements KeyListener {
```

Internally, Seeder stores the seed value in a byte array, called mSeed. An integer, mBitIndex, serves as the current bit index. The mDone member variable indicates whether the Seeder is done gathering seed bits. Seeder also keeps track of the last key character it received. It rejects repeating keys because the timing of repeated keys may be predictable, and this would mess up our supposed random seed value. Seeder uses an ActionListener member variable to keep track of who gets notified when seed generation is complete. And finally, a Counter member variable keeps track of the object that measures the time between keyboard events. You'll see the Counter class later.

```
protected byte[] mSeed;
protected int mBitIndex;
protected boolean mDone;
protected char mLastKeyChar;
protected ActionListener mListenerChain;
protected Counter mCounter;
```

Seeder has only one constructor, which accepts the number of bytes of seed that are to be generated. The constructor simply calls the reset() method, which initializes the Seeder.

```
public Seeder(int seedBytes) { reset(seedBytes); }

public void reset(int seedBytes) {
  mSeed = new byte[seedBytes];
```

```
        mBitIndex = seedBytes * 8 - 1;
        mDone = false;
        mLastKeyChar = '\0';
        mListenerChain = null;
        mCounter = new Counter();
    }
```

The following methods provide useful information about the `Seeder`:

```
    public byte[] getSeed() { return mSeed; }
    public int getBitLength() { return mSeed.length * 8; }
```

Internally, the `mBitIndex` member variable counts down to zero. The `getCurrentBitIndex()` method actually returns a value that counts up from zero to `getBitLength()`.

```
    public int getCurrentBitIndex() {
        return mSeed.length * 8 - 1 - mBitIndex;
    }
```

Objects that wish to be notified when the seed is generated will register and unregister using `addActionListener()` and `removeActionListener()`. These calls are handled using the static methods of `AWTEventMulticaster`.

```
    public void addActionListener(ActionListener al) {
        mListenerChain = AWTEventMulticaster.add(mListenerChain, al);
    }

    public void removeActionListener(ActionListener al) {
        mListenerChain = AWTEventMulticaster.remove(mListenerChain, al);
    }
```

As a `KeyListener`, `Seeder` is notified of key press and release events. A matched key press and release is transmitted as a "typed" key. `Seeder` filters out repeated keys and calls `grabTimeBit()` for the events we receive in `keyTyped()`.

```
    public void keyPressed(KeyEvent ke) {}
    public void keyReleased(KeyEvent ke) {}
    public void keyTyped(KeyEvent ke) {
        char keyChar = ke.getKeyChar();
        if (keyChar != mLastKeyChar)
            grabTimeBit();
        mLastKeyChar = keyChar;
    }
```

In `grabTimeBit()`, we first examine `mDone`. If we're finished gathering seed bits, we return immediately. Otherwise, `grabTimeBit()` pulls off a bit from the `Counter` and adds it to the seed value.

```
    protected void grabTimeBit() {
        if (mDone) return;
```

```
int t = mCounter.getCount();
int bit = t & 0x0001;
```

If the bit is not zero, the seed value needs to be updated, as follows:

```
if (bit != 0) {
  int seedIndex = mBitIndex / 8;
  int shiftIndex = mBitIndex % 8;
  mSeed[seedIndex] |= (bit << shiftIndex);
}
```

Regardless of the bit value, the index variable is decremented.

```
mBitIndex--;
```

If the bit index is less than zero, we're finished. We stop the Counter, first of all. Then we reset the bit index to zero, so the getCurrentBitIndex() method returns a valid value. Setting the mDone flag to true signifies that seed generation is complete.

```
if (mBitIndex < 0) {
  mCounter.stop();
  mBitIndex = 0; // Reset this so getCurrentBitIndex() works.
  mDone = true;
```

Finally, we notify any registered ActionListeners that the seed value is ready. This concludes both the grabTimeBit() method and the Seeder class.

```
      if (mListenerChain != null) {
        mListenerChain.actionPerformed(
            new ActionEvent(this, 0, "Your seed is ready."));
      }
    }
  }
}
```

There are three steps involved in using Seeder. First, create a Seeder for the desired number of seed bytes, as follows:

```
Seeder s = new Seeder(20);
```

Then hook up a source of KeyEvents to the Seeder.

```
theComponent.addKeyListener(s);
```

Finally, to be notified when the seed generation is through, register an object to listen for ActionEvents from the Seeder.

```
s.addActionListener(this);
```

Counter

The Counter class that Seeder uses is presented below. It creates a thread for itself and counts as fast as it can.

What Is AWTEventMulticaster?

You may be mystified by Seeder's use of AWTEventMulticaster. And why, if Seeder keeps track of multiple ActionListeners, is there only a single member variable to represent them?

The mListenerChain member variable actually keeps track of a chain of ActionListeners. When a new listener is added, using addActionListener(), AWTEventMulticaster handles adding the new listener. It creates a new object that encapsulates all the previous ActionListeners and the new ActionListener. When an ActionEvent is sent to this object, it propagates the event to all its contained ActionListeners. Even though there is only a single ActionListener variable, mListenerChain, this variable references an object that may contain a whole chain of listeners.

```
package oreilly.jonathan.util;

public class Counter
    implements Runnable {
  protected boolean mTrucking;
  protected int mCounter;

  public Counter() {
    mTrucking = true;
    mCounter = 0;
    Thread t = new Thread(this);
    t.start();
  }

  public void run() {
    while (mTrucking){
      mCounter++;
      try { Thread.sleep(1); }
      catch (InterruptedException ie) {}
    }
  }

  public void stop() { mTrucking = false; }
  public int getCount() { return mCounter; }
}
```

Pitfalls

Two issues governed the design of Seeder:

Timing is tricky

Counter runs in its own thread, but without knowing how Java threads work in detail, we can't be sure that there might be some regularity in the values that

Counter returns to Seeder. Originally I wrote this class to use the value of the system clock instead of a value from Counter. On my Windows 95 machine, however, the system clock (as returned by System.currentTimeMillis()) had a resolution of only 10 ms, which I felt was too coarse for comfort. I use Counter instead because it has a higher resolution than the system clock. Note, however, that this is really a variation on the thread-timing method that Sun uses as the default SecureRandom seed generation process.

Repeated keys are dangerous

The timing of repeated keys is very regular. Seeder dodges this trap by explicitly filtering out repeated keys. But are there other traps like this lurking in the Seeder class? Could you produce even timing by quickly alternating two keys? Does the keyboard device itself have some coarse interval for generating key events, so that you might be able to type faster than the keyboard could process the events?

How can you tell if Seeder's results are truly random? There are many statistical tests for randomness, but even data that passes these tests may not be random. For interesting discussions on the mathematics and philosophy of random numbers, try these resources:

http://random.mat.sbg.ac.at/

This site, hosted at the University of Salzburg, contains information on random number generators and tests for random numbers, as well as links to literature and other web sites on randomness.

http://www.cs.berkeley.edu/~daw/netscape-randomness.html

This site contains a no-nonsense list of links to papers, source code, and hardware specifications relating to random numbers.

http://lavarand.sgi.com/

For a lighter look at random numbers, try this cartoonish site. It describes how Lava Lites® can be used to generate random numbers.

Without a review of Seeder's design by security professionals, and without statistical analysis of its output, you shouldn't trust Seeder too much. It does demonstrate the basic principle of gathering random bits from timed events, however. You could modify this class to gather timing information from other sources as well, like the mouse. If you use more sources of supposedly random events, you're more likely to get a truly unpredictable stream of data.

SeederDialog

Wouldn't it be nice if there were a modal dialog that used a Seeder to generate a seed value? And wouldn't it be nice if the dialog had a progress bar that showed how far along the generation was? I'll develop this nice dialog now.

`SeederDialog` is designed to make it easy to integrate `Seeder` into your application. Create one, show it, and retrieve the seed value as follows:

```
SeederDialog sd = new SeederDialog(this, 20);
sd.show();
byte[] seed = sd.getSeed();
```

The dialog itself is shown in Figure 4-1. As the user types characters, the progress bar fills up. When the seed is fully generated, the dialog goes away.

Figure 4-1: SeederDialog in action

`SeederDialog` is both an `ActionListener` and a `KeyListener`. It receives an `ActionEvent` from its `Seeder` when the seed is fully generated. It receives the same KeyEvents as the `Seeder`, which allows it to update the progress bar.

```
package oreilly.jonathan.awt;

import java.awt.*;
import java.awt.event.*;

import oreilly.jonathan.util.*;

public class SeederDialog
    extends Dialog
    implements ActionListener, KeyListener {
```

Internally, the dialog contains a `Seeder` object and a progress bar. (The progress bar is type `oreilly.jonathan.awt.ProgressBar`. I'll present the code at the end of this section.)

```
ProgressBar mProgressBar;
Seeder mSeeder;
```

`SeederDialog`'s constructor accepts a parent `Frame` and a number of seed bytes. It creates itself as a modal dialog (`true` in the call to `super()`) and uses the `setupWindow()` method to configure the dialog.

```
public SeederDialog(Frame parent, int seedBytes) {
    super(parent, "Seeder Dialog", true);
    setupWindow(seedBytes);
}
```

The getSeed() method returns the seed value from the underlying Seeder object.

```
public byte[] getSeed() { return mSeeder.getSeed(); }
```

The dialog receives an **ActionEvent** from the **Seeder** when it is done. In this case, it simply shuts itself down.

```
public void actionPerformed(ActionEvent ae) { dispose(); }
```

SeederDialog receives the same KeyEvents that are sent to the Seeder. They are used to set the current level of the progress bar.

```
public void keyPressed(KeyEvent ke) {}
public void keyReleased(KeyEvent ke) {}
public void keyTyped(KeyEvent ke) {
    mProgressBar.setLevel(mSeeder.getCurrentBitIndex());
}
```

Finally, the setupWindow() method configures the user interface of the dialog and wires up the event handling.

```
protected void setupWindow(int seedBytes) {
    setFont(new Font("TimesRoman", Font.PLAIN, 12));
    setLayout(new GridLayout(4, 1));
    Label t1 = new Label("Please type some keys");
    Label t2 = new Label("to initialize the random");
    Label t3 = new Label("number generator.");
    add(t1);
    add(t2);
    add(t3);
    mProgressBar = new ProgressBar();
    Panel p = new Panel();
    p.add(mProgressBar);
    add(p);

    setSize(200, 200);
    setLocation(100, 100);
    pack();

    mSeeder = new Seeder(seedBytes);
    mProgressBar.setMaximum(mSeeder.getBitLength());
    mSeeder.addActionListener(this);

    t1.addKeyListener(mSeeder);
    t1.addKeyListener(this);
    t1.requestFocus();
  }
}
```

As promised, here is the code for the progress bar that SeederDialog uses.

```
package oreilly.jonathan.awt;
```

```java
import java.awt.*;

public class ProgressBar
    extends Canvas {
  int mLevel;
  int mMaximum;
  Color mFrameColor;

  public ProgressBar() { this(100); }

  public ProgressBar(int max) {
    setForeground(Color.blue);
    mFrameColor = Color.black;
    setMaximum(max);
    setLevel(0);
  }

  public void setMaximum(int max) {
    mMaximum = max;
    repaint();
  }

  public void setLevel(int level) {
    mLevel = (level > mMaximum) ? mMaximum : level;
    repaint();
  }

  public void update(Graphics g) { paint(g); }

  public void paint(Graphics g) {
    Dimension d = getSize();
    double ratio = (double)((double)mLevel / (double)mMaximum);
    int x = (int)((double)d.width * ratio);

    g.setColor(mFrameColor);
    g.drawRect(0, 0, d.width - 1, d.height - 1);

    g.setColor(getForeground());
    g.fillRect(1, 1, x, d.height - 2);

    g.setColor(getBackground());
    g.fillRect(x + 1, 1, d.width - 2 - x, d.height - 2);
  }

  public Dimension getMinimumSize() { return new Dimension(10, 1); }
  public Dimension getPreferredSize() { return new Dimension(100, 10); }
}
```

5

Key Management

Key management is the biggest challenge for developers who wish to use public key cryptography in their applications. Even Sun wasn't quite sure how to tackle this problem. Between JDK 1.1 and JDK 1.2, they shifted their strategy so there are now two key management paradigms you can use.

In this chapter, I'll cover the key management concepts represented by classes and interfaces in the JDK. These concepts include the following:

- Keys

- Key generators and translators

- Key agreement protocols

- Identity-based key management, including identities, signers, and scopes

- Keystore-based key management, including the KeyStore class and the key-tool utility

One of our examples is a general-purpose identity-based key management class, KeyManager, that I'll use in the examples in Chapter 10, *SafeTalk*, and Chapter 11, *CipherMail.*

Keys

The java.security.Key interface encapsulates a cryptographic key. It defines only three methods:

public String getAlgorithm()
> This method returns the name of the cryptographic algorithm for which this key is used. An example is DSA, the Digital Signature Algorithm.

public byte[] getEncoded()
> You can retrieve the encoded value of the key by calling this method. Encoding is a process of mapping the key's value into an array of bytes. The getFormat() method will return the name of the format used to encode the key.

public String getFormat()
> This method returns the name of the format used to encode the key. An example is X.509.

Several interfaces extend the Key interface. These child interfaces define different flavors of keys, but none of them defines any additional methods; they are used for clarity and type safety. As we saw in Chapter 2, *Concepts*, keys are used differently for symmetric ciphers, asymmetric ciphers, and signatures. Semantic extensions to the Key interfaces keep the concepts clear. In the JDK, there are two such interfaces:

java.security.PublicKey
> This interface represents the public key of a key pair, suitable for use with a signature or an asymmetric cipher (see Chapter 6, *Authentication*, and Chapter 7, *Encryption*, respectively). When used with a signature, a PublicKey is used to verify a signature (see initVerify() in the Signature class).

java.security.PrivateKey
> This interface represents the other half of a key pair. Just like a public key, a private key can be used with a signature or an asymmetric cipher. When used with a signature, however, the private key is used to generate the signature (see initSign() in Signature).

The JCE includes another semantic extension of Key:

javax.crypto.SecretKey
> This interface represents a secret (or private, or session) key that is used for a symmetric cipher. With a symmetric cipher, the same secret key is used to encrypt and decrypt data.

Public and private keys are always created in matched pairs. The JDK includes a class, java.security.KeyPair, that encapsulates a matched public and private key. It's a very simple class:

public KeyPair(PublicKey publicKey, PrivateKey privateKey)
> This constructor creates a KeyPair with the given public and private keys.

public PublicKey getPublic()
> This method returns the public key.

public PrivateKey getPrivate()
> This method returns the private key.

Key Generators

How are keys created? A special class, called a *key generator*, is used to create new, random keys. Three steps are involved in creating cryptographic keys:

1. Obtain a key generator object for the algorithm you want to use.

2. Initialize the key generator.

3. Ask the key generator to generate a key or key pair.

There are two varieties of key generators. The first generates key pairs for use with asymmetric ciphers and signatures. The second kind generates a single key for use with a symmetric cipher.

KeyPairGenerator

The `java.security.KeyPairGenerator` class creates a matched public and private key and returns them as a `KeyPair`. You can create a `KeyPairGenerator` using one of the `getInstance()` factory methods, as described in Chapter 3, *Architecture*. For example, to generate a key pair for ElGamal signing, you obtain a `KeyPairGenerator` as follows:

```
KeyPairGenerator kpg = KeyPairGenerator.getInstance("ElGamal");
```

Like any other `getInstance()` method, this one may throw a `NoSuchAlgorithm-Exception` if the given algorithm is not found.

Next, the generator needs to be initialized. There are two methods for this:

public abstract void initialize(int strength, SecureRandom random)
> When keys are generated, they will be created for the given strength using the supplied source of random bits. Although the strength of a key almost always refers to its bit length, the interpretation of the strength parameter is algorithm dependent.

public void initialize(int strength)
> This method is the same as the last one, except it creates a new Secure-Random to serve as a source of random bits. If you haven't created a new SecureRandom previously in your application, this call may take some time to complete as SecureRandom attempts to seed itself.

Once the `KeyPairGenerator` is initialized, you can ask it to generate a new, random key pair:

public abstract KeyPair genKeyPair()
> This method generates a key pair using the strength and random bit source specified in a previous call to `initialize()`.

If you wanted to generate a 1024-bit key pair suitable for DSA signatures, you would do the following:

```
KeyPairGenerator kpg = KeyPairGenerator.getInstance("DSA");
kpg.initialize(1024);
KeyPair pair = kpg.genKeyPair();
```

Depending on the algorithm, key size, and your hardware, you may have to wait 10 or 20 seconds for the key pair generation to work. (Remember that it takes a while for the `KeyPairGenerator` to initialize `SecureRandom`, as we discussed in Chapter 4, *Random Numbers*.)

KeyGenerator

Symmetric ciphers use a single key instead of a key pair. The JCE, therefore, includes a class called `javax.crypto.KeyGenerator` that is suitable for randomly generating a single key. Like its cousin, `KeyPairGenerator`, it can be created using a `getInstance()` factory method. To create a `KeyGenerator` for the DES cipher, use this:

```
KeyGenerator kg = KeyGenerator.getInstance("DES");
```

To initialize the `KeyGenerator`, give it a source of random data, a strength, or both. Some symmetric ciphers algorithms have a fixed key size, while others are variable. (See Chapter 2 for more discussion of algorithms and key sizes.) Once the `KeyGenerator` is initialized, you can create a new key with `generateKey()`.

public final void init(SecureRandom random)[*]
> This method tells the `KeyGenerator` to use the given source of random bits to create keys.

public final void init(int strength)
> This method initializes the `KeyGenerator` to create keys of the specified length.

public final void init(int strength, SecureRandom random)
> This method initializes the `KeyGenerator` with the supplied key strength and source of randomness.

public final SecretKey generateKey()
> This method generates a new, random `SecretKey`.

For example, to generate a new DES key, do this:

```
KeyGenerator kg = KeyGenerator.getInstance("DES");
kg.init(new SecureRandom());
SecretKey key = kg.generateKey();
```

---

[*] `KeyPairGenerator` has an `initialize()` method, while `KeyGenerator` has an `init()` method. Go figure.

Algorithm-Specific Initialization

Both `java.security.KeyPairGenerator` and `javax.crypto.KeyGenerator`
support the concept of *algorithm-specific initialization*. This means that if you know
what algorithm you'll be using, you can use parameters that are useful for that
particular algorithm to initialize a key generator.

The thing that makes algorithm-specific initialization work is a little interface with
a long name, `java.security.spec.AlgorithmParameterSpec`. This interface
defines no methods or constants. Think of it as a box for parameters. You can pass
an `AlgorithmParameterSpec` to a key generator to initialize it; it's up to the key
generator to extract parameters from whatever object was passed to it.

`java.security.KeyPairGenerator` contains one method for algorithm-specific
initialization:

public void initialize(AlgorithmParameterSpec params) throws
InvalidAlgorithmParameterException

> This method initializes the `KeyPairGenerator` using the supplied parameters. If
> the `AlgorithmParameterSpec` object is not recognized, an exception is thrown.

And in `javax.crypto.KeyGenerator`, there are two algorithm-specific initialization methods:

public final void init(AlgorithmParameterSpec params) throws
InvalidAlgorithmParameterException

> This method initializes the `KeyGenerator` using the supplied parameters. If the
> `AlgorithmParameterSpec` object is not recognized, an exception is thrown.

public final void init(AlgorithmParameterSpec params, SecureRandom random) throws
InvalidAlgorithmParameterException

> This method is the same as `init(AlgorithmParameterSpec)`, but the
> `KeyGenerator` will use the supplied source of randomness to generate keys.

Algorithm-specific initialization can also be used with `Signatures` and `Ciphers`, as
you'll see in Chapters 6 and 7, respectively.

Key Translators

How do you store a key on disk? How do you transmit a key over a network
connection? One solution is to use object serialization, as we did in the `Secret-`
`Writing` example in Chapter 1, *Introduction*. It's more common, however, simply
to store or transmit the key as an array of bytes. To do this, we need a way to translate a `Key` object into a `byte` array and vice versa.

The `javax.crypto.spec.SecretKeySpec`, `javax.crypto.SecretKeyFactory`,
and `java.security.KeyFactory` classes fill this niche. Although the last two

classes are called factories, they function as translators. Let's look at `SecretKey-Spec` first because it's simplest.

SecretKeySpec

The simplest way to convert an array of bytes to a secret key is the `javax.crypto.spec.SecretKeySpec` class. This class implements the `SecretKey` interface. You can create it from an array of bytes using one of the two constructors:

public SecretKeySpec(byte[] key, String algorithm)
> This constructor creates a `SecretKeySpec` using the supplied byte array. The key will have the supplied algorithm.

public SecretKeySpec(byte[] key, int offset, int len, String algorithm)
> This constructor creates a `SecretKeySpec` using `len` bytes of the supplied byte array, starting at `offset`. The key will have the supplied algorithm.

This class is useful for creating keys for `Macs`, as I demonstrate in Chapter 6. For example, the following code creates a MAC key from an array of random data:

```
SecureRandom sr = new SecureRandom();
byte[] keyBytes = new byte[20];
sr.nextBytes(keyBytes);
SecretKey key = new SecretKeySpec(keyBytes, "HmacSHA1");
```

If you need to do more complicated translations between `SecretKeys` and other key representations, use the `SecretKeyFactory` class instead.

SecretKeyFactory

You can create a `SecretKeyFactory` using one of its `getInstance()` methods:

public static final SecretKeyFactory getInstance(String algorithm) throws NoSuchAlgorithmException
> Use this method to create a new `SecretKeyFactory` for the given algorithm. The algorithm name should correspond to a symmetric cipher algorithm name, for example, "DES."

public static final SecretKeyFactory getInstance(String algorithm, String provider) throws NoSuchAlgorithmException, NoSuchProviderException
> This method creates a new `SecretKeyFactory`, using the implementation supplied by the named provider.

Having obtained a `SecretKeyFactory`, you are free to translate keys. `SecretKeyFactory` knows how to translate between `javax.crypto.SecretKey` objects and `javax.crypto.spec.KeySpec` objects. `KeySpec` is a lot like `AlgorithmParameterSpec`; it's an interface that defines no methods and no constants. Just think of it as a box that holds key data. For example, the JCE comes with a class that represents

DES key data as a byte array, `javax.crypto.spec.DESKeySpec`. You can create a KeySpec that represents DES key data as follows:

```
// obtain key data in keyBytes
KeySpec spec = new DESKeySpec(keyBytes);
```

From things to keys

To translate a `KeySpec` into a `SecretKey`, use `SecretKeyFactory`'s `generate-Secret()` method:

public final SecretKey generateSecret(KeySpec keySpec) throws InvalidKeySpecException
> This method uses the key information in `keySpec` to create a `SecretKey`. If the `KeySpec` is not recognized, an exception is thrown.

A simple method to create a DES key from an array of bytes looks like this:

```
public SecretKey makeDESKey(byte[] input, int offset)
    throws NoSuchAlgorithmException, InvalidKeyException,
    InvalidKeySpecException {
  SecretKeyFactory desFactory = SecretKeyFactory.getInstance("DES");
  KeySpec spec = new DESKeySpec(input, offset);
  return desFactory.generateSecret(spec);
}
```

There are three simple steps in the `makeDESKey()` method:

1. Obtain a key factory for DES keys using `SecretKeyFactory.getInstance()`.

2. Create a `KeySpec` representing DES key data from the supplied byte array.

3. Create a `SecretKey` from the `KeySpec` using `generateSecret()`.

Where do all those exceptions come from? The `getInstance()` method may throw a `NoSuchAlgorithmException`. If the byte array passed to `DESKeySpec`'s constructor is not the right length, it will throw an `InvalidKeyException`. And finally, the `generateSecret()` method will throw an `InvalidKeySpecException` if it doesn't recognize the `KeySpec` type it receives.

From keys to things

`SecretKeyFactory` also knows how to create a `KeySpec` from a `SecretKey`:

public final KeySpec getKeySpec(SecretKey key, Class keySpec) throws
InvalidKeySpecException
> This method creates a `KeySpec` from the given `SecretKey`. The `keySpec` parameter determines the type of object returned by this method. If the `SecretKeyFactory` doesn't recognize the requested class represented by `keySpec`, or if the `SecretKey` itself is not recognized, this method throws an `InvalidKeySpecException`.

For example, the following method shows how to translate a DES key into an array
of bytes:

```
public byte[] makeBytesFromDESKey(SecretKey key)
    throws NoSuchAlgorithmException, InvalidKeySpecException {
  SecretKeyFactory desFactory = SecretKeyFactory.getInstance("DES");
  DESKeySpec spec =
      (DESKeySpec)desFactory.getKeySpec(key, DESKeySpec.class);
  return spec.getKey();
}
```

This time we use getKeySpec() to create a DESKeySpec from the supplied
SecretKey. We request that the returned object be a DESKeySpec by passing
DESKeySpec.class to getKeySpec(). If the key factory doesn't know how to
create this kind of KeySpec, or if it doesn't recognize the SecretKey we passed it,
an exception is thrown.

KeyFactory

java.security.KeyFactory is a lot like SecretKeyFactory, except that it deals
with public and private keys instead of secret keys. As usual, you obtain a KeyFactory using one of its getInstance() methods:

public static final KeyFactory getInstance(String algorithm) throws
NoSuchAlgorithmException

> Use this method to create a new KeyFactory for the given algorithm. The
> algorithm name should be an asymmetric cipher algorithm name or a signa-
> ture algorithm name, like "DSA."

public static final KeyFactory getInstance(String algorithm, String provider) throws
NoSuchAlgorithmException, NoSuchProviderException

> This method creates a new KeyFactory, using the implementation supplied
> by the named provider.

To convert from a KeySpec to a PublicKey or a PrivateKey, use the generate-
Public() and generatePrivate() methods:

public final PublicKey generatePublic(KeySpec keySpec) throws InvalidKeySpecException

> Use this method to create a PublicKey from the supplied KeySpec. If the
> KeySpec is not recognized by this KeyFactory, an exception is thrown.

public final PrivateKey generatePrivate(KeySpec keySpec) throws InvalidKeySpecException

> Use this method to create a PrivateKey from the supplied KeySpec.

KeyFactory has a getKeySpec() method that handles both public and private
keys:

public final KeySpec getKeySpec(Key key, Class keySpec) throws InvalidKeySpecException
This method creates a KeySpec from the given Key. The object returned will be an instance of the supplied keySpec class. If the KeyFactory doesn't recognize the given key or the requested return type, an exception is thrown.

Key Agreement

A *key agreement* is a protocol whereby two or more parties can agree on a secret value. The neat thing about key agreements is that they can agree on a secret value even while talking on an insecure medium (like the Internet). These protocols are called key agreement protocols because they are most often used to settle on a session key that will be used to encrypt a conversation.

Diffie-Hellman

The most famous key agreement protocol is Diffie-Hellman (DH). Diffie-Hellman was originally published in 1976, in a paper that is widely considered to be the genesis of public key cryptography. In this section, I'll explain the mathematics behind the algorithm. In the next section, I'll show how the javax.crypto .KeyAgreement class encapsulates key agreement algorithms like Diffie-Hellman. Here's how it works, mathematically, for a hypothetical exchange between Maid Marian and Robin Hood:

1. First, some central authority chooses a *base*, g, and a *modulus*, p, such that g is *primitive* mod p. This means that for every value, b, from 1 to p −1, there is some value, a, that satisfies g^a mod p = b. The base and modulus values are used by a group of users, or perhaps as part of another standard. At any rate, they may be freely published; knowing them won't do an attacker much good. Both Marian and Robin know g and p.

2. Marian randomly chooses a value, x, and computes y = g^x mod p. We'll call these values x_m and y_m, because they belong to Marian.

3. Robin randomly chooses an x and calculates a y. We'll call these values x_r and y_r.

4. Marian sends Robin y_m. Robin, in turn, sends Marian y_r. These values may be transmitted over an insecure channel, but they cannot be used to authenticate either Robin or Marian.

5. Marian calculates $k_m = y_r^{x_m}$ mod p, which is the same as $g^{x_r x_m}$ mod p.

6. Robin calculates $k_r = y_m^{x_r}$ mod p, which is equal to $g^{x_m x_r}$ mod p. This is the same as k_m.

And presto! Marian and Robin have calculated the same secret value, k, without exchanging it directly. They don't even have to know anything about each other, except to be using the same values for g and p. But note that Robin and Marian can't authenticate each other using this protocol. All they really know is that someone at the other end of the wire knows how to use Diffie-Hellman. What they do with the secret value is up to them. Usually, it's used to construct a session key to encrypt a subsequent conversation.

Diffie-Hellman can easily be expanded to include three or more participants. Let's step through an exchange between Maid Marian, Robin Hood, and Will Scarlet. Imagine them sitting around a card table; it will help you visualize the flow of information:

1. As before, some central authority picks values for g and p. All three parties will use the same values of g and p.

2. Each party randomly chooses an x and calculates a y from it.

3. Each person passes his or her y value to the person sitting to his or her right. Marian gives y_m to Robin, Robin gives y_r to Will, and Will passes y_w to Marian.

4. Now, each person calculates another y value using his or her x value. Marian calculates $y_{mw} = y_w^{x_m} \bmod p$, Robin calculates $y_{rm} = y_m^{x_r} \bmod p$, and Will calculates $y_{wr} = y_r^{x_w} \bmod p$.

5. Each person passes his or her freshly calculated y value to the right. Marian gives y_{mw} to Robin, Robin gives y_{rm} to Will, and Will gives y_{wr} to Marian.

6. Now the participants calculate the secret value. Marian calculates $k_m = y_{wr}^{x_m} \bmod p$, Robin calculates $k_r = y_{mw}^{x_r} \bmod p$, and Will calculates $k_w = y_{rm}^{x_w} \bmod p$. If you do the substitutions, you'll see that all of these quantities are equal to $g^{x_m x_r x_w} \bmod p$.

If there are n participants, n − 1 exchanges of information are required before the secret value can be calculated.

javax.crypto.KeyAgreement

In JCE 1.2, `javax.crypto.KeyAgreement` encapsulates key agreement protocols. The SunJCE provider includes a `KeyAgreement` implementation based on Diffie-Hellman. In this implementation, x and y are treated as the private and public keys (respectively) in a key pair. You can supply g and p as parameters to the Diffie-Hellman `KeyPairGenerator`.

To obtain a `KeyAgreement` object, use one of the `getInstance()` methods:

public static final KeyAgreement getInstance(String algorithm) throws NoSuchAlgorithmException

This method creates a new `KeyAgreement` for the given algorithm. The name should be a key agreement name, like "DH" for Diffie-Hellman.

public static final KeyAgreement getInstance(String algorithm, String provider) throws NoSuchAlgorithmException, NoSuchProviderException

This method creates a new `KeyAgreement`, using the implementation supplied by the named provider.

`KeyAgreements` are initialized with a private key, which is used to calculate the secret value. In addition, you can initialize a `KeyAgreement` with a source of randomness, a set of algorithm-specific parameters, or both:

public final void init(Key key) throws InvalidKeyException

This method initializes the `KeyAgreement` using the supplied key. An exception is thrown if the key is not the right type.

public final void init(Key key, SecureRandom random) throws InvalidKeyException

This method initializes the `KeyAgreement` with the supplied key and `SecureRandom`.

public final void init(Key key, AlgorithmParameterSpec params) throws InvalidKeyException, InvalidAlgorithmParameterException

This method initializes the `KeyAgreement` with the given key and algorithm-specific parameters.

public final void init(Key key, AlgorithmParameterSpec params, SecureRandom random) throws InvalidKeyException, InvalidAlgorithmParameterException

This is the `init()` that does it all. Use this method to initialize the `KeyAgreement` with the given key, algorithm-specific parameters, and source of randomness.

A key agreement protocol passes through distinct phases. In Diffie-Hellman, for example, a key pair (x and y) is first created. The private key is used to initialize the `KeyAgreement`; it is used to calculate the secret value. The private key is also used to calculate the intermediate y values for Diffie-Hellman with three or more parties. All the y values are treated as public keys. These are passed to the `doPhase()` method along with a flag that indicates if the last phase has been reached. In Diffie-Hellman with more than two parties, the `doPhase()` method returns a new `Key` representing an intermediate y value. If you think of everyone sitting around a table, you receive intermediate y values (public keys) from your left, perform a calculation on these values (`doPhase()`), and pass the new y values (public keys) to your right:

public final Key doPhase(Key key, boolean lastPhase) throws InvalidKeyException, IllegalStateException

This method executes a phase of the key agreement protocol, using the supplied key. If appropriate, the result of the phase is returned as another key. In Diffie-Hellman with three or more parties, the intermediate key values are returned as public keys. The `lastPhase` parameter indicates whether the final phase of the key agreement is being performed.

When all phases of the key agreement protocol have been performed using `doPhase()`, the secret value can be calculated. You can retrieve this value using `generateSecret()`:

public final byte[] generateSecret() throws IllegalStateException

> This method returns the secret value of the key agreement protocol as a byte array. If the `KeyAgreement` has not executed all its phases, an `Illegal-StateException` is thrown.

public final int generateSecret(byte[] sharedSecret, int offset) throws IllegalStateException, ShortBufferException

> This method writes the secret value of the key agreement protocol into the supplied array, starting at `offset`. If the array is not long enough, a `Short-BufferException` is thrown. The number of bytes written is returned.

public final SecretKey generateSecret(String algorithm) throws InvalidKeyException, IllegalStateException, NoSuchAlgorithmException

> This method returns the secret value of the key agreement as a `SecretKey` with the given algorithm. If the requested key algorithm is not available, a `NoSuchAlgorithmException` is thrown.

SKIP

As I said, the base and modulus used in Diffie-Hellman may be dictated by a standard. One such standard is Simple Key Management for Internet Protocols (SKIP).[*] SKIP uses Diffie-Hellman so that Internet hosts can agree on a session key that will be used to encrypt each data packet that is sent between them. It can be used in firewalls, to secure communications on a local network, or to create a *Virtual Private Network* (VPN). In this section, I'll demonstrate how to use Java's `KeyAgreement` class to agree on a secret value using the SKIP Diffie-Hellman base and modulus.[†] SKIP defines base and modulus values for three different sizes of Diffie-Hellman keys. We'll use the 1024-bit base and modulus.

First, let's create a class that contains the Diffie-Hellman base and modulus values that SKIP defines. Don't take my word for it: You can check these values at *http://skip.incog.com/spec/numbers.html*. In the `Skip` class, I first define a string that

---

[*] See *http://skip.incog.com/*.

[†] Note that these examples do not provide an authenticated connection; they are still vulnerable to a man-in-the-middle attack. The examples presented here demonstrate how to use Diffie-Hellman to agree on a secret value. Creating an authenticated, confidential communications channel requires a more complicated protocol. You could, for example, use cryptographic signatures to authenticate each party. The secret value could be used as a DES session key to encrypt subsequent communications.

represents the modulus value in hexadecimal. Then I create a `BigInteger` from it and another `BigInteger` representing the base. Finally, the base and modulus are placed in a `DHParameterSpec` object that I will use later when I generate Diffie-Hellman key pairs.

```java
import java.math.BigInteger;

import javax.crypto.spec.*;

public class Skip {
  // SKIP's 1024 DH parameters
  private static final String skip1024String =
      "F488FD584E49DBCD20B49DE49107366B336C380D451D0F7C88B31C7C5B2D8EF6" +
      "F3C923C043F0A55B188D8EBB558CB85D38D334FD7C175743A31D186CDE33212C" +
      "B52AFF3CE1B1294018118D7C84A70A72D686C40319C807297ACA950CD9969FAB" +
      "D00A509B0246D3083D66A45D419F9C7CBD894B221926BAABA25EC355E92F78C7";

  // Modulus
  private static final BigInteger skip1024Modulus = new BigInteger
      (skip1024String, 16);

  // Base
  private static final BigInteger skip1024Base = BigInteger.valueOf(2);

  public static final DHParameterSpec sDHParameterSpec =
      new DHParameterSpec(skip1024Modulus, skip1024Base);
}
```

SkipServer

This example takes the form of a client/server application. The client connects to the server and sends its Diffie-Hellman public key. The server sends the client its own public key. Then the client and server calculate the secret values and print them out. If everything works, the values are the same. Let's start with the server.

```java
import java.io.*;
import java.net.*;
import java.security.*;
import java.security.spec.*;

import javax.crypto.*;
import javax.crypto.spec.*;

import Skip;

public class SkipServer {
  public static void main(String[] args) throws Exception {
    int port = Integer.parseInt(args[0]);
```

We begin by creating a Diffie-Hellman key pair, using the SKIP parameters.

```
// Create a Diffie-Hellman key pair.
KeyPairGenerator kpg = KeyPairGenerator.getInstance("DH");
kpg.initialize(Skip.sDHParameterSpec);
KeyPair keyPair = kpg.genKeyPair();
```

Then we wait for a network connection. You can specify the port number to listen on in the command line.

```
// Wait for a connection.
ServerSocket ss = new ServerSocket(port);
System.out.println("Listening on port " + port + "...");
Socket s = ss.accept();
DataOutputStream out = new DataOutputStream(s.getOutputStream());
DataInputStream in = new DataInputStream(s.getInputStream());
```

First, the client will send us an encoded Diffie-Hellman public key as an array of bytes. A KeyFactory is used to reconstruct the key.

```
// Receive a public key.
byte[] keyBytes = new byte[in.readInt()];
in.readFully(keyBytes);
KeyFactory kf = KeyFactory.getInstance("DH");
X509EncodedKeySpec x509Spec = new X509EncodedKeySpec(keyBytes);
PublicKey theirPublicKey = kf.generatePublic(x509Spec);
```

Then we send our public key to the client.

```
// Send the public key.
keyBytes = keyPair.getPublic().getEncoded();
out.writeInt(keyBytes.length);
out.write(keyBytes);
```

Now we can calculate the secret value, using our private key and the client's public key. The secret value is as long as the modulus used to generate the Diffie-Hellman keys. In this case, the secret value is 1024 bits long.

```
// Generate the secret value.
KeyAgreement ka = KeyAgreement.getInstance("DH");
ka.init(keyPair.getPrivate());
ka.doPhase(theirPublicKey, true);
byte[] secret = ka.generateSecret();

// Clean up.
out.close();
in.close();
```

Finally, we print out the secret value in base64. (If you didn't type in the oreilly.jonathan.util.Base64 class yet, you can find it in Appendix B, *Base64*.)

```
// Print out the secret value
System.out.println(oreilly.jonathan.util.Base64.encode(secret));
```

```
    }
  }
```

You can run `SkipServer` by telling it what port to use. After it initializes itself, it will print a message indicating it's ready to receive a connection:

```
C:\ java SkipServer 7999
Listening on port 7999...
```

SkipClient

The client is very similar to the server. It begins by generating a Diffie-Hellman key pair.

```
import java.io.*;
import java.net.*;
import java.security.*;
import java.security.spec.*;

import javax.crypto.*;
import javax.crypto.spec.*;

import Skip;

public class SkipClient {
  public static void main(String[] args) throws Exception {
    String host = args[0];
    int port = Integer.parseInt(args[1]);

    // Create a Diffie-Hellman key pair.
    KeyPairGenerator kpg = KeyPairGenerator.getInstance("DH");
    kpg.initialize(Skip.sDHParameterSpec);
    KeyPair keyPair = kpg.genKeyPair();
```

Then we connect to the server, using the host and port number specified on the command line.

```
    // Open the network connection.
    Socket s = new Socket(host, port);
    DataOutputStream out = new DataOutputStream(s.getOutputStream());
    DataInputStream in = new DataInputStream(s.getInputStream());
```

In `SkipServer`, we waited for a public key and then sent our own. In the client, the process is reversed.

```
    // Send the public key.
    byte[] keyBytes = keyPair.getPublic().getEncoded();
    out.writeInt(keyBytes.length);
    out.write(keyBytes);
```

```
// Receive a public key.
keyBytes = new byte[in.readInt()];
in.readFully(keyBytes);
KeyFactory kf = KeyFactory.getInstance("DH");
X509EncodedKeySpec x509Spec = new X509EncodedKeySpec(keyBytes);
PublicKey theirPublicKey = kf.generatePublic(x509Spec);
```

As in the server, we generate the secret value using our private key and the other party's public key.

```
// Generate the secret value.
KeyAgreement ka = KeyAgreement.getInstance("DH");
ka.init(keyPair.getPrivate());
ka.doPhase(theirPublicKey, true);
byte[] secret = ka.generateSecret();

// Clean up.
out.close();
in.close();
```

We end by printing out the secret value. It is exactly the same as the value that the server prints out.

```
// Print out the secret value
System.out.println(oreilly.jonathan.util.Base64.encode(secret));
    }
}
```

You can run `SkipClient` by telling it where the server can be found. In the following example, `SkipClient` connects to the server and prints out the secret value.

```
C:\ java SkipClient 172.16.0.2 7999
uo9Ke+tSyrSN2Q4p9HJ/OVpD7IIWf1PSj1j4D6ZBwgF46bnS9quuKRsVr52FjvdKBe1aAzqxy/e
gVZXpdIyp9nfqw36yfQXThCNt0O0wLyHfhPcC3fuup900PATahi/5B/8+QT7Q1T/KXgFWWup7fs
PnKQdwhIgosJjgrsdreXE=

C:\
```

Skipper: Multiparty key agreement

It's a little tricky to use Diffie-Hellman with three or more parties because of the timing involved. Imagine all the parties sitting around a table. Each party listens for keys coming from the left, performs a phase of the key agreement, and passes the resulting key to the right.

The following example, `Skipper`, listens for connections from the left in a separate thread. `Skipper` needs five pieces of information to run: the number of parties involved, a name, a network port number for incoming connections (from the left), and an address and a port for outgoing connections (to the right).

Skipper's constructor saves this information in member variables and kicks off a separate thread to listen for incoming connections.

```java
import java.io.*;
import java.net.*;
import java.security.*;
import java.security.spec.*;

import javax.crypto.*;
import javax.crypto.spec.*;

public class Skipper
    implements Runnable {
  protected int mCount;
  protected String mName;
  protected int mListenPort;
  protected String mConnectAddress;
  protected int mConnectPort;

  protected DataInputStream mIn;
  protected DataOutputStream mOut;

  public Skipper(int count, String name, int listenPort,
      String connectAddress, int connectPort) throws Exception {
    mCount = count;
    mName = name;
    mListenPort = listenPort;
    mConnectAddress = connectAddress;
    mConnectPort = connectPort;

    // Listen for incoming keys in a separate thread.
    Thread t = new Thread(this);
    t.start();
  }
```

It's in the run() method that Skipper listens for incoming connections.

```java
  public void run() {
    try {
      // Create ServerSocket.
      ServerSocket ss = new ServerSocket(mListenPort);
      // Wait for an incoming connection.
      Socket s = ss.accept();
      mIn = new DataInputStream(s.getInputStream());
    }
    catch (IOException ioe) {
      System.out.println(mName + ": " + ioe.toString());
    }
  }
```

Skipper's `agree()` method contains the bulk of the multiple-party key agreement algorithm. After creating a key pair and a `KeyAgreement` object, this method sends and receives keys until the key agreement is complete. Then it calculates the secret value and prints it out as a base64 string.

```
public void agree() throws Exception {
  // Generate a SKIP key pair.
  KeyPairGenerator kpg = KeyPairGenerator.getInstance("DH");
  kpg.initialize(Skip.sDHParameterSpec);
  KeyPair keyPair = kpg.generateKeyPair();

  // Create the KeyAgreement.
  KeyAgreement ka = KeyAgreement.getInstance("DH");
  ka.init(keyPair.getPrivate());

  waitForOutput();

  PublicKey publicKey = keyPair.getPublic();
  // For each party...
  for (int i = 1; i < mCount; i++) {
    // Send the current public key.
    byte[] keyBytes = publicKey.getEncoded();
    mOut.writeInt(keyBytes.length);
    mOut.write(keyBytes);
    mOut.flush();
    // Receive a public key.
    waitForInput();
    keyBytes = new byte[mIn.readInt()];
    mIn.readFully(keyBytes);
    KeyFactory kf = KeyFactory.getInstance("DH");
    X509EncodedKeySpec x509Spec = new X509EncodedKeySpec(keyBytes);
    publicKey = kf.generatePublic(x509Spec);
    // Do a key agreement phase.
    Key resultKey = ka.doPhase(publicKey, i == (mCount - 1));
    if (resultKey instanceof PublicKey)
      publicKey = (PublicKey)resultKey;
  }
  // Clean up.
  mOut.close();
  mIn.close();
  // Calculate the secret value.
  byte[] secretValue = ka.generateSecret();
  System.out.print(mName + ": Secret value = ");
  System.out.println(
      oreilly.jonathan.util.Base64.encode(secretValue));
}
```

The `waitForOutput()` and `waitForInput` methods are utility methods that wait for the outgoing and incoming connections to be established.

```
protected void waitForOutput() throws IOException {
  boolean connected = false;
  while (connected == false) {
    try {
      // Connect to the next party.
      Socket s = new Socket(mConnectAddress, mConnectPort);
      mOut = new DataOutputStream(s.getOutputStream());
      connected = true;
    }
    catch (ConnectException ce) {
      try { Thread.sleep(1000); }
      catch (InterruptedException ie) {}
      System.out.println(mName + ": couldn't connect, retrying...");
    }
  }
}

protected void waitForInput() throws IOException {
  while (mIn == null) {
    try { Thread.sleep(1000); }
    catch (InterruptedException ie) {}
    System.out.println(mName +
      ": no incoming connection, waiting...");
  }
}
```

Finally, `Skipper`'s `main()` method accepts parameters from the command line and constructs a `Skipper` instance from them.

```
public static void main(String[] args) throws Exception {
  if (args.length != 5) {
    System.out.println("Usage: Skipper count name listenPort " +
        "connectAddress connectPort");
    return;
  }
  int count = Integer.parseInt(args[0]);
  String name = args[1];
  int listenPort = Integer.parseInt(args[2]);
  String connectAddress = args[3];
  int connectPort = Integer.parseInt(args[4]);
  Skipper skipper = new Skipper(count, name, listenPort,
      connectAddress, connectPort);
  skipper.agree();
}
```

You can test this program by starting up different Skipper instances in different command line windows. For example, to test a three party key agreement on a single machine, I used the following command lines:

```
C:\ java Skipper 3 Marian 801 localhost 802
C:\ java Skipper 3 Robin 802 localhost 803
C:\ java Skipper 3 Will 803 localhost 801
```

The Identity Key Management Paradigm

JDK 1.1's solution to the thorny problem of key management is a set of classes clustered around java.security.Identity. The javakey command-line utility is based on java.security.IdentityScope, a subclass of Identity. You can read about javakey in Appendix D, *Javakey*. In JDK 1.2, identity-based key management is replaced by keystore-based key management, which we'll discuss later in this chapter. javakey is replaced by keytool, which we'll also be discussing later. Both approaches have their merits, and I'll cover each of them in this chapter.

JDK 1.1's approach to key management centers around the Identity class, which represents something that possesses a public key. An IdentityScope represents a group of Identity objects. IdentityScopes can contain other, nested Identity-Scopes. Finally, an extension of Identity, java.security.Signer, is an Identity that also possesses a private key. Figure 5-1 shows an example. The large IdentityScope (Marian's computer) contains a Signer, Marian, and an Identity, Sheriff. It also contains another IdentityScope, Merry Men. This IdentityScope contains three Identity objects, one each for Will, Tuck, and Robin. Each Identity contains a PublicKey and other relevant information (name, address, phone number, etc.). Each Signer contains a matched PublicKey and PrivateKey and other useful information.

Key Holders

Keys usually belong to something—a person, a group of people, a company, a computer, a thread of execution, or almost anything else. In the JDK, the java.security.Identity class represents something that possesses a key.

Principal

Identity implements the java.security.Principal interface. A principal is simply something with a name:

public abstract String getName()

This method returns the Principal's name.

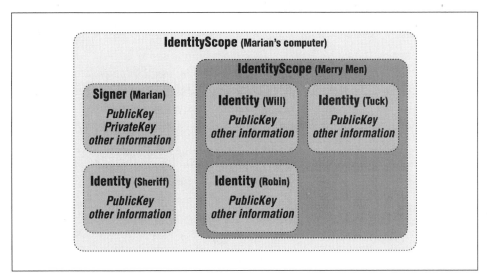

Figure 5-1: Identity-based key management

The `Principal` interface is used throughout the `java.security.acl` package. Because it implements the `Principal` interface, the `Identity` class serves as a bridge between the access control constructs of `java.security.acl` and the key management concepts of `java.security`. For more information on access control, see O'Reilly's book, *Java Security.*

Identity

An `Identity` represents a person, an organization, or anything else that has an associated public key. In other words, an `Identity` is a `Principal` with a public key. It's useful for holding information about other people, like an entry in an address book. An `Identity` has a name, and as you'll see, can also have a *scope*. A scope is a way of grouping identities so that no two identities in a scope have the same name or public key. I'll talk more about scope later. `Identity`'s two constructors allow you to specify a name and, optionally, a scope:

public Identity(String name)
>   This constructor creates an unscoped identity.

public Identity(String name, IdentityScope scope) throws KeyManagementException
>   This constructor creates an identity in the given scope. No two identities in the same scope can have the same name. If you try to create a new `Identity` with the same name as one that exists in `scope`, a `KeyManagementException` is thrown.

A set of methods allows manipulation of the identity's public key:

public PublicKey getPublicKey()

> This method returns the identity's public key.

public void setPublicKey(PublicKey key) throws KeyManagementException

> This method sets the identity's public key. No two identities in the same scope can have the same public key. If you try to use this method to set the public key of an `Identity` to a nonunique value, an exception is thrown.

Let's say you wanted to examine an identity's public key. You could print the key's algorithm and format like this:

```
public void printKey(Identity i) {
  PublicKey k = i.getPublicKey();
  System.out.println("  Public key uses " + k.getAlgorithm() +
      " and is encoded with " + k.getFormat() + ".");
}
```

`Identity` also has methods for managing certificates. An `Identity` can hold a list of certificates that vouch for the authenticity of its public key. This is akin to a real person carrying around several forms of identification. You can manage an `Identity`'s certificate list with a trio of methods:[*]

public void addCertificate(Certificate certificate) throws KeyManagementException

> You can add a certificate to the `Identity`'s certificate list using this method. If the `Identity` has no public key, its public key is set using the key contained by the given certificate. If the `Identity` already has a public key defined, it must be the same as the key in the certificate; otherwise, an exception is thrown.

public void removeCertificate(Certificate certificate) throws KeyManagementException

> This method removes the given certificate from this `Identity`. It throws an exception if the given certificate is not in this `Identity`'s certificate list.

public Certificate[] getCertificates()

> This method returns an array containing the certificate list.

`Identity`, useful as it seems, is defined as an abstract class and may not be instantiated directly. It has no abstract methods, however, so it's trivial to create a concrete subclass:

```
import java.security.*;

public class ConcreteIdentity extends Identity {
```

---

[*] As we'll see in Chapter 6, there are actually two kinds of certificates, which makes life very confusing. The `java.security.Certificate` interface was introduced in JDK 1.1 and is now deprecated. In JDK 1.2, `java.security.cert.Certificate` is the official certificate class. The certificate management methods I present here for `Identity` correspond to the new certificate class. Although `Identity` has methods that use the old certificate interface, they are deprecated.

```
        public ConcreteIdentity(String name) { super(name); }
    }
```

I'll use this technique later in this chapter, in the section on KeyManager.

Signer

java.security.Signer is a subclass of Identity that adds support for private key management. Two additional methods are defined:

public PrivateKey getPrivateKey()
> This method returns the signer's private key.

public final void setKeyPair(KeyPair pair) throws InvalidParameterException, KeyException
> This method sets the signer's public and private keys. If something goes wrong, an exception is thrown. This method is provided instead of a setPrivateKey() because public and private keys always come in pairs.

IdentityScope

Identities can have a *scope*. The identity of Marian, for example, might have the scope of the Royal Castle. There might be a different Marian identity within the scope of the Village, with a different set of keys and certificates. An Identity-Scope represents this concept in the Security API. An IdentityScope has a name and contains Identity objects. In a tricky twist of object-oriented design, IdentityScope actually descends from Identity.[*] This means that scopes can be nested; one IdentityScope can contain another. No two identities in a given scope can have the same public key or name.

JDK 1.1 comes with a command line tool, javakey, that manages a special Identi-tyScope, the *system scope*. The class used as the system scope is determined by the system.scope property in the *lib/security/java.security* file found in the JDK installation directory. The default class is sun.security.provider.IdentityDatabase, which is a subclass of IdentityScope. It is this class that knows how to serialize itself to and from the *identitydb.obj* file. All identities that are managed by javakey live in the flat namespace of the system scope. Appendix D has more information on using javakey.

In JDK 1.2, javakey has disappeared in a puff of smoke. It is replaced by two new utilities, keytool and jarsigner. I'll talk about keytool later in this chapter in the section on keystore-based key management. jarsigner will be discussed in Chapter 8, *Signed Applets*. Even though javakey is gone in JDK 1.2, however, the Identity and IdentityScope classes still exist. In JDK 1.1, you can access the

---

[*] Actually, this is a standard design pattern, but if you haven't seen it before, it takes a while to get used to it.

system scope using the `getSystemScope()` static method in the `IdentityScope` class. In JDK 1.2, this method returns `null`.

If you're still running JDK 1.1, here's a simple program that prints out the algorithm and encoding of the public key of the identity named on the command line. It pulls information about the named identity from the system identity scope.

```
import java.security.*;
import java.util.*;

public class ShowKey {
  public static void main(String[] args) {
    if (args.length < 1) {
      System.out.println("Usage: ShowKey name");
      return;
    }

    IdentityScope systemScope = IdentityScope.getSystemScope();
    Identity i = systemScope.getIdentity(args[0]);
    Key k = i.getPublicKey();
    if (k != null) {
      System.out.println("  Public key uses " + k.getAlgorithm() +
          " and is encoded by " + k.getFormat() + ".");
    }
  }
}
```

In this example, we use `getIdentity()` to retrieve an `Identity` from the system scope. `IdentityScope` defines a complete set of `Identity`-manipulating methods:

public abstract void addIdentity(Identity identity) throws KeyManagementException
> This method adds the given `Identity` to this scope. If the `Identity`'s name or public key is already used in this scope, an exception is thrown.

public abstract void removeIdentity(Identity identity) throws KeyManagementException
> Use this method to remove the given `Identity` from this scope. If the identity does not exist in this scope, an exception is thrown.

public abstract int size()
> Use this method to get the number of identities within this scope.

public abstract Enumeration identites()
> This method returns an `Enumeration` of the identities within this scope.

public abstract Identity getIdentity(String name)
> This method returns the named `Identity` or `null` if it is not contained in this scope.

public abstract Identity getIdentity(PublicKey key)
> This method returns the `Identity` with the given public key or `null` if it is not contained in this scope.

public Identity getIdentity(Principal principal)
>   This method returns the `Identity` with the same name as the given `Principal` or `null` if it is not contained in this scope.

Because an `IdentityScope` is an `Identity`, it can belong to another scope. Furthermore, it can have a public key and certificates. Is this useful? Perhaps. For example, you might create an `IdentityScope` that represented an entire company. Each employee of the company would be represented by an `Identity` inside the company `IdentityScope`. But the company itself has an identity; it might make sense that it would have a public key, too, especially if the company sells software that is cryptographically signed. A logical place to store the public key for the company would be in the company's `IdentityScope`.

Note that an `IdentityScope` cannot be a `Signer` because both classes descend from `Identity`.

KeyManager

In this section, I'll develop a class to manage keys and identities. It encapsulates the following information:

*   A public and private key pair
*   A list of identities

Essentially, `KeyManager` is an `IdentityScope` with a private key. Internally, it uses a `Hashtable` to keep track of its contained identities. Additionally, the `KeyManager` class knows how to save and load itself from a file. I'll use this class in Chapter 10, for the `SafeTalk` application, and in Chapter 11, for the `CipherMail` application.

JDK 1.2 includes a more full-featured key management class, `java.security.KeyStore`, which I'll talk about a little later. The `KeyManager` class I'll develop here is similar to `KeyStore`, but it doesn't include any support for certificates. Although this limits its usefulness, it also makes `KeyManager` a simpler class.

To make `KeyManager` a generally useful tool, I've included a command-line interface for managing keys and identities. You can create a new `KeyManager` file, import and export keys, remove identities, and list the contents of the `KeyManager` file:

`java KeyManager -c` *keyfile signer algorithm strength*
>   The `-c` option creates a new `KeyManager` instance and saves it in a file named *keyfile*. It generates a new key pair using the given *algorithm* and *strength* and assigns the key pair to the named *signer*.

java KeyManager -e *keyfile idname outfile*

> The -e option exports a public key. First, a KeyManager instance is created from the given file, *keyfile*. Then the public key belonging to *idname* is exported to the given file, *outfile*.

java KeyManager -i *keyfile infile*

> The -i option imports a public key from the given file, *infile*. The key and its owner's name are added to the KeyManager contained in *keyfile*.

java KeyManager -r *keyfile idname*

> The -r option removes the named identity, *idname*, from the KeyManager contained in *keyfile*.

java KeyManager -l *keyfile*

> The -l option lists the contents of the KeyManager contained in *keyfile*.

The class itself is not complicated. As I said, it's basically an IdentityScope with a private key, and thus KeyManager descends from IdentityScope. Most of the class deals with implementing the methods of IdentityScope and the KeyManager command-line interface. Member variables are used to keep track of the KeyManager's identities (using a Hashtable) and the private key.

```
package oreilly.jonathan.security;

import java.io.*;
import java.security.*;
import java.text.NumberFormat;
import java.util.*;

public class KeyManager
    extends IdentityScope {
  protected PrivateKey mPrivateKey;
  protected Hashtable mIdentities;
```

KeyManager saves itself to a file using object serialization. It doesn't make much sense, however, to save the name of the file as part of the KeyManager. Thus, the variable representing the filename, mKeyFile, is marked transient so it doesn't get serialized along with the rest of the KeyManager's data.

```
  protected transient String mKeyFile;
```

KeyManager's only constructor is protected. Later on, I'll develop a static method, getInstance(), to create KeyManager instances from files. KeyManagers are created with a name and a key pair that belongs to the name.

```
  protected KeyManager(String name, KeyPair pair) {
    super(name);
    try { setPublicKey(pair.getPublic()); }
    catch (KeyManagementException kme) {}
    mPrivateKey = pair.getPrivate();
```

```
    mIdentities = new Hashtable();
}
```

The next six methods are implementations of abstract `IdentityScope` methods. They use the internal `Hashtable` to manage the list of identities.

```
public int size() { return mIdentities.size(); }
public Enumeration identities() { return mIdentities.elements(); }

public synchronized Identity getIdentity(String name) {
  Enumeration e = mIdentities.elements();
  while (e.hasMoreElements()) {
    Identity i = (Identity)e.nextElement();
    if (i.getName().equals(name))
      return i;
  }
  return null;
}

public Identity getIdentity(PublicKey key) {
  return (Identity)mIdentities.get(key);
}

public synchronized void addIdentity(Identity identity)
    throws KeyManagementException {
  if (mIdentities.contains(identity))
    throw new KeyManagementException("This KeyManager already contains "
        + identity.getName() + ".");
  if (mIdentities.containsKey(identity.getPublicKey()))
    throw new KeyManagementException("This KeyManager already contains "
        + identity.getName() + "'s key.");
  mIdentities.put(identity.getPublicKey(), identity);
}

public synchronized void removeIdentity(Identity identity)
    throws KeyManagementException {
  PublicKey key = identity.getPublicKey();
  if (mIdentities.containsKey(key))
    mIdentities.remove(key);
  else
    throw new KeyManagementException("This KeyManager does not contain "
        + identity.getName() + ".");
}
```

As a convenience, `KeyManager` will return the public key corresponding to a given name, even if the name is the name of the whole `KeyManager`.

```
public synchronized PublicKey getPublicKey(String name) {
  if (name.equals(getName()))
    return getPublicKey();
```

```
      return getIdentity(name).getPublicKey();
}
```

The private key can be retrieved using getPrivateKey().

```
      public PrivateKey getPrivateKey() { return mPrivateKey; }
```

KeyManager includes an overloaded version of addIdentity() that accepts a name and a public key. It creates a KeyManagerIdentity and adds it to the KeyManager. KeyManagerIdentity is a private inner class, a concrete subclass of Identity, which is abstract. I'll come to it in a little while.

```
      public void addIdentity(String name, PublicKey key)
          throws KeyManagementException {
        Identity i = new KeyManagerIdentity(name);
        i.setPublicKey(key);
        addIdentity(i);
      }
```

The getInstance() static method is used to obtain a KeyManager from a file. It attempts to deserialize a KeyManager from the given file. If it is successful, it sets the mKeyFile member variable so that the KeyManager will know how to save itself (see save() later in this section).

```
      public static KeyManager getInstance(String file)
          throws IOException, ClassNotFoundException {
        ObjectInputStream in = new ObjectInputStream(
            new FileInputStream(file));
        KeyManager km = (KeyManager)in.readObject();
        in.close();
        km.mKeyFile = file;
        return km;
      }
```

Brand-new KeyManagers must be created with a name and a key pair. The static method create() takes care of this by calling the protected KeyManager constructor. Like getInstance(), create() sets the mKeyFile variable.

```
      public static KeyManager create(String file, String name, KeyPair pair) {
        KeyManager km = new KeyManager(name, pair);
        km.mKeyFile = file;
        return km;
      }
```

The save() method simply attempts to serialize the KeyManager to the file named by mKeyFile.

```
      public synchronized void save() {
        try {
          ObjectOutputStream out = new ObjectOutputStream(
              new FileOutputStream(mKeyFile));
          out.writeObject(this);
```

```
        out.close();
      }
      catch (Exception e) {
        System.out.println("KeyManager.save: " + e.toString());
      }
    }
```

The `KeyManagerIdentity` inner class is used in `addIdentity()`, shown previously. It subclasses the abstract `Identity` class and provides a single constructor that accepts a name.

```
    private static class KeyManagerIdentity
        extends Identity {
      public KeyManagerIdentity(String name) { super(name); }
    }
```

The `main()` method in `KeyManager` implements the command-line interface.

```
    public static void main(String[] args) throws Exception {
      if (args.length < 2) {
        usage();
        return;
      }
      String option = args[0];
      String keyfile = args[1];
```

The `-c` option creates a new `KeyManager` file. It generates a key pair using the given algorithm and key size and uses `KeyManager`'s `create()` method to create a new `KeyManager` instance. The instance is saved to disk using `save()`.

```
      if (option.indexOf("c") != -1) {
        if (args.length < 5) { usage(); return; }
        String signer = args[2];
        String algorithm = args[3];
        int strength = NumberFormat.getInstance().parse(args[4]).intValue();
        System.out.println("Initializing the KeyPairGenerator...");
        KeyPairGenerator kpg = KeyPairGenerator.getInstance(algorithm);
        kpg.initialize(strength);
        System.out.println("Generating the key pair...");
        KeyPair pair = kpg.genKeyPair();
        KeyManager km = create(keyfile, signer, pair);
        km.save();
        System.out.println("Done.");
      }
```

The `-e` option exports a public key. After constructing a `KeyManager` instance from the given file, the named key is retrieved. Then the identity's name and public key are serialized to the given output file.

```
      else if (option.indexOf("e") != -1) {
        if (args.length < 4) { usage(); return; }
        String idname = args[2];
```

```
    String outfile = args[3];
    KeyManager km = getInstance(keyfile);
    ObjectOutputStream out = new ObjectOutputStream(
        new FileOutputStream(outfile));
    PublicKey key = km.getPublicKey(idname);
    out.writeObject(idname);
    out.writeObject(key);
    out.close();
    System.out.println("Done.");
}
```

Exported keys can be imported using the -i option. A KeyManager is obtained, as before, using getInstance(). Then the input file is deserialized and the name and public key are added to the KeyManager instance.

```
else if (option.indexOf("i") != -1) {
  if (args.length < 3) { usage(); return; }
  String infile = args[2];
  KeyManager km = getInstance(keyfile);
  ObjectInputStream in = new ObjectInputStream(
      new FileInputStream(infile));
  String idname = (String)in.readObject();
  PublicKey key = (PublicKey)in.readObject();
  in.close();
  km.addIdentity(idname, key);
  km.save();
  System.out.println("Done.");
}
```

The -r option is used to remove an identity from a KeyManager.

```
else if (option.indexOf("r") != -1) {
  if (args.length < 3) { usage(); return; }
  String idname = args[2];
  KeyManager km = getInstance(keyfile);
  Identity i = km.getIdentity(idname);
  km.removeIdentity(i);
  km.save();
  System.out.println("Done.");
}
```

Finally, the -l option lists the contents of a KeyManager file.

```
else if (option.indexOf("l") != -1) {
  if (args.length < 2) { usage(); return; }
  KeyManager km = getInstance(keyfile);
  System.out.println("KeyManager contents of " + keyfile + ":");
  System.out.println("  public and private key for " + km.getName());
  Enumeration e = km.identities();
  while (e.hasMoreElements()) {
    Identity i = (Identity)e.nextElement();
```

```
        System.out.println("  public key for " + i.getName());
      }
    }
  }
```

The last method in KeyManager, usage(), is a helper method that prints out the command-line options for KeyManager.

```
protected static void usage() {
  System.out.println("Options:");
  System.out.println("  create: -c keyfile signer algorithm strength");
  System.out.println("  export: -e keyfile idname outfile");
  System.out.println("  import: -i keyfile infile");
  System.out.println("  remove: -r keyfile idname");
  System.out.println("  list  : -l keyfile");
  }
}
```

In Chapters 10 and 11, I'll use KeyManager as part of cryptographic applications.

The KeyStore Key Management Paradigm

JDK 1.2 offers a new method for key management, based on java.security.KeyStore. A KeyStore is a handy box that holds keys and certificates. One KeyStore contains all the information a single person (or application, or identity) needs for authentication. Usually, you have two distinct uses for authentication:

- You need to prove to others who you are.

- You need to make sure that other people are legitimate.

In the first case, you can use a private key to sign data. A certificate that contains the matching public key can be used to prove your identity. In the second case, you can use other people's certificates to prove to yourself that they are who they say they are. I'll talk more about certificates in Chapter 6. For now, just think of them as containers for someone's public key and information about that person.

You may have more than one private/public key pair that you need to manage. For example, you might have a key pair that you use for day-to-day Internet shopping and a different key pair that you use for signing software you've written. (The KeyManager class, presented earlier in this chapter, holds only a single key pair.)

A KeyStore contains two types of entries. The first type contains a private key and a chain of certificates that correspond to the matching public key. I'll call this type of entry a *private key entry*. This is useful for signing and distributing code and other data. The private key is used to sign data; the certificates can be presented as credentials backing up the signature. The second type of keystore entry contains a certificate from someone you trust. I'll call this type of entry a *trusted certificate entry*.

This can be used in tandem with the security policy utility, `policytool`, to define a security policy for a trusted code signer.

`KeyStore` holds all this information, organized by *aliases*, or short names. Entries are stored and retrieved using an alias, similar to the way a `Hashtable` or `Properties` object works. Figure 5-2 shows an example `KeyStore` that Maid Marian might find useful. It contains two key pair entries, one for signing applets and one for signing email messages. It also contains three different certificate chains, corresponding to Will, Tuck, and Robin. These certificate chains are used to associate the people Marian knows and their public keys. Each entry is identified by an alias; for example, "CodeKeys" or "WillScarlet."

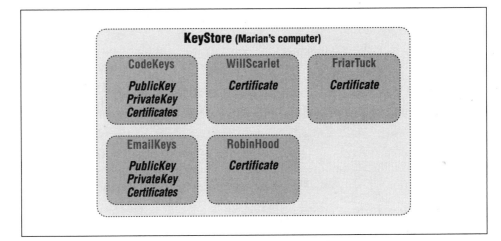

Figure 5-2: Keystore-based key management

KeyStore

Getting

`KeyStore` is an abstract class, but you can obtain a concrete subclass using `getInstance()`:

public static final KeyStore getInstance() throws KeyStoreException
> This method returns a `KeyStore` instance.

`KeyStore`'s `getInstance()` method uses a line in the *java.security* properties file to decide what subclass of `KeyStore` to create. The line might look like this:

```
keystore=oreilly.jonathan.security.SuperDuperKeyStore
```

If the line is missing, `getInstance()` uses the default `KeyStore` implementation, `sun.security.tools.JavaKeyStore`.

Loading and saving

Two methods support loading and saving KeyStores. A passphrase checks the integrity of the data:

public abstract void store(OutputStream stream, String password) throws IOException, NoSuchAlgorithmException, CertificateException

> Use this method to save the KeyStore's data to the given stream. The format of the data depends entirely on the KeyStore implementation. The supplied passphrase generates an integrity check for the keystore's data, which should also be stored.

public abstract void load(InputStream stream, String password) throws IOException, NoSuchAlgorithmException, CertificateException

> This method loads keystore data from the given InputStream. Again, the format of the data depends on the KeyStore implementation. This method should be able to load data written using the store() method. It should also perform a check on the data's integrity, using the supplied passphrase.

The integrity check is important because, properly implemented, it provides some assurance that no one has monkeyed with the keystore data. The simplest case would be to store a message digest of the keystore along with the keystore. When loading, you could compare the stored message digest with a freshly computed message digest based on the keystore's data. This scheme is subject to attack, however, as it would be easy to substitute new keystore data and a new message digest value. The password (or passphrase) is used to foil this attack. Typically, the passphrase is digested with the rest of the keystore data; the resulting digest value is stored with the keystore. When loading, the same password is needed to generate the same digest value. If the two digest values don't match, then either the wrong password was used or the keystore data has been modified.

Adding private key entries

Let's say, for example, that you had a key pair that you wanted to add to a KeyStore. Instead of adding the keys directly, you add a private key and a certificate chain that represents the corresponding public key. If you have a self-signed certificate that contains your public key, you can add it as a certificate chain that contains just the one certificate.

public abstract void setKeyEntry(String alias, PrivateKey key, String passphrase, Certificate[] chain) throws KeyStoreException

> This method assigns the given private key and certificate chain to alias. If the alias already exists, its current key and certificate information is replaced with the new values. The private key is "protected" using the supplied passphrase.

It's up to subclasses of KeyStore to decide what protection will be used for the private key.

Note that KeyStore doesn't specify exactly how a passphrase should be used to protect a private key in the database. This implementation is left to subclasses. This means that the security provided from this passphrase can range from totally ineffective to moderately strong. Let's examine a few possibilities:

Brain-dead protection

The simplest possible scheme might be to store the private key and the passphrase in plaintext when the KeyStore is saved. That way, you could recover the key and the passphrase easily; the key could be accessed only if a matching passphrase was supplied. This system is not secure at all: it's a piece of cake for anyone who examines the KeyStore's file to recover both the private key and the passphrase.

Weak encryption

It's possible to encrypt the private key by scrambling the passphrase and combining it with the private key. This won't foil real cryptanalysis, but it is probably effective in preventing casual snoops and amateur crackers from recovering your private key. This is the scheme used by Sun's implementation of KeyStore, sun.security.tools.JavaKeyStore.

Strong encryption

The best solution would be to use passphrase-based encryption (described in Chapter 7). In this scheme, a passphrase is used to generate a session key; the session key is used with a symmetric cipher to encrypt the original private key before it is saved with the KeyStore. Depending on the cipher algorithm, this can be quite effective in hiding the private key.

This is a different use of a passphrase from what we saw earlier, with store() and load(). In those methods, a passphrase is used to protect the integrity of the keystore data as a whole. Here, a passphrase is used for confidentiality, to obscure a private key.

Adding trusted certificate entries

KeyStore can also hold certificates containing other people's public keys. You can add a certificate to the KeyStore using setCertificateEntry():

public abstract setCertificateEntry(String alias, Certificate cert) throws KeyStoreException

This method associates alias with the given certificate. If the alias already exists, the current certificate is replaced with the new one.

You can't add a whole certificate chain. If you receive a certificate chain corresponding to someone's public key, you can add each certificate in the chain as a trusted certificate entry.

Retrieving entries

Once you have entered information into the KeyStore, you may retrieve it with several get methods:

public abstract PrivateKey getPrivateKey(String alias, String passphrase) throws NoSuchAlgorithmException, UnrecoverableKeyException
> You can use this method to retrieve the private key associated with alias. The given passphrase is used to undo whatever protection has been applied to the private key.

public abstract Certificate[] getCertificateChain(String alias)
> This method returns the certificate chain associated with alias.

public abstract Certificate getCertificate(String alias)
> This method returns the certificate associated with alias.

keytool

keytool is a command-line interface to the java.security.KeyStore class. As we've seen, a KeyStore is a simple database for private keys, public keys, and certificates. Each entry in the KeyStore has an *alias* that identifies it. Entries are always referenced using an alias.

By default, KeyStores are saved in files on your hard disk. One KeyStore fits in one file. keytool can be used to manage any number of KeyStore files. If you don't specify a KeyStore file when using keytool, the default file will be used. This is a file called *.keystore*, located in the directory determined by the HOMEDRIVE and HOMEPATH environment variables. The values of these variables are concatenated; if they form a valid path, then the default *.keystore* file is located in this directory. Otherwise, *.keystore* is located in the JDK installation directory.

KeyStores don't necessarily have to be stored in files; this is just the default implementation. You can change this default implementation; I'll get to this later.

Creating a key pair

You can create a key pair using the –genkey command option.[*]

```
C:\ keytool -genkey -alias Jonathan -keyalg DSA -keysize 1024 -dname
"CN=Jonathan Knudsen, OU=Technical Publications, O=O'Reilly & Associates,
C=US" -keypass buendia -storepass buendia

C:\
```

---

[*] My Win95 machine won't let me type a command line this long. I had to put the command line in a batch file and run the batch file.

I'll explain each of the options in detail:

`-genkey`

> This command option tells `keytool` to generate a new key pair. This key pair is used to create a private key entry in the keystore. The public key is placed inside a self-signed certificate.

`-alias`

> Just as you'd think, this option is used to associate an alias with the keystore entry.

`-keyalg`

> This option specifies the algorithm for which you want keys generated.

`-keysize`

> Use this option to specify the size of the key pair you are generating. Here, I specified the maximum size for DSA keys, 1024 bits.

`-dname`

> This entry is used to specify a *distinguished name* (DN).[*] A DN contains your name and places you in a hierarchy based on countries and organizations (companies, universities, etc.). In the preceding example, I've identified my real name, my company, my group within the company (Technical Publications), and the country I live in. Here is a complete list of DN fields that `keytool` recognizes:
>
> - CN (common name): your name
>
> - OU (organizational unit): the part of your organization to which you belong
>
> - O (organization): your organization
>
> - L (locality): usually, a city
>
> - S (state): a state or province
>
> - C (country): a country
>
> You don't have to include every DN field. In the example, I left out both the L and S fields. At the very least, you need to specify a common name, the CN field. Also, you should specify the fields in order, as shown in the preceding list.
>
> You'll notice that the DN is enclosed in quotes in the example just shown. This ensures that the entire DN string is treated as a single command-line argument to `keytool`.

`-keypass`

> This passphrase is used to protect the private key of the new key pair. Note that anyone peeking over your shoulder will be able to see this password. Also,

---

[*] Distinguished names are described in X.500, a document published by the International Telecommunications Union (ITU). To order the document online, visit *http://www.itu.ch/*.

the actual protection applied depends on the KeyStore implementation you're using (see the description of KeyStore earlier in this section). You will have to type the same passphrase to access the private key at a later date.

-storepass

> This passphrase protects the integrity of the entire keystore. Because I am using the -genkey option to create a new keystore, I am setting the keystore's passphrase with this option. Later operations on this keystore require that I type the same passphrase.

I could have used a few other options:

-sigalg

> When you generate a key pair using -genkey, the public key is automatically placed in a self-signed certificate. This option is used to specify the algorithm that will be used to sign the certificate. Because the newly created private key is used to sign the certificate, -sigalg will always be the same as -keyalg.

-validity

> The -validity option tells keytool how long the certificate should be valid. Specify a number of days.

-keystore

> This option is used to specify the keystore file to use. If you leave off this option (as we did earlier), the default keystore file will be used. This is the *.keystore* file, usually located in your home directory. In Windows, check in the *\windows* directory.

-v

> This option tells keytool to be verbose, that is, to print out detailed information about what it's doing. You can use this option with every keytool command.

Ubiquitous options and defaults

Several of keytool's options can be used with any command. These are -keystore, -storepass, and -v.

keytool is forgiving if you forget an option that it needs; in many cases, there is a default value. If there is not, keytool will prompt you for the missing information. The default values are shown in Table 5-1.

Table 5-1: Default Values for keytool Options

Option	Default Value
-alias	mykey
-keyalg	DSA

Table 5-1: Default Values for keytool Options (continued)

Option	Default Value
-keysize	1024
-sigalg	DSA/SHA-1
-validity	90
-keystore	Default *.keystore* file
-file	Standard input or output

Inspecting the keystore

To see the contents of a keystore, use the -list command:

```
C:\ keytool -list -storepass buendia

Your keystore contains 1 entry:

jonathan, Mon Jan 12 16:16:59 EST 1998, keyEntry,
Certificate MD5 Fingerprint: 56:E0:FD:24:13:6C:51:C0:D9:57:B4:33:7F:79:A8:4E


C:\
```

If you use the -v option in conjunction with -list, you'll get a much more detailed report:

```
C:\ keytool -list -storepass buendia -v

Your keystore contains 1 entry:

ALIAS: jonathan
Creation Date: Mon Jan 12 16:16:59 EST 1998

Entry type: keyEntry

CERT CHAIN Length: 1

CERT[1]:
Owner: CN=Jonathan Knudsen, OU=Technical Publications, O=O'Reilly &
Associates, C=US
Issuer: CN=Jonathan Knudsen, OU=Technical Publications, O=O'Reilly &
Associates, C=US
Serial Number: 34ba884a
Valid from: Mon Jan 12 16:16:58 EST 1998 until: Mon Jan 19 16:16:58 EST 1998
Certificate Fingerprints:
     MD5:  56:E0:FD:24:13:6C:51:C0:D9:57:B4:33:7F:79:A8:4E
     SHA1: 6C:04:8A:AC:02:13:0B:55:7C:4C:BD:E5:57:4C:83:4D:1E:B5:BF:3B
```

****

```
*********************************************
```

```
C:\
```

Finally, you can use the -alias option to view a single keystore entry:

```
C:\ keytool -list -alias Jonathan -storepass buendia
Jonathan, Mon Jan 12 16:16:59 EST 1998, keyEntry,
Certificate MD5 Fingerprint: 56:E0:FD:24:13:6C:51:C0:D9:57:B4:33:7F:79:A8:4E
```

```
C:\
```

Generating a CSR

To get a real certificate, signed by a Certificate Authority (CA), you need to generate a Certificate Signing Request (CSR). The CSR is a special file that contains your public key and information about you. It is signed with your private key. When you send a CSR to a CA, the CA will make some effort to verify your identity and to verify the authenticity of the CSR. Then it can issue you a certificate, signed with the CA's private key, that verifies your public key. We'll talk about how to import the returned certificate later.

To generate the CSR, use the -csr command option:

```
C:\ keytool -csr -alias Jonathan -file Jonathan.csr -keypass buendia
    -storepass buendia -v
Certification request stored in file <Jonathan.csr>.
Submit this to your certificate authority.
```

```
C:\
```

The options for -csr are as follows:

-alias

The certificate request is generated for the specified alias. The public key of the given alias will be contained in the certificate returned from the CA. The private key of the alias is used to sign the CSR itself.

-sigalg

This option tells keytool which algorithm to use to sign the CSR. It defaults to DSA.

-file

Use this option to specify a file for the CSR. In the example, the CSR is written to *Jonathan.csr.*

-keypass

The CSR is signed with the private key of the named alias. To access this private key, you must supply the key's password using the -keypass option.

As before, the -keystore, -keypass, and -v options are all available.

So what does the CSR look like? Basically it's just a long string of base64 data. You can send it to your CA via FTP, HTTP, or email. The format is specified in PKCS#10, one of RSA's PKCS documents.[*]

```
C:\ type Jonathan.csr
-----BEGIN NEW CERTIFICATE REQUEST-----
MIICbTCCAisCAQAwaTELMAkGA1UEBhMCVVMxHjAcBgNVBAoTFU8nUmVpbGx5ICYgQXNzb2NpYXRl
czEfMB0GA1UECxMWVGVjaG5pY2FsIFB1YmxpcY2F0aW9uczEZMBcGA1UEAxMQSm9uYXRoYW4gS251
ZHNlbjCCAbcwggEsBgcqhkjOOAQBMIIBHwKBgQD9f1OBHXUSKVLfSpwu7OTn9hG3UjzvRADDHj+A
tlEmaUVdQCJR+1k9jVj6v8X1ujD2y5tVbNeBO4AdNG/yZmC3a5lQpaSfn+gEexAiwk+7qdf+t8Yb
+DtX58aophUPBPuD9tPFHsMCNVQTWhaRMvZ1864rYdcq7/IiAxmd0UgBxwIVAJdgUI8VIwvMspK5
gqLrhAvwWBz1AoGBAPfhoIXWmz3ey7yrXDa4V7l5lK+7+jrqgvlXTAs9B4JnUVlXjrrUWU/mcQcQ
gYCOSRZxI+hMKBYTt88JMozIpuE8FnqLVHyNKOCjrh4rs6Z1kW6jfwv6ITVi8ftiegEkO8yk8b6o
UZCJqIPf4VrlnwaSi2ZegHtVJWQBTDv+z0kqA4GEAAKBgHpPfSlmQI63akljC8SqBiBiELUtEsTW
jgKzWVJcJdMsJuz1sWl8BF5wEt5YkjMX2xubZ9NkobqHVVf9UT+exaUigVX76h+qFfAvTJIaWwsP
WqvlijaxtxLDYNcp21MWp7KMamCCsZ1CXI4HjeHsWj2IezEycgtCpg6O341o+KQyoAAwCwYHKoZI
zjgEAwUAAy8AMCwCFDRgtj16NUIvbsKW+8MLHp6gKMW6AhQdP3+nfkUtzo8OGIOgrDUBUj2oDA==
-----END NEW CERTIFICATE REQUEST-----

C:\
```

Importing certificates

There are two reasons for importing a certificate to a keystore. First, you may be receiving a certificate from a CA in response to a CSR. In this case, you want to associate the certificate with the private key entry that was used to generate the CSR. The second case is when you import someone else's certificate to make a trusted certificate entry.

In either case, you will use keytool's -import command option. keytool knows how to import X.509 certificates in "printable encoding," as described in RFC 1421.[†] This format has a header line, a footer line, and a body of base64 data. (For more information about base64, see Appendix B or the sidebar in Chapter 1.) Here's an example certificate file:

```
-----BEGIN CERTIFICATE-----
MIICMTCCAZoCAS0wDQYJKoZIhvcNAQEEBQAwXDELMAkGA1UEBhMCQ1oxETAPBgNV
BAoTCFBWVCBhLnMuMRAwDgYDVQQDEwdDQS1QV1QxMSgwJgYJKoZIhvcNAQkBFhlj
YS1vcGVyQHA3MHgwMy5icm4ucHZZ0LmN6MB4XDTk3MDgwNDA1MDQ1NloXDTk4MDIw
MzA1MDQ1NlowgakxCzAJBgNVBAYTAkNaMQowCAYDVQQIEwEyMRkwFwYDVQQHEwBD
ZXNrZSBCdWRlam92aWNlMREwDwYDVQQKEwhQV1QsYS5zLjEMMAoGA1UECxMDVkNV
MRcwFQYDVQQDEw5MaWJvci5iEb3N0YWxlazEfMB0GCSqGSIb3DQEJARYQZG9zdGFs
```

---

* You can find the PKCS documents at *http://www.rsa.com/rsalabs/pubs/PKCS/*.

† See *ftp://ds.internic.net/rfc/rfc1421.txt* for the whole story on printable encoding. This encoding scheme is also sometimes called Privacy Enhanced Mail (PEM) format because it is used in the PEM standard.

ZWtAcHZOLm51dDEYMBYGA1UEDBMPKzQyIDM4IDc3NDcgMzYxMFwwDQYJKoZIhvcN
AQEBBQADSwAwSAJBAORQnnnaTGhwrWBGK+qdvIGiBGyaPNZfnqXlbtXuSUqRHXhE
acIYDtMVfK4wdROe6lmdlr3DuMc747/oT7SjO2UCAwEAATANBgkqhkiG9w0BAQQF
AAOBgQBxfebIQCCxnVtyY/YVfsAct1dbmxrBkeb9Z+xN7i/Fc3XYLig8rag3cfWg
wDqbnt8LKzvFt+FzlrO1qIm7miYlWNq26rlY3KGpWPNoWGJTkyrqX80/WAhU5B91
QOqgL9zXHhE65Qq0Wu/3ryRgyBgebSiFem10RZVavBHjgVcejw==
-----END CERTIFICATE-----

To import a certificate to a private key entry, simply name the entry and the file
that contains the certificate. Let's say that I sent off the CSR from the previous
section to my CA, and it sent back a certificate. If the certificate is stored in
Jonathan.x509, we can import the certificate as follows:

```
C:\ keytool -import -alias Jonathan -file Jonathan.x509 -keypass buendia
    -storepass buendia
```

Notice that you must specify the password for the entry's private key to import a
certificate for it.

Importing a certificate to create a trusted certificate entry is just as easy. Suppose
we get Marian's certificate in a file called *Marian.x509*. We can create a trusted
certficate entry as follows:

```
C:\ keytool -import -alias Marian -file Marian.x509 -storepass buendia
Owner: CN=Maid Marian, OU=Overprotected daughters, O=Royal Castle, C=GB
Issuer: CN=Certificates R Us, OU=Fables and Legends, O=CRU, C=US
Serial Number: 34ba884a
Valid from: Mon Jan 12 16:16:58 EST 1998 until: Mon Jan 19 16:16:58 EST 1998
Certificate Fingerprints:
       MD5:  56:E0:FD:24:13:6C:51:C0:D9:57:B4:33:7F:79:A8:4E
       SHA1: 6C:04:8A:AC:02:13:0B:55:7C:4C:BD:E5:57:4C:83:4D:1E:B5:BF:3B
Trust this certificate? [no]: yes

C:\
```

Note that `keytool` prints out the certificate's fingerprints and asks us whether the
certificate should be trusted or not. You should verify the fingerprint with the
certificate's owner before typing "yes." If you don't want to be prompted this way,
add the −noprompt option. (I'll talk more about certificates and fingerprints in
Chapter 6.)

Other options

`keytool`'s remaining command options are briefly discussed here:

−selfcert

This command option tells `keytool` to regenerate a self-signed certificate for
a private key entry. You could use it to change the Distinguished Name of a

private key entry. This command option accepts most of the same options as
-genkey, as shown in Table 5-2.

Table 5-2: Self-Signed Certificate Options

Option	Description
-alias	The entry's alias
-sigalg	The signature algorithm
-dname	A distinguished name
-validity	The validity period for the certificate, in days
-keypass	The password for the private key entry

-export
> Export (save) a certificate to a file. Use the -alias option to specify the entry
> and the -file option to specify an output file.

-printcert
> Print information about a certificate contained in a file. Simply specify the file-
> name using -file. This command does not use or modify any keystore data.

-keyclone
> Copy a private key keystore entry. It accepts the options listed in Table 5-3.

Table 5-3: Key Cloning Options

Option	Description
-alias	The original entry's alias
-dest	The alias for the new (copied) entry
-keypass	The password for the original entry
-new	The password for the new entry

-storepasswd
> Change the password on a keystore. As with all other commands, the original
> keystore password is specified using -storepass. The new keystore password
> is specified using the -new option.

-keypasswd
> Change the password on a private key entry in a keystore. It uses the options
> listed in Table 5-4.

Table 5-4: Key Password Options

Option	Description
-alias	The entry's alias
-keypass	The original key password
-new	The new password

`-delete`

Remove an entry from a keystore. Specify the entry using the `-alias` option.

`-help`

This command option prints a list of all of `keytool`'s options.

Changing the default keystore class

By default, `keytool` uses `sun.security.tools.JavaKeyStore` to do its work. If you write your own `KeyStore` implementation, you can still use `keytool` to manage your keys and certificates. You'll need to change a line in the *java.security* file, found in the *lib/security* directory underneath the JDK installation directory. The line reads as follows:

```
keystore=sun.security.tools.JavaKeyStore
```

If your `KeyStore` implementation is `oreilly.jonathan.security.Super-DuperKeyStore`, for example, you would need to change the line as follows:

```
keystore=oreilly.jonathan.security.SuperDuperKeyStore
```

6

Authentication

The first challenge of building a secure application is *authentication*. Let's look at some examples of authentication from everyday life:

- At an automated bank machine, you identify yourself using your bank card. You authenticate yourself using a personal identification number (PIN). The PIN is a *shared secret*, something that both you and the bank know. Presumably, you and the bank are the *only* ones who know this number.

- When you use a credit card, you identify yourself with the card. You authenticate yourself with your signature. Most store clerks never check the signature; in this situation, possession of the card is authentication enough. This is true when you order something over the telephone, as well; simply knowing the credit card number is proof of your identity.

- When you rent a movie at a video store, you prove your identity with a card or by saying your telephone number.

Authentication is tremendously important in computer applications. The program or person you communicate with may be in the next room or on another continent; you have none of the usual visual or aural clues that are helpful in everyday transactions. Public key cryptography offers some powerful tools for proving identity.

In this chapter, I'll describe three cryptographic concepts that are useful for authentication:

- *Message digests* produce a small "fingerprint" of a larger set of data.

- *Digital signatures* can be used to prove the integrity of data.

- *Certificates* are used as cryptographically safe containers for public keys.

A common feature of applications, especially custom-developed "enterprise" applications, is a login window. Users have to authenticate themselves to the application before they use it. In this chapter, we'll examine several ways to implement this with cryptography.[*] In the next section, for instance, I'll show two ways to use a message digest to avoid transmitting a password in cleartext from a client to a server. Later on, we'll use digital signatures instead of passwords.

Message Digests

As you saw in Chapter 2, *Concepts,* a message digest takes an arbitrary amount of input data and produces a short, digested version of the data. The Java Cryptography Architecture (JCA) makes it very easy to use message digests. The java .security.MessageDigest class encapsulates a cryptographic message digest.

Getting

To obtain a MessageDigest for a particular algorithm use one of its getInstance() factory methods:

public static MessageDigest getInstance(String algorithm) throws NoSuchAlgorithmException
> This method returns a MessageDigest for the given algorithm. The first provider supporting the given algorithm is used.

public static MessageDigest getInstance(String algorithm, String provider) throws NoSuchAlgorithmException, NoSuchProviderException
> This method returns a MessageDigest for the given algorithm, using the given provider.

Feeding

To feed data into the MessageDigest, use one of the update() methods:

public void update(byte input)
> This method adds the specified byte to the message digest's input data.

public void update(byte[] input)
> Use this method to add the entire input array to the message digest's input data.

public void update(byte[] input, int offset, int len)
> This method adds len bytes of the given array, starting at offset, to the message digest's input data.

---

* These methods are based on the authentication procedures outlined in the X.509 standard, published by the International Telecommunications Union (ITU). Although X.509 is best known for its certificate definition, the document concerns the general problem of authentication. For more information, you can download the document from the ITU at *http://www.itu.ch/*.

You can call the update() methods as many times as you want before calculating the digest value.

Digesting

To find out the digest value, use one of the digest() methods:

public byte[] digest()
> The value of the message digest is returned as a byte array.

public byte[] digest(byte[] input)
> This method is provided for convenience. It is equivalent to calling update(input), followed by digest().

If you use a MessageDigest to calculate a digest value for one set of input data, you can reuse the MessageDigest for a second set of data by clearing its internal state first.

public void reset()
> This method clears the internal state of the MessageDigest. It can then be used to calculate a new digest value for an entirely new set of input data.

One, Two, Three!

Thus, you can calculate a message digest value for any input data with just a few lines of code:

```
// Define byte[] inputData first.
MessageDigest md = MessageDigest.getInstance("SHA");
md.update(inputData);
byte[] digest = md.digest();
```

Message digests are one of the building blocks of digital signatures. Message digests alone, however, can be useful, as you'll see in the following sections.

Digest Streams

The java.security package comes with two classes that make it easy to calculate message digests on stream data. These classes are DigestInputStream and DigestOutputStream, descendants of the FilterInputStream and FilterOutputStream classes in java.io.

Let's apply DigestInputStream to the Masher class from Chapter 1, *Introduction*. In that class, we read a file and calculated its message digest value as follows:

```
// Obtain a message digest object.
MessageDigest md = MessageDigest.getInstance("MD5");

// Calculate the digest for the given file.
```

```
FileInputStream in = new FileInputStream(args[0]);
byte[] buffer = new byte[8192];
int length;
while ((length = in.read(buffer)) != -1)
    md.update(buffer, 0, length);
byte[] raw = md.digest();
```

Now let's wrap a `DigestInputStream` around the `FileInputStream`, as follows. As we read data from the file, the `MessageDigest` will automatically be updated. All we need to do is read the entire file.

```
// Obtain a message digest object.
MessageDigest md = MessageDigest.getInstance("MD5");

// Calculate the digest for the given file.
DigestInputStream in = new DigestInputStream(
    new FileInputStream(args[0]), md);
byte[] buffer = new byte[8192];
while (in.read(buffer) != -1)
    ;
byte[] raw = md.digest();
```

`DigestOutputStream` works the same way; all bytes written to the stream are automatically passed to the `MessageDigest`.

Protected Password Login

A basic problem in client/server applications is that the server wants to know who its clients are. In a password-based scheme, the client prompts the user for his or her name and password. The client relays this information to the server. The server checks the name and password and either allows the user into the system or denies access. The password is a *shared secret* because both the user and the server must know it. The obvious solution is to send the user's name and password directly to the server. Most computer networks, however, are highly susceptible to eavesdropping, so this is not a very secure solution.

To avoid passing a cleartext password from client to server, you can send a message digest of the password instead. The server can create a message digest of its copy of the password. If the two message digests are equal, then the client is authenticated. This simple procedure, however, is vulnerable to a *replay attack*. A malicious user could listen to the digested password and replay it later to gain illicit access to the server. To avoid this problem, some session-specific information is added to the message digest. In particular, the client generates a random number and a timestamp and includes them in the digest. These values must also be sent, in the clear, to the server, so that the server can use them to calculate a matching digest value. The server must be programmed to receive the extra information and include it in its message digest calculations. Figure 6-1 shows how this works on the client side.

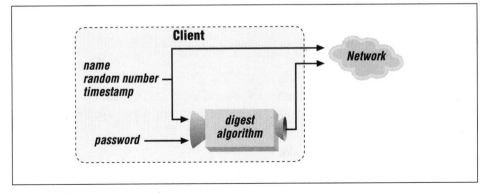

Figure 6-1: Protecting a password

The server uses the given name to look up the password in a private database. Then it uses the given name, random number, timestamp, and the password it just retrieved to calculate a message digest. If this digest value matches the digest sent by the client, the client has been authenticated.

The following program shows the procedure from the client's point of view:

```
import java.io.*;
import java.net.*;
import java.security.*;
import java.util.Date;

import Protection;

public class ProtectedClient {
    public void sendAuthentication(String user, String password,
        OutputStream outStream) throws IOException, NoSuchAlgorithmException {
      DataOutputStream out = new DataOutputStream(outStream);
      long t1 = (new Date()).getTime();
      double q1 = Math.random();
      byte[] protected1 = Protection.makeDigest(user, password, t1, q1);

      out.writeUTF(user);
      out.writeLong(t1);
      out.writeDouble(q1);
      out.writeInt(protected1.length);
      out.write(protected1);
      out.flush();
    }

    public static void main(String[] args) throws Exception {
      String host = args[0];
      int port = 7999;
      String user = "Jonathan";
```

```
        String password = "buendia";
        Socket s = new Socket(host, port);

        ProtectedClient client = new ProtectedClient();
        client.sendAuthentication(user, password, s.getOutputStream());

        s.close();
    }
}
```

The bulk of the algorithm is in the SendAuthentication() method, in these lines:

```
out.writeUTF(user);
out.writeLong(t1);
out.writeDouble(q1);
out.writeInt(protected1.length);
out.write(protected1);
```

Here we write the user string, timestamp, and random number as cleartext. Instead of writing the message digest right away, we first write out its length. This makes it easier for the server to read the message digest. Although we could code the server to always read a 20-byte SHA digest, we might decide to change algorithms some time in the future. Writing the digest length into the stream means we don't have to worry about the length of the digest, whatever algorithm we use.

Also note that ProtectedClient is not Socket-specific. You could use it to write authentication information to a file or an email message.

Some of the digestion that ProtectedClient performs will be mirrored in the server class. Therefore, ProtectedClient's sendAuthentication() method uses a static utility method, makeDigest(), that is defined in the Protection class. This class is shown below:

```
import java.io.*;
import java.security.*;

public class Protection {
    public static byte[] makeDigest(String user, String password,
        long t1, double q1) throws NoSuchAlgorithmException {
    MessageDigest md = MessageDigest.getInstance("SHA");
    md.update(user.getBytes());
    md.update(password.getBytes());
    md.update(makeBytes(t1, q1));
    return md.digest();
    }

    public static byte[] makeBytes(long t, double q) {
        try {
            ByteArrayOutputStream byteOut = new ByteArrayOutputStream();
            DataOutputStream dataOut = new DataOutputStream(byteOut);
```

```
        dataOut.writeLong(t);
        dataOut.writeDouble(q);
        return byteOut.toByteArray();
      }
    catch (IOException e) {
      return new byte[0];
      }
    }
  }
```

Protection defines two static methods. The makeDigest() method creates a message digest from its input data. It uses a helper method, makeBytes(), whose purpose is to convert a long and a double into an array of bytes.

On the server side, the process is similar. The ProtectedServer class has a method, lookupPassword(), that returns the password of a supplied user. In our implementation, it is hardcoded to return one password. In a real application, this method would probably connect to a database or a password file to find the user's password.

```
import java.io.*;
import java.net.*;
import java.security.*;

import Protection;

public class ProtectedServer {
  public boolean authenticate(InputStream inStream)
      throws IOException, NoSuchAlgorithmException {
    DataInputStream in = new DataInputStream(inStream);

    String user = in.readUTF();
    long t1 = in.readLong();
    double q1 = in.readDouble();
    int length = in.readInt();
    byte[] protected1 = new byte[length];
    in.readFully(protected1);

    String password = lookupPassword(user);
    byte[] local = Protection.makeDigest(user, password, t1, q1);
    return MessageDigest.isEqual(protected1, local);
  }

  protected String lookupPassword(String user) { return "buendia"; }

  public static void main(String[] args) throws Exception {
    int port = 7999;
    ServerSocket s = new ServerSocket(port);
    Socket client = s.accept();
```

```
    ProtectedServer server = new ProtectedServer();
    if (server.authenticate(client.getInputStream()))
      System.out.println("Client logged in.");
    else
      System.out.println("Client failed to log in.");

    s.close();
  }
}
```

To test the protected password login, first start up the server:

C:\ **java ProtectedServer**

Then run the client, pointing it to the machine where the server is running. I run both these programs on the same machine, so I type this in a different command-line window:

C:\ **java ProtectedClient localhost**

The server will print out a message indicating whether the client logged in. Then both programs exit.

Double-Strength Password Login

There is a stronger method for protecting password information using message digests. It involves an additional timestamp and random number, as shown in Figure 6-2.

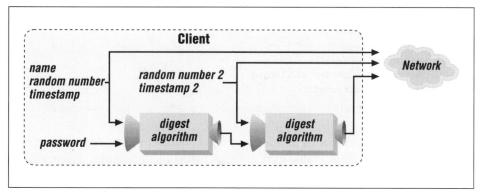

Figure 6-2: A doubly protected password

First, a digest is computed, just as in the previous example. Then, the digest value, another random number, and another timestamp are fed into a second digest. Then the server is sent the second digest value, along with the timestamps and random numbers.

Why is this better than the simpler scheme we outlined earlier? To understand why, think about how you might try to break the protected password scheme. Recall that a message digest is a *one-way function*; ideally, this means that it's impossible to figure out what input produced a given digest value.[*] Thus, your best bet is to launch a dictionary attack. This means that you try passwords, one at a time, running them through the simple protection algorithm just described and attempting to log in each time. In this process, it's important to consider how much time it takes to test a single password. In the double-strength protection scheme, two digest values must be computed instead of just one, which should double the time required for a dictionary attack.

We can implement the double protection scheme with a few minimal changes to the `ProtectedClient` and `ProtectedServer` classes. First, `ProtectedClient`'s `sendAuthentication()` method needs some additional logic. The new lines are shown in bold.

```
public void sendAuthentication(String user, String password,
    OutputStream outStream) throws IOException, NoSuchAlgorithmException {
DataOutputStream out = new DataOutputStream(outStream);
long t1 = (new Date()).getTime();
double q1 = Math.random();
byte[] protected1 = Protection.makeDigest(user, password, t1, q1);
long t2 = (new Date()).getTime();
double q2 = Math.random();
byte[] protected2 = Protection.makeDigest(protected1, t2, q2);

out.writeUTF(user);
out.writeLong(t1);
out.writeDouble(q1);
out.writeLong(t2);
out.writeDouble(q2);
out.writeInt(protected2.length);
out.write(protected2);
out.flush();
}
```

You probably noticed that there's a new helper method in the `Protection` class. It takes a message digest value (an array of bytes), a timestamp, and a random number and generates a new digest value. This new static method in the `Protection` class is shown next:

```
public static byte[] makeDigest(byte[] mush, long t2, double q2)
    throws NoSuchAlgorithmException {
MessageDigest md = MessageDigest.getInstance("SHA");
md.update(mush);
```

---

[*] In practice, it just takes a very, very long time to figure out what input produced a given digest value.

```
            md.update(makeBytes(t2, q2));
            return md.digest();
        }
```

Finally, the server needs to be updated to accept the additional protection information. `ProtectedServer`'s modified `authenticate()` method is shown here, with the new lines indicated in bold:

```
        public boolean authenticate(InputStream inStream)
            throws IOException, NoSuchAlgorithmException {
        DataInputStream in = new DataInputStream(inStream);

        String user = in.readUTF();
        long t1 = in.readLong();
        double q1 = in.readDouble();
        long t2 = in.readLong();
        double q2 = in.readDouble();
        int length = in.readInt();
        byte[] protected2 = new byte[length];
        in.readFully(protected2);

        String password = lookupPassword(user);
        byte[] local1 = Protection.makeDigest(user, password, t1, q1);
        byte[] local2 = Protection.makeDigest(local1, t2, q2);
        return MessageDigest.isEqual(protected2, local2);
        }
```

Neither the regular or double-strength login methods described here prevent a dictionary attack on the password. For a method that does prevent a dictionary attack, see *http://srp.stanford.edu/srp/*.

MACs

A message authentication code (MAC) is basically a keyed message digest. Like a message digest, a MAC takes an arbitrary amount of input data and creates a short digest value. Unlike a message digest, a MAC uses a key to create the digest value. This makes it useful for protecting the integrity of data that is sent over an insecure network. The `javax.crypto.Mac` class encapsulates a MAC.

Setting Up

To create a `Mac`, use one of its `getInstance()` methods:

public static final Mac getInstance(String algorithm) throws NoSuchAlgorithmException
    This method returns a new `Mac` for the given algorithm.

public static final Mac getInstance(String algorithm, String provider) throws NoSuchAlgorithmException, NoSuchProviderException

> This method returns a new Mac for the given algorithm using the supplied provider.

Once you have obtained the Mac, you need to initialize it with a key. You can also use algorithm-specific initialization information, if you wish.

public final void init(Key key) throws InvalidKeyException

> Use this method to initialize the Macwith the supplied key. An exception is thrown if the key cannot be used.

public final void init(Key key, AlgorithmParameterSpec params) throws InvalidKeyException, InvalidAlgorithmParameterException

> This method initializes the Mac with the supplied key and algorithm-specific parameters.

Feeding

A Mac has several update() methods for adding data. These are just like the update() methods in MessageDigest:

public final void update(byte input) throws IllegalStateException

> This method adds the given byte to the Mac's input data. If the Mac has not been initialized, an exception is thrown.

public final void update(byte[] input) throws IllegalStateException

> Use this method to add the entire input array to the Mac.

public final void update(byte[] input, int offset, int len) throws IllegalStateException

> This method adds len bytes of the given array, starting at offset, to the Mac.

Calculating the Code

To actually calculate the MAC value, use one of the doFinal() methods:

public final byte[] doFinal() throws IllegalStateException

> This method returns the MAC value and resets the state of the Mac. You can calculate a fresh MAC value using the same key by calling update() with new data.

public final void doFinal(byte[] output, int outOffset) throws IllegalStateException, ShortBufferException

> This method places the MAC value into the given array, starting at outOffset, and resets the state of the Mac.

public final byte[] doFinal(byte[] input) throws IllegalStateException
> This method adds the entire input array to this Mac. Then the MAC value is calculated and returned. The internal state of the Mac is reset.

To clear the results of previous calls to update() without calculating the MAC value, use the reset() method:

public final void reset()
> This method clears the internal state of the Mac. If you wish to use a different key to calculate a MAC value, you can reinitialize the Mac using init().

For Instance

The following example shows how to create a MAC key and calculate a MAC value:

```
SecureRandom sr = new SecureRandom();
byte[] keyBytes = new byte[20];
sr.nextBytes(keyBytes);
SecretKey key = new SecretKeySpec(keyBytes, "HmacSHA1");
Mac m = Mac.getInstance("HmacSHA1");
m.init(key);
m.update(inputData);
byte[] mac = m.doFinal();
```

Signatures

A *signature* provides two security services, authentication and integrity. A signature gives you assurance that a message has not been tampered with and that it originated from a certain person. As you'll recall from Chapter 2, a signature is a message digest that is encrypted with the signer's private key. Only the signer's public key can decrypt the signature, which provides authentication. If the message digest of the message matches the decrypted message digest from the signature, then integrity is also assured.

Signatures do not provide confidentiality. A signature accompanies a plaintext message. Anyone can intercept and read the message. Signatures are useful for distributing software and documentation because they foil forgery.

The Java Security API provides a class, java.security.Signature, that represents cryptographic signatures. This class operates in two distinct modes, depending on whether you wish to generate a signature or verify a signature.

Like the other cryptography classes, Signature has two factory methods:

public static Signature getInstance(String algorithm) throws NoSuchAlgorithmException
> This method returns a Signature for the given algorithm. The first provider supporting the given algorithm is used.

public static Signature getInstance(String algorithm, String provider) throws
NoSuchAlgorithmException, NoSuchProviderException

> This method returns a `Signature` for the given algorithm, using the given provider.

One of two methods initializes the `Signature`:

public final void initSign(PrivateKey privateKey) throws InvalidKeyException

> If you want to generate a signature, use this method to initialize the `Signature` with the given private key.

public final void initVerify(PublicKey publicKey) throws InvalidKeyException

> To verify a signature, call this method with the public key that matches the private key that was used to generate the signature.

If you want to set algorithm-specific parameters in the `Signature` object, you can pass an `AlgorithmParameterSpec` to `setParameter()`.

public final void setParameter(AlgorithmParameterSpec params) throws
InvalidAlgorithmPararmeterException

> You can pass algorithm-specific parameters to a `Signature` using this object. If the `Signature` does not recognize the `AlgorithmParameterSpec` object, an exception is thrown.

You can add data to a `Signature` the same way as for a message digest, using the `update()` methods. A `SignatureException` is thrown if the `Signature` has not been initialized.

public final void update(byte input) throws SignatureException

> You can add a single byte to the `Signature`'s input data using this method.

public final void update(byte[] input) throws SignatureException

> This method adds the given array of bytes to the `Signature`'s input data.

public final void update(byte[] input, int offset, int len) throws SignatureException

> This method adds `len` bytes from the given array, starting at `offset`, to the `Signature`'s input data.

Generating a Signature

Generating a signature is a lot like generating a message digest value. The `sign()` method returns the signature itself:

public final byte[] sign() throws SignatureException

> This method calculates a signature, based on the input data as supplied in calls to `update()`. A `SignatureException` is thrown if the `Signature` is not properly initialized.

To generate a signature, you will need the signer's private key and the message that you wish to sign. The procedure is straightforward:

1. Obtain a `Signature` object using the `getInstance()` factory method. You'll need to specify an algorithm. A signature actually uses two algorithms—one to calculate a message digest and one to encrypt the message digest. The SUN provider shipped with the JDK 1.1 supports DSA encryption of an SHA-1 message digest. This is simply referred to as DSA.

2. Initialize the `Signature` with the signer's private key using `initSign()`.

3. Use the `update()` method to add the data of the message into the signature. You can call `update()` as many times as you would like. Three different overloads allow you to update the signature with byte data.

4. Calculate the signature using the `sign()` method. This method returns an array of bytes that are the signature itself. It's up to you to store the signature somewhere.

Verifying a Signature

You can use `Signature`'s `verify()` method to verify a signature:

public final boolean verify(byte[] signature) throws SignatureException
This method verifies that the supplied byte array, `signature`, matches the input data that has been supplied using `update()`. If the signature verifies, `true` is returned. If the `Signature` is not properly initialized, a `Signature-Exception` is thrown.

Verifying a signature is similar to generating a signature. In fact, Steps 1 and 3 are identical. It's assumed that you already have a signature value. The process here verifies that the message you've received produces the same signature:

1. Obtain a `Signature` using the `getInstance()` factory method.

2. Initialize the `Signature` with the signer's public key using `initVerify()`.

3. Use `update()` to add message data into the signature.

4. Check if your signatures match using the `verify()` method. This method accepts an array of bytes that are the signature to be verified. It returns a `boolean` value that is `true` if the signatures match and `false` otherwise.

Hancock

Let's examine a complete program, called `Hancock`, that generates and verifies signatures. We'll use a file for the message input, and we'll pull keys out of a `KeyStore`. (You can manipulate keystores with the `keytool` utility, described in Chapter 5, *Key Management*. To run this example, you'll have to have created a keystore with at least one key pair.) Hancock is a command-line utility that accepts parameters as follows:

```
java Hancock -s|-v keystore storepass alias messagefile signaturefile
```

The -s option is used for signing. The private key of the given alias is used to create a signature from the data contained in *messagefile*. The resulting signature is stored in *signaturefile*. The *keystore* parameter is the filename of a keystore, and storepass is the password needed to access the keystore.

The -v option tells Hancock to verify a signature. The signature is assumed to be in *signaturefile*. Hancock verifies that the signature is from the given alias for the data contained in *messagefile*. Again, *keystore* is a keystore file, and storepass is used to access the keystore.

Let's begin by checking our command-line arguments:

```
import java.io.*;
import java.security.*;

public class Hancock {
  public static void main(String[] args) throws Exception {
    if (args.length != 6) {
      System.out.println(
          "Usage: Hancock -s|-v keystore storepass alias " +
          "messagefile signaturefile");
      return;
    }

    String options = args[0];
    String keystorefile = args[1];
    String storepass = args[2];
    String alias = args[3];
    String messagefile = args[4];
    String signaturefile = args[5];
```

Our first step, as you'll recall, is the same for signing and verifying: We need to get a Signature object. We use DSA because it's supplied with the Sun provider:

```
Signature signature = Signature.getInstance("DSA");
```

Next, the Signature needs to be initialized with either the public key or the private key of the named alias. In either case, we need a reference to the keystore, which we obtain as follows:

```
KeyStore keystore = KeyStore.getInstance();
keystore.load(new FileInputStream(keystorefile), storepass);
```

To sign, we initialize the `Signature` with a private key. The password for the private key is assumed to be the same as the keystore password. To verify, we initialize the `Signature` with a public key.

```
if (options.indexOf("s") != -1)
    signature.initSign(keystore.getPrivateKey(alias, storepass));
else
    signature.initVerify(keystore.getCertificate(alias).getPublicKey());
```

The next step is to update the signature with the given message. This step is the same whether we are signing or verifying. We open the message file and read it in 8K chunks. The signature is updated with every byte read from the message file.

```
FileInputStream in = new FileInputStream(messagefile);
byte[] buffer = new byte[8192];
int length;
while ((length = in.read(buffer)) != -1)
    signature.update(buffer, 0, length);
in.close();
```

Finally, we're ready to sign the message or verify a signature. If we're signing, we simply generate a signature and store it in a file.

```
if (options.indexOf("s") != -1) {
    FileOutputStream out = new FileOutputStream(signaturefile);
    byte[] raw = signature.sign();
    out.write(raw);
    out.close();
}
```

Otherwise, we are verifying a signature. All we need to do is read in the signature and check if it verifies. We'll print out a message to the user that tells if the signature verified.

```
else {
    FileInputStream sigIn = new FileInputStream(signaturefile);
    byte[] raw = new byte[sigIn.available()];
    sigIn.read(raw);
    sigIn.close();
    if (signature.verify(raw))
        System.out.println("The signature is good.");
    else
        System.out.println("The signature is bad.");
    }
  }
}
```

You can use `Hancock` to sign any file with any private key that's in a keystore. A friend who has your public key can use `Hancock` to verify a file he or she has downloaded from you.

Login, Again

Passwords are a simple solution to authentication, but they are not considered very secure. People choose easy-to-guess passwords, or they write down passwords in obvious places. A sly malcontent, pretending to be a system administrator, can usually convince a user to tell his or her password.

If you want a stronger form of authentication, and you are willing to pay the price in complexity, then you should use a signature-based authentication scheme.

The basic procedure is very similar to the password-based schemes examined earlier, in the section on message digests. The client generates a timestamp and a random number. This time, the client creates a signature of this data and sends it to the server. The server can verify the signature with the client's public key.

How does the client access your private key, to generate a signature? In a real application, you would probably point the client to a disk file that contained your key (preferably on removable media, like a floppy disk or a smart card). In this example, we'll just pull a private key out of a keystore.

The hard part is in creating and maintaining the public key database. The server needs to have a public key for every possible person who will log in. Furthermore, the server needs to obtain these public keys in a secure way. Certificates solve this problem; I'll discuss them a bit later.

We'll look at the simple case, with a pair of programs called `StrongClient` and `StrongServer`. `StrongClient` creates a timestamp and a random number and sends them along with the user's name and a signature to the server. The length of the signature is sent before the signature itself, just as it was with the message digest login examples.

The `main()` method attempts to use a private key extracted from a keystore. The keystore location, password, alias, and private key password are all command-line parameters. For this to work, you'll need to have created a pair of DSA keys in a keystore somewhere. See Chapter 5 if you're not sure how to do this.

```
import java.io.*;
import java.net.*;
import java.security.*;
import java.util.Date;

import Protection;

public class StrongClient {
    public void sendAuthentication(String user, PrivateKey key,
        OutputStream outStream) throws IOException, NoSuchAlgorithmException,
        InvalidKeyException, SignatureException {
    DataOutputStream out = new DataOutputStream(outStream);
```

```
        long t = (new Date()).getTime();
        double q = Math.random();

        Signature s = Signature.getInstance("DSA");
        s.initSign(key);
        s.update(Protection.makeBytes(t, q));
        byte[] signature = s.sign();

        out.writeUTF(user);
        out.writeLong(t);
        out.writeDouble(q);
        out.writeInt(signature.length);
        out.write(signature);
        out.flush();
    }

    public static void main(String[] args) throws Exception {
        if (args.length != 5) {
            System.out.println(
                "Usage: StrongClient host keystore storepass alias keypass");
            return;
        }

        String host = args[0];
        String keystorefile = args[1];
        String storepass = args[2];
        String alias = args[3];
        String keypass = args[4];

        int port = 7999;
        Socket s = new Socket(host, port);

        StrongClient client = new StrongClient();
        KeyStore keystore = KeyStore.getInstance();
        keystore.load(new FileInputStream(keystorefile), storepass);
        PrivateKey key = keystore.getPrivateKey(alias, keypass);
        client.sendAuthentication(alias, key, s.getOutputStream());

        s.close();
    }
}
```

The server version of this program simply reads the information from the stream and verifies the given signature, using a public key from the keystore named in the command line. Note that the client sends the alias name to the server. This implies that the correct keys must be referenced by the same alias in both the keystore that the client uses and the keystore that the server uses.

```
import java.io.*;
import java.net.*;
```

```java
import java.security.*;

import Protection;

public class StrongServer {
  protected KeyStore mKeyStore;

  public StrongServer(KeyStore keystore) { mKeyStore = keystore; }

  public boolean authenticate(InputStream inStream)
      throws IOException, NoSuchAlgorithmException,
        InvalidKeyException, SignatureException {
    DataInputStream in = new DataInputStream(inStream);

    String user = in.readUTF();
    long t = in.readLong();
    double q = in.readDouble();
    int length = in.readInt();
    byte[] signature = new byte[length];
    in.readFully(signature);

    Signature s = Signature.getInstance("DSA");
    s.initVerify(mKeyStore.getCertificate(user).getPublicKey());
    s.update(Protection.makeBytes(t, q));
    return s.verify(signature);
  }

  public static void main(String[] args) throws Exception {
    if (args.length != 2) {
      System.out.println("Usage: StrongServer keystore storepass");
      return;
    }

    String keystorefile = args[0];
    String storepass = args[1];

    int port = 7999;
    ServerSocket s = new ServerSocket(port);
    Socket client = s.accept();

    KeyStore keystore = KeyStore.getInstance();
    keystore.load(new FileInputStream(keystorefile), storepass);
    StrongServer server = new StrongServer(keystore);
    if (server.authenticate(client.getInputStream()))
      System.out.println("Client logged in.");
    else
      System.out.println("Client failed to log in.");

    s.close();
  }
}
```

Run the server by pointing it to the keystore you wish to use, as follows:

```
C:\ java StrongServer c:\windows\.keystore buendia
```

Then run the client, telling it the server's IP address, the keystore location, the alias, and the private key password. Because I'm running the server and client on the same machine, I use *localhost* for the server's address:

```
C:\ java StrongClient localhost c:\windows\.keystore buendia Jonathan
     buendia
```

The server prints a message indicating if the client logged in. Then the server and client exit.

SignedObject

JDK 1.2 offers a utility class, java.security.SignedObject, that contains any Serializable object and a matching signature. You can construct a SignedObject with a Serializable object, a private key, and a Signature:

public SignedObject(Serializable object, PrivateKey signingKey, Signature signingEngine) throws IOException, InvalidKeyException, SignatureException

This constructor creates a SignedObject that encapsulates the given Serializable object. The object is serialized and stored internally. The serialized object is signed using the supplied Signature and private key.

You can verify the signature on a SignedObject with the verify() method:

public final boolean verify(PublicKey verificationKey, Signature verificationEngine) throws InvalidKeyException, SignatureException

This method verifies that the SignedObject's internal signature matches its contained object. It uses the supplied public key and Signature to perform the verification. As before, the Signature does not need to be initialized. This method returns true if the SignedObject's signature matches its contained object; that is, the contained object's integrity is verified.

You can retrieve the SignedObject's contained object using the getObject() method:

public Object getObject() throws IOException, ClassNotFoundException

This method returns the object contained in this SignedObject. The object is stored internally as a byte array; this method deserializes the object and returns it. To be assured of the object's integrity, you should call verify() before calling this method.

One possible application of SignedObject is in the last example. We might write a simple class, AuthorizationToken, that contained the user's name, the timestamp, and the random value. This object, in turn, could be placed inside a SignedObject that could be passed from client to server.

Certificates

To verify a signature, you need the signer's public key. So how are public keys distributed securely? You could simply download the key from a server somewhere, but how would you know you got the right file and not a forgery? Even if you get a valid key, how do you know that it belongs to a particular person?

Certificates answer these questions. A certificate is a statement, signed by one person, that the public key of another person has a particular value. In some ways, it's like a driver's license. The license is a document issued by your state government that matches your face to your name, address, and date of birth. When you buy alcohol, tobacco, or dirty magazines, you can use your license to prove your identity (and your age).

Note that the license only has value because you and your local shopkeepers trust the authority of the state government. Digital certificates have the same property: You need to trust the person who issued the certificate (who is known as a *Certificate Authority,* or CA).

In cryptographic terminology, a certificate associates an identity with a public key. The identity is called the *subject.* The identity that signs the certificate is the *signer.* The certificate contains information about the subject and the subject's public key, plus information about the signer. The whole thing is cryptographically signed, and the signature becomes part of the certificate, too. Because the certificate is signed, it can be freely distributed over insecure channels.

At a basic level, a certificate contains these elements:

- Information about the subject
- The subject's public key
- Information about the issuer
- The issuer's signature of the above information

Sun recognized that certificate support was anemic in JDK 1.1. Things are improved in JDK 1.2. You can now import X.509v3 certificates and verify them. You still can't generate a certificate using the public API.

In this section, I'll talk about the JDK 1.2 classes that represent certificates and Certificate Revocation Lists (CRLs).

java.security.cert.Certificate

JDK 1.1 introduced support for certificates, based around the `java.secu-rity.Certificate` interface. In JDK 1.2, this interface is deprecated; we won't be covering it. It is replaced by an abstract class, `java.security.cert.Certifi-cate`. This class is a little simpler than its predecessor, and it includes the ability to verify a certificate. Support for X.509 certificates is provided in a separate class, which I'll explain in a moment.

First, of course, `java.security.cert.Certificate` is a container for a public key:

public abstract PublicKey getPublicKey()
 This method returns the public key that is contained by this certificate.

You can get an encoded version of the certificate using `getEncoded()`. The data returned by this method could be written to a file:

public abstract byte[] getEncoded() throws CertificateEncodingException
 This method returns an encoded representation of the certificate.

Generating a Certificate

Oddly enough, there is still no programmatic way to generate a certificate from scratch, even with the new classes in JDK 1.2. You can, however, load an X.509 certificate from a file using the `getInstance()` method in the `X509Certificate` class. I'll talk about this later.

NOTE　　Working with certificates in JDK 1.2 is sometimes difficult because there are two things named `Certificate`. The `java.security.Certificate` interface was introduced in JDK 1.1, but it's now deprecated. The "official" certificate class in JDK 1.2 is `java.security.cert.Certificate`. Whenever you see `Certificate` in source code, make sure you understand what it refers to. And be careful if you import both `java.security.*` and `java.security.cert.*`.

Verifying a Certificate

To verify the contents of the certificate, use one of the `verify()` methods:

public abstract void verify(PublicKey key) throws CertificateException, NoSuchAlgorithmException, InvalidKeyException, NoSuchProviderException, SignatureException
 This method uses the supplied public key to verify the certificate's contents. The public key should belong to the certificate's issuer (and has nothing to do with the public key contained in this certificate). The supplied issuer's public key is used to verify the internal signature that protects the integrity of the certificate's data.

public abstract void verify(PublicKey key, String sigProvider) throws CertificateException,
NoSuchAlgorithmException, InvalidKeyException, NoSuchProviderException,
SignatureException

> This is the same as the previous method, but specifically uses the given
> provider to supply the signing algorithm implementation.

X.509

Several standards specify the contents of a certificate. One of the most popular is
X.509, published by the International Telecommunications Union (ITU). Three
versions of this standard have been published. Table 6-1 shows the contents of an
X.509 certificate.

Support for X.509 certificates is provided by a subclass of `Certificate`, `java.secu-`
`rity.cert.X509Certificate`. This class is also abstract although it defines a
`getInstance()` method that returns a concrete subclass. Most of the methods in this
class return the fields of an X.509 certificate: `getVersion()`, `getSerialNumber()`,
`getIssuerDN()`, and so on. Table 6-1 shows the `X509Certificate` methods corresponding to the certificate fields.

Table 6-1: X.509 Certificate Contents

Field	Description	Method
Version	X.509 v1, v2, or v3	`int getVersion()`
Serial number	A number unique to the issuer	`BigInteger getSerial-Number()`
Signature algorithm	Describes the cryptographic algorithm used for the signature	`String getSigAlgName()`
Issuer	The issuer's name	`Principal getIssuerDN()`
Validity period	A range of time when the certificate is valid	`Date getNotBefore()`, `Date getNotAfter()`
Subject	The subject's name	`Principal getSubjectDN()`
Subject's public key	The subject's public key	`PublicKey getPublicKey()` (inherited from `Certificate`)
Issuer's unique identifier	A unique identifier representing the issuer (versions 2 and 3)	`boolean[] getIssuer-UniqueID()`
Subject's unique identifier	A unique identifier representing the subject (versions 2 and 3)	`boolean[] getSubject-UniqueID()`
Extensions	Additional data (version 3)	`boolean[] getKeyUsage()`, `int getBasicConstraints()`
Signature	A signature of all of the previous fields	`byte[] getSignature()`

To load an X.509 certificate from a file, you can use `getInstance()`:

public static final X509Certificate getInstance(InputStream inStream) throws CertificateException
> This method instantiates a concrete subclass of `X509Certificate` and initializes it with the given input stream.

public static final X509Certificate getInstance(byte[] certData) throws CertificateException
> This method works as above, except the new certificate is initialized using the supplied byte array.

The way that `getInstance()` works is a little convoluted. The actual object that is created is determined by an entry in the *java.security* properties file. This file is found in the *lib/security* directory underneath the JDK installation directory. By default, the relevant line looks like this:

```
cert.provider.x509=sun.security.x509.X509CertImpl
```

Let's say you call `getInstance()` with an input stream. A `sun.security` `.x509.X509CertImpl` will be created, using a constructor that accepts the input stream. It's up to the `X509CertImpl` to read data from the input stream to initialize itself. `X509CertImpl` knows how to construct itself from a DER-encoded certificate. What is DER? In the X.509 standard, a certificate is specified as a data structure using the ASN.1 (Abstract Syntax Notation) language. There are a few different ways that ASN.1 data structures can be reduced to a byte stream, and DER (Distinguished Encoding Rules) is one of these methods. The net result is that an `X509CertImpl` can recognize an X.509 certificate if it is DER-encoded.

Spill

Let's look at an example that uses `X509Certificate`. We'll write a tool that displays information about a certificate contained in a file, just like `keytool -printcert`. Like `keytool`, we'll recognize certificate files in the format described by RFC 1421. An RFC 1421 certificate representation is simply a DER representation, converted to base64, with a header and a footer line. Here is such a file:

```
-----BEGIN CERTIFICATE-----
MIICMTCCAZoCAS0wDQYJKoZIhvcNAQEEBQAwXDELMAkGA1UEBhMCQ1oxETAPBgNV
BAoTCFBWVCBhLnMuMRAwDgYDVQQDEwdDQS1QV1QxMSgwJgYJKoZIhvcNAQkBFhlj
YS1vcGVyYQHA3MHgwMy5icm4ucHZ0LmN6MB4XDTk3MDgwNDA1MDQ1NloXDTk4MDIw
MzA1MDQ1NlowgakxCzAJBgNVBAYTAkNaMQowCAYDVQQIEwEyMRkwFwYDVQQHExBD
ZXNrZSBCdWRlam92aWNlMREwDwYDVQQKEwhQV1QsYS5zLjEMMAoGA1UECxMDVkNV
MRcwFQYDVQQDEw5MaWJvciBEb3N0YWxlazEfMB0GCSqGSIb3DQEJARYQZG9zdGFs
ZWtAcHZ0Lm51dDEYMBYGA1UEDBMPKzQyIDM4IDc3NDcgMzYxMFwwDQYJKoZIhvcN
AQEBBQADSwAwSAJBAORQnnnaTGhwrWBGK+qdvIGiBGyaPNZfnqXlbtXuSUqRHXhE
acIYDtMVfK4wdROe6lmdlr3DuMc747/oT7SjO2UCAwEAATANBgkqhkiG9w0BAQQF
```

```
AAOBgQBxfebIQCCxnVtyY/YVfsActldbmxrBkeb9Z+xN7i/Fc3XYLig8rag3cfWg
wDqbnt8LKzvFt+FzlrOlqIm7miYlWNq26rlY3KGpWPNoWGJTkyrqX80/WAhU5B9l
QOqgL9zXHhE65Qq0Wu/3ryRgyBgebSiFem1ORZVavBHjgVcejw==
-----END CERTIFICATE-----
```

Our class performs three tasks:

1. We need to read the file, strip off the header and footer, and convert the body from a base64 string to a byte array. The `oreilly.jonathan.util.Base64` class is used to perform the base64 conversion. This class is presented in Appendix B, *Base64*.

2. We'll use this byte array (a DER-encoded certificate) to create a new `X509Certificate`. We can then print out some basic information about the certificate.

3. Finally, we'll calculate certificate fingerprints and print them.

`Spill` begins by checking its command-line arguments:

```java
import java.io.*;
import java.security.KeyStore;
import java.security.MessageDigest;
import java.security.cert.X509Certificate;

import oreilly.jonathan.util.Base64;

public class Spill {
  public static void main(String[] args) throws Exception {
    if (args.length != 1) {
      System.out.println("Usage: Spill file");
      return;
    }
```

Next, `Spill` creates a `BufferedReader` for reading lines of text from the file. If the first line doesn't contain the certificate header, an exception is thrown. Otherwise, subsequent lines are read and accumulated as one large base64 string. We stop reading lines when we encounter the footer line. This done, we convert the base64 string to a byte array:

```java
BufferedReader in = new BufferedReader(new FileReader(args[0]));
String begin = in.readLine();
if (begin.equals("-----BEGIN CERTIFICATE-----") == false)
  throw new IOException("Couldn't find certificate beginning");
String base64 = new String();
boolean trucking = true;
while (trucking) {
  String line = in.readLine();
  if (line.startsWith("-----")) trucking = false;
  else base64 += line;
}
```

```
in.close();
byte[] certificateData = Base64.decode(base64);
```

We now have the raw certificate data and can create a new certificate using getIn-stance() in the X509Certificate class:

```
X509Certificate c = X509Certificate.getInstance(certificateData);
```

Having obtained an X509Certificate, Spill prints out various bits of information about it.

```
System.out.println("Subject: " + c.getSubjectDN().getName());
System.out.println("Issuer : " + c.getIssuerDN().getName());
System.out.println("Serial number: " +
    c.getSerialNumber().toString(16));
System.out.println("Valid from " + c.getNotBefore() +
    " to " + c.getNotAfter());
```

We also want to print out the certificate's fingerprints. It's a little tricky to format the fingerprints correctly, so a helper method, doFingerprint(), is used:

```
System.out.println("Fingerprints:");
doFingerprint(certificateData, "MD5");
doFingerprint(certificateData, "SHA");
    }
```

The doFingerprint() method calculates a fingerprint (message digest value) and prints it out. First, it obtains a message digest for the requested algorithm and calculates the digest value:

```
protected static void doFingerprint(byte[] certificateBytes,
    String algorithm) throws Exception {
System.out.print("  " + algorithm + ": ");
MessageDigest md = MessageDigest.getInstance(algorithm);
md.update(certificateBytes);
byte[] digest = md.digest();
```

Now doFingerprint() will print out the digest value as a series of two-digit hexa-decimal numbers. We loop through the digest value. Each byte is converted to a two-digit hex string. Colons separate the hex values.

```
for (int i = 0; i < digest.length; i++) {
    if (i != 0) System.out.print(":");
    int b = digest[i] & 0xff;
    String hex = Integer.toHexString(b);
    if (hex.length() == 1) System.out.print("0");
    System.out.print(hex);
}
System.out.println();
    }
}
```

Let's take it for a test drive. Let's say you have a certificate in a file named *ca1.x509*. You would run Spill as follows:

```
C:\ java Spill ca1.x509
Subject: T="+42 38 7747 361", OID.1.2.840.113549.1.9.1=dostalek@pvt.net,
CN=Libor Dostalek, OU=VCU, O="PVT,a.s.", L=Ceske Budejovice, S=2, C=CZ
Issuer : OID.1.2.840.113549.1.9.1=ca-oper@p70x03.brn.pvt.cz, CN=CA-PVT1,
O=PVT a.s., C=CZ
Serial number: 2d
Valid from Mon Aug 04 01:04:56 EDT 1997 to Tue Feb 03 00:04:56 EST 1998
Fingerprints:
   MD5: d9:6f:56:3e:e0:ec:35:70:94:bb:df:05:75:d6:32:0e
   SHA: db:be:df:e5:ff:ec:f9:53:98:dc:88:dd:6b:ba:cf:2e:2a:68:0c:44
```

If you run keytool -printcert on the same file, you'll see the same information:

```
C:\ keytool -printcert -file ca1.x509
Owner: T="+42 38 7747 361", OID.1.2.840.113549.1.9.1=dostalek@pvt.net,
CN=Libor Dostalek, OU=VCU, O="PVT,a.s.", L=Ceske Budejovice, S=2, C=CZ
Issuer: OID.1.2.840.113549.1.9.1=ca-oper@p70x03.brn.pvt.cz, CN=CA-PVT1, O=PVT
a.s., C=CZ
Serial Number: 2d
Valid from: Mon Aug 04 01:04:56 EDT 1997 until: Tue Feb 03 00:04:56 EST 1998
Certificate Fingerprints:
        MD5:  D9:6F:56:3E:E0:EC:35:70:94:BB:DF:05:75:D6:32:0E
        SHA1: DB:BE:DF:E5:FF:EC:F9:53:98:DC:88:DD:6B:BA:CF:2E:2A:68:0C:44
```

Certificate Revocation Lists

JDK 1.2 addresses another shortcoming of the JDK 1.1 certificate support: Certificate Revocation Lists (CRLs). CRLs answer the question of what happens to certificates when they're lost or stolen. A CRL is simply a list of certificates that are no longer valid. (Unfortunately, there aren't yet any standards for how CRLs are issued; presumably they're published in some way by the CAs.) JDK 1.2 provides two classes that support CRLs. First, java.security.cert.X509CRL represents a CRL as specified in the X.509 standard. You can create an X509CRL from a file using getInstance(), just as with X509Certificate:

public static final X509CRL getInstance(InputStream inStream) throws CRLException, X509ExtensionException

   This method instantiates a concrete subclass of X509CRL and initializes it with the given input stream.

public static final X509CRL getInstance(byte[] crlData) throws CRLException, X509ExtensionException

   This method works like the preceding method except it uses the supplied byte array to initialize the X509CRL.

X509CRL's getInstance() works in much the same way as X509Certificate. The actual subclass of X509CRL that is returned by getInstance() is determined, again, by an entry in the *java.security* file. The relevant entry for CRLs is this:

```
crl.provider.x509=sun.security.x509.X509CRLImpl
```

X509CRL is similar to X509Certificate in many ways. It includes getEncoded() and verify() methods that accomplish the same thing as in X509Certificate. It also includes methods that return information about the CRL itself, like getIssuerDN() and getSigAlgName().

To find out if a particular certificate has been revoked, you can use the isRevoked() method:

public abstract boolean isRevoked(BigInteger serialNumber)
> This method returns true if the certificate matching the given serial number has been revoked. Serial numbers are unique to a Certificate Authority (CA). Each CA issues its own CRLs. Thus, this method is used to correlate certificate serial numbers from the same CA.

If you want more information about a revoked certificate, you can use the getRevokedCertificate() and getRevokedCertificates() methods. These return instances of java.security.cert.RevokedCertificate, which can be used to check the revocation date:

public abstract RevokedCertificate getRevokedCertificate(BigInteger serialNumber) throws CRLException
> This method returns a RevokedCertificate corresponding to the given serial number.

public abstract Set getRevokedCertificates() throws CRLException
> This method returns a collection of all the revoked certificates contained in this X509CRL.

7

Encryption

Encryption is a tool you can use to protect secrets. You might encrypt files on your hard drive so that the loss or theft of your computer would not compromise your data. You might also want to encrypt your network communications, especially the ones to your bank, or your doctor, or your friends.

A *cipher* encrypts or decrypts data. Ciphers comes in three flavors:

- *Symmetric*, or *private key*, ciphers use a single secret key to encrypt and decrypt data. Symmetric keys can be useful in applications like hard-disk file encryption, when the same person encrypts and decrypts data.

- *Asymmetric*, or *public key*, ciphers use a pair of keys. One key is public and may be freely distributed. The other key is private and should be kept secret. Data encrypted with either key can be decrypted using the other key.

- *Hybrid* systems use a combination of symmetric and asymmetric ciphers. Asymmetric ciphers are much slower than their symmetric counterparts. In a hybrid system, an asymmetric cipher is used to exchange a private key (also called a secret key or a session key). The secret key is used with a symmetric cipher for data encryption and decryption.

This list mixes apples and oranges a little bit. Symmetric and asymmetric ciphers are described by algorithms. A hybrid system is at a higher level; it's a protocol that uses both public and private key algorithms.

In this chapter, I'll cover the following topics:

- Stream and block ciphers

- Padding for block ciphers

- Cipher modes, or the different ways a block cipher can be used

- Cipher algorithms

- The `javax.crypto.Cipher` class

- Utility classes based on ciphers

- Passphrase encryption, in which a key is derived from a passphrase

- How to write your own cipher implementations

- Hybrid systems

Remember, this is the dangerous stuff; to play with ciphers, you'll have to download and install the nonexportable Java Cryptography Extension. See Chapter 3, *Architecture*, for more details.

Streams and Blocks

Symmetric ciphers come in two varieties. *Block ciphers* encrypt and decrypt fixed-size blocks of data, usually 64 bits long. *Stream ciphers* operate on a stream of bits or bytes. The distinction is blurry, however. A block cipher can be made to work like a stream cipher, using the appropriate mode (CFB). I'll talk about this soon. Asymmetric ciphers are block ciphers.

Before computers, encryption was accomplished using stream ciphers, which are ciphers that operate on one character of a message at a time. The use of computers in cryptography has led to the creation of block ciphers, in which a message is broken into blocks. The cipher encrypts or decrypts one block at a time. When would you choose a block or stream cipher? It depends on the application. In a cryptographically enabled Telnet application, for example, using a block cipher would be awkward. In telnet, the server should receive each character that the client types, as it is typed. If you were encrypting the data between the client and server with a block cipher, you'd have to wait until the client typed enough characters to fill a block. In this case, a stream cipher is better suited to the task.

Be that as it may, block cipher algorithms are much more prevalent than stream cipher algorithms. If you need a stream cipher (as you will in Chapter 10, *Safe-Talk*), then use a block cipher in CFB mode.

Block Ciphers

Padding

The implementation of block ciphers raises an interesting problem: The plaintext you wish to encrypt will not always be a multiple of the block size (usually 64 bits). To compensate for the last incomplete block, *padding* is needed. A padding scheme specifies exactly how the last block of plaintext is filled with data before it is encrypted. A corresponding procedure on the decryption side removes the padding and restores the plaintext's original length.

PKCS#5

PKCS#5 is one possible padding scheme. PKCS#5 is a Public-Key Cryptography Standard, a self-proclaimed standard published by RSA Data Security, Inc. The padding method is straightforward: Fill the remainder of the block with bytes containing the number of remaining bytes.[*] For example, in a 64-bit block, if there are five leftover plaintext bytes in the block, three bytes with a value of 3 pad the block. Data that ends on a block boundary has a whole block of padding added. In a 64-bit block, a whole block of padding is eight bytes with a value of 8. This method allows the padding to be unambiguously removed after decryption, restoring the original size of the plaintext. Figure 7-1 shows some examples of PKCS#5-style padding in 64-bit blocks.[†]

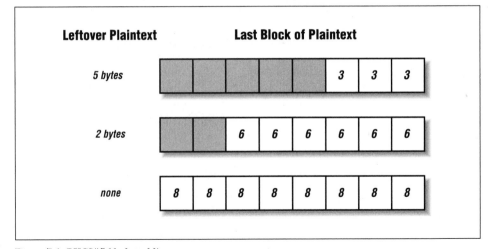

Figure 7-1: PKCS#5 block padding

At first glance, it doesn't seem necessary to add the entire block of padding when the plaintext is a multiple of the block size. Consider, however, some plaintext that is a multiple of the block length and ends with three bytes with the value 3. Suppose it is encrypted without adding any padding. When the corresponding ciphertext is decrypted, it appears to have three bytes of padding. But these are really part of the original plaintext! To avoid this ambiguity, padding is *always*

---

[*] Strictly speaking, blocks are made of *octets*, not bytes. In some obscure cases, a byte is not eight bits long. An octect is always eight bits. I use the more familiar term byte with the assumption that it's eight bits long.

[†] PKCS#5 is actually a standard for passphrase-based encryption. Part of the standard specifies this padding scheme. You can get PKCS#5 from RSA Data Security, Inc., at *http://www.rsa.com/rsal-abs/pubs/PKCS/*.

added when encrypting, no matter what the original plaintext length. When the ciphertext is decrypted, the padding is always removed.

You can find out the padding scheme of a `Cipher` using the `getPadding()` method. In the SunJCE provider, the name for PKCS#5 padding is "PKCS5Padding."

Other padding schemes

There are other padding schemes. You could fill out the remainder of a block with random data or a pattern of data. Basically, you just need to have some way to remove the padding when the ciphertext is decrypted. This implies that somewhere in the padding, there is some data that describes the length of the padding. In PKCS#5, for example, the padding length is distributed throughout the padding data.

Modes

The *mode* of a cipher determines how blocks of plaintext are encrypted into blocks of ciphertext, and vice versa. You can find out the mode of a `Cipher` by calling `getMode()`. The SunJCE provider supports ECB, CBC, CFB, OFB, and PCBC modes, which I will describe here.

ECB

The simplest case is *electronic code book* (ECB) mode, in which each block of plaintext encrypts to a block of ciphertext. ECB mode has the disadvantage that the same plaintext will always encrypt to the same ciphertext, if you use the same key. Consider, for example, the `SecretWriting` program from Chapter 1, *Introduction*. Using this program,

```
Hello, world!
```

encrypts to

```
1Sk5ElK+QKw4ZItlFen4Hg==
```

Using the same key,

```
Hello, world!  Mamma mia!
```

encrypts to

```
1Sk5ElK+QKzJ75LKMLS/zSoVlOn6pfjcEZR7aP3fvpA=
```

Note that the first block of the ciphertext is the same.[*] This is a weakness that can be exploited by a cryptanalyst. This kind of repetition often occurs in messages:

---

[*] The ciphertext is represented in base64, which uses 6 bits per digit. Thus, the first 10 digits make up 60 bits of the first 64-bit ciphertext block, and these digits are the same for both ciphertexts. For more on base64, see Appendix B, *Base64*.

A common salutation, header, or footer can all aid cryptanalysis. If your data is more "random looking," like a key or a message digest, then ECB may be appropriate. Otherwise, you should consider a different mode.

CBC

Cipher block chaining (CBC) mode overcomes the weakness of ECB mode. Each block of plaintext is combined with the previous block's ciphertext, using XOR; the result is encrypted to form a block of ciphertext. Because there is no previous ciphertext block for the first block of plaintext, an *initialization vector* (IV) is used for the first block of plaintext. The IV is usually just random data. The decrypting cipher must be initialized with the same IV to correctly decrypt the data. Encryption in CBC mode is shown in Figure 7-2.

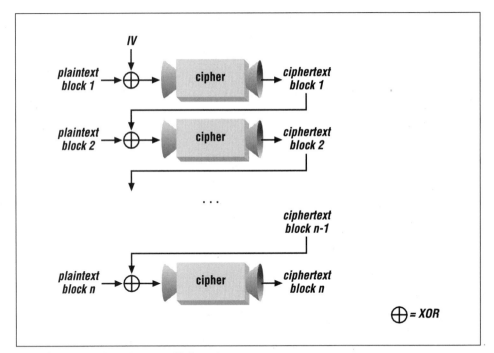

Figure 7-2: Cipher block chaining (CBC) mode

CBC decryption is the reverse of the encryption process. As each block of ciphertext is decrypted, it is XORed with the previous ciphertext block. This produces the plaintext. Again, the cipher must be initialized with an IV to get the ball rolling.

In a way, the IV is a kind of key. On the encrypting side, the cipher is initialized using both a key and the IV. On the decrypting end, the cipher is initialized with a key and the same IV. The IV must be transmitted with the ciphertext to anyone interested in decrypting the ciphertext.

PCBC

Propagating cipher block chaining (PCBC) mode is a lot like CBC mode. When a plaintext block is encrypted, however, it is XORed with both the previous plaintext block and the previous ciphertext block. Likewise, decrypted blocks are XORed with the previous plaintext and ciphertext blocks.

CFB

Cipher feedback (CFB) mode allows a block cipher to act like a stream cipher. Like CBC, it uses an IV, but the internal process is more involved. The net result is that a block cipher in CFB mode can encrypt pieces of data that are smaller than the block size. In fact, CFB can be used to encrypt any data size, from one bit to the block size. Usually, CFB is used to encrypt or decrypt one byte (eight bits) at a time, which is called CFB8.

Figure 7-3 shows how a byte is encrypted using CFB8.

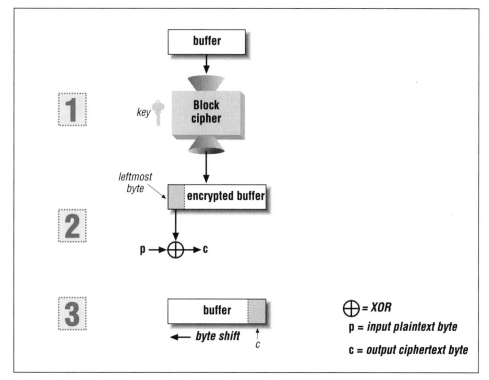

Figure 7-3: Cipher feedback (CFB) mode encrypting eight bits at a time

A plaintext byte, p, is encrypted to a ciphertext byte, c, in three steps:

1. A buffer as large as the block size of the underlying cipher is encrypted using the block cipher. This buffer is filled, initially, with the initialization vector (IV).

2. The desired number of leftmost bits of the encrypted buffer are XORed with the plaintext. The result is the ciphertext output. The remainder of the encrypted buffer is discarded. In CFB8, the leftmost byte of the encrypted buffer is XORed with the plaintext byte, producing a ciphertext byte.

3. The original buffer is shifted to the left by the desired number of bits. In CFB8, the buffer is shifted one byte to the left. The ciphertext is used to fill in the empty space on the right side of the buffer. This buffer will be used again in the next encryption. As this process continues, the buffer will become entirely filled with ciphertext.

Decryption follows the same process, except for Step 2:

1. The buffer is encrypted using the block cipher. Even though we are *decrypting* a ciphertext byte, we still use the block cipher to *encrypt* the buffer.

2. The leftmost bits of the encrypted buffer are XORed with the ciphertext, producing the plaintext output. Again, the remainder of the encrypted buffer is discarded.

3. The original buffer is shifted left and filled in with the ciphertext. The buffer will be used again in the next decryption.

Why does this work? Let's call the leftmost bits of the encrypted buffer b. Whether you are encrypting or decrypting, CFB mode produces the same sequence of b values if you start with the same IV. This is because the underlying cipher always encrypts the internal buffer, and the internal buffer is always shifted to the left and filled on the right with the ciphertext. This happens regardless of whether the CFB mode cipher is encrypting or decrypting. In encryption, the ciphertext is produced by XORing the plaintext with the leftmost bits of the encrypted buffer: $c = p \oplus b$. When decrypting, the plaintext is calculated from $c \oplus b$. Substituting for c, we get $c \oplus b = p \oplus b \oplus b = p$.

As you might have noticed, CFB mode is not particularly efficient. Each time a piece of plaintext is encrypted, an entire block is encrypted by the underlying cipher. Likewise, each piece of decrypted ciphertext comes at the cost of an entire encrypted block. For a cipher with a block size of 64 bits, CFB8 will be about eight times slower than ECB or CBC. As the number of bits encrypted in CFB mode approaches the block size of the underlying cipher, the efficiency improves. CFB64 (also called CFB) will be just as efficient as CBC for a cipher with a 64-bit block size.

You can use CFB mode with any symmetric block cipher. Interestingly, you can use CFB mode with an asymmetric cipher algorithm, too, but it will behave like a symmetric cipher. To understand why, remember that a block cipher in CFB mode always encrypts the internal buffer, regardless of whether you are encrypting or decrypting data. The asymmetric cipher will have to be initialized with the same key each time, whether you are encrypting or decrypting. This is the behavior of a symmetric cipher.

OFB

Output feedback (OFB) mode works just like CFB mode, except in how the internal buffer is updated. When the internal buffer is shifted left, the space on the right side is filled with the leftmost bits of the encrypted buffer (instead of the ciphertext, which was used in CFB). In theory, OFB can be used with any bit size less than or equal to the cipher's block size. However, OFB is weak when the feedback size is less than the block size of the underlying cipher. Only use OFB with a feedback size equal to the cipher's block size.

Other modes

There are other cipher modes; for details, see Bruce Schneier's *Applied Cryptography*. When you use a cipher, make sure you understand what mode it's using. The mode affects the cipher's resistance to cryptanalysis and its ability to recover from transmission errors.

For example, in ECB mode, one block of plaintext corresponds to one block of ciphertext. A transmission error in one block of ciphertext results in only one bad block of decrypted plaintext. In CBC mode, a bad block of ciphertext will result in two bad blocks of decrypted plaintext because the previous ciphertext block is used in decrypting a current plaintext block. In CFB mode, using an underlying cipher with a 64-bit block size, a bad byte of ciphertext will result in eight more bad bytes of plaintext, as the bogus ciphertext byte works its way through CFB's internal buffer. OFB doesn't exhibit this property; a single bad bit in OFB mode results in a single bad decrypted plaintext bit.

In cipher modes, there's a trade-off between making the ciphertext resistant to cryptanalyis and making the ciphertext robust in the face of transmission errors. ECB, for example, is the easiest mode to break, but it also has no error propagation.

Algorithms

One of the nice features of the provider architecture in the Security API is that it's possible to use different cryptographic algorithms without having to rewrite your program. The SunJCE provider includes three cipher algorithms. Other providers include other algorithms; you can select one according to your needs and budget.

Table 7-1 lists cipher algorithms and the providers that support them. Table 7-2 gives details on the providers.

Table 7-1: Cipher Algorithms

Name	Provider(s)
DES	SunJCE, Cryptix, IAIK, JCP
DESede (triple DES)	SunJCE, Cryptix (DES-EDE3), IAIK (3DES), JCP
PBEWithMD5AndDES	SunJCE
RSA	Cryptix, IAIK, JSAFE
Blowfish	Cryptix
IDEA	Cryptix, IAIK, JCP
SPEED	Cryptix
RC2	IAIK, Cryptix
RC4	IAIK, Cryptix, JCP
CAST5	Cryptix
LOKI91	Cryptix
SAFER	Cryptix
Square	Cryptix

Table 7-2: Cipher Algorithm Providers

Name	Full name	Location	Free?	U.S. only?
SunJCE	Sun JCE Security Provider v1.0	*http://java.sun.com/products/jdk/1.2/jce/*	Yes	Yes
Cryptix	Cryptix for Java (3.0 or later)	*http://www.systemics.com/software/ cryptix-java/*	Yes	No
IAIK	IAIK Security Provider	*http://wwwjce.iaik.tu-graz.ac.at/*	No	No
JSAFE	RSA's Java Crypto Toolkit	*http://www.rsa.com/rsa/products/jsafe/*	No	Yes
JCP	JCP Crypto Development Kit	*http://www.jcp.co.uk/products/*	No	No

javax.crypto.Cipher

The `javax.crypto.Cipher` class encapsulates a cipher algorithm. A `Cipher` either encrypts data or decrypts data. The `Cipher` class encompasses both asymmetric (public key) and symmetric (private key) algorithms.

This class is part of the JCE, a piece of software that cannot be exported from the United States. For a description of the JCE, refer to Chapter 3. Groups outside the

United States have implemented the JCE based on its documentation. Two such implementations are Cryptix (*http://www.systemics.com/software/cryptix-java/*) and IAIK-JCE (*http://wwwjce.iaik.tu-graz.ac.at/*).

Cipher is an abstract class, so you can't instantiate it directly. Like the classes in the JCA, it provides factory methods that return useful instances. Using a Cipher is a three-step process:

1. Obtain a Cipher using the getInstance() factory method.

2. Initialize the Cipher for encryption or decryption using init(). These methods accept a mode (either Cipher.ENCRYPT_MODE or Cipher.DECRYPT_MODE) and a Key. The type of key you use, public, private, or secret, depends on the Cipher's algorithm.

3. Encrypt or decrypt data using the update() and doFinal() methods.

In the SecretWriting example from Chapter 1, for the encrypting case, these steps look like:

```
Cipher cipher = Cipher.getInstance("DES/ECB/PKCS5Padding");
cipher.init(Cipher.ENCRYPT_MODE, key);
byte[] raw = cipher.doFinal(stringBytes);
```

You probably noticed that the call to getInstance() specifies more than just an algorithm name. As a matter of fact, we've specified an algorithm (DES), a *mode* (ECB), and a *padding scheme* (PKCS5Padding). The getInstance() methods for Cipher recognize two types of strings:

algorithm

You can pass the algorithm name by itself. Whichever provider supplies the algorithm implementation will also supply a default mode and padding scheme.

algorithm/mode/padding

You've seen this already. If you wish, you can specify an algorithm, a cipher mode, and a padding scheme in your call to getInstance().

Getting a Cipher

Cipher's factory methods look like all the factory methods in the JCA, so you already know how to use them:

public static Cipher getInstance(String algorithm) throws NoSuchAlgorithmException, NoSuchPaddingException

This factory method returns a Cipher for the given algorithm. The algorithm name usually includes additional information, like a padding scheme and a cipher mode.

public static Cipher getInstance(String algorithm, String provider) throws
NoSuchAlgorithmException, NoSuchProviderException, NoSuchPaddingException

> This method is the same as above, but it uses the named provider's implementation of the given algorithm.

Just as there are standard algorithm names, there are standard names for the cipher modes and padding schemes supported by the JCE. These are shown in Table 7-3. Note that you can specify a bit size with OFB and CFB mode. If no bit size is specified, the cipher's block size is used. All of the padding schemes apply to the JCE's cipher algorithms, DES and DESede.

Table 7-3: Standard Names for Cipher Modes and Padding Schemes

Name	Description
ECB	Electronic code book mode
CBC	Cipher block chaining mode
PCBC	Propagating cipher block chaining mode
CFBn	Cipher feedback mode, using n bits per operation
OFBn	Output feedback mode, using n bits per operation[a]
NoPadding	No padding
PKCS5Padding	PKCS#5-style padding

[a] As I mentioned, you should not use OFB unless the feedback size is the same as the cipher block size. This is the default behavior if you request OFB mode without specifying a feedback size.

Basic Information

Several of `Cipher`'s methods return basic information about the cipher:

public final Provider getProvider()

> This method returns the cryptographic provider of this `Cipher`.

public final int getBlockSize()

> This method returns the block size of the cipher, measured in bytes.

public final int getOutputSize(int inputLen) throws IllegalStateException

> This method calculates the output size for the next call to `update()` or `doFinal()`, given an input length. The lengths are measured in bytes. If the `Cipher` has not been initialized, an exception is thrown. This method returns a maximum length; calling `update()` or `doFinal()` with the same length of input data may actually result in a shorter output length than reported by this method.

public final byte[] getIV()

> This method returns the IV used to encrypt data. It is only for cipher modes that use an IV. A `Cipher` in ECB mode, for example, will return `null` from

this method. You can call this method immediately after initializing a `Cipher` for encryption to retrieve the `Cipher`'s IV. The same IV should be used, later, to initialize the `Cipher` for decryption.

Initializing a Cipher

The `Cipher` can be initialized for encryption or decryption, using constants defined in the `Cipher` class:

public static final int ENCRYPT_MODE
public static final int DECRYPT_MODE

> Use one of these constants with an `init()` method to initialize the `Cipher` for encryption or decryption.

`Cipher` provides four overloaded `init()` methods. You can completely reinitialize the `Cipher` at any time by calling one of the `init()` methods.

Generic

Two of `Cipher`'s `init()` methods are algorithm independent. If you use these methods and program carefully, you should be able to switch the algorithms that you're using without rewriting any of your application. Given the modular nature of the provider architecture, it would be nice if your users could choose the strongest installed algorithm to use with your application.

public final void init(int opmode, Key key) throws InvalidKeyException

> This method initializes the `Cipher` to encrypt or decrypt data, using the supplied key. opmode should be `ENCRYPT_MODE` or `DECRYPT_MODE`. An exception is thrown if the wrong type of key is supplied.

public final void init(int opmode, Key key, SecureRandom random) throws
InvalidKeyException

> This method is the same as above, except the `Cipher` will use the supplied `SecureRandom` to generate random numbers internally.

Name brand

Sometimes you may not be able to correctly initialize a `Cipher` in an algorithm-independent way. In these cases, the `Cipher` can be initialized by a set of algorithm-specific parameters encapsulated by an `java.security.spec.AlgorithmParameterSpec` object. Later in this chapter, there's an example of this technique based on passphrase encryption.

public final void init(int opmode, Key key, AlgorithmParameterSpec params) throws
InvalidKeyException, InvalidAlgorithmParameterException

> You can initialize a `Cipher` with algorithm-specific parameters using this method.

public final void init(int opmode, Key key, AlgorithmParameterSpec params, SecureRandom random) throws InvalidKeyException, InvalidAlgorithmParameterException

> This method is the same as above, but it tells the `Cipher` to use the supplied `SecureRandom` for generating random numbers.

Feedback ciphers need to be set up with an IV to decrypt data properly. For these ciphers, a special parameter object, `javax.crypto.spec.IvParameterSpec`, holds the IV. The following code demonstrates how to initialize a `Cipher` for decryption using a particular IV:

```
// First obtain iv, a byte array, and sessionKey, a DES key.
Cipher cipher = Cipher.getInstance("DES/CBC/PKCS5Padding");
IvParameterSpec spec = new IvParameterSpec(iv);
cipher.init(Cipher.DECRYPT_MODE, sessionKey, spec);
```

You'll see feedback ciphers and IVs in action in Chapter 10 and Chapter 11, *CipherMail.*

Feeding Data to a Cipher

A `Cipher` transforms one block of data into another block of data, either encrypting or decrypting. Two methods, `update()` and `doFinal()`, are used to feed data into the `Cipher`. There are four overloaded versions of `update()`:

public final byte[] update(byte[] input) throws IllegalStateException

> This method adds the given array of input data to the `Cipher`. If the `Cipher` has accumulated enough data to transform one or more blocks, it does so, returning the transformed blocks. Leftover data that does not fill an entire block is stored for use with the next call to `update()` or `doFinal()`.

public final byte[] update(byte[] input, int inputOffset, int inputLen) throws IllegalStateException

> This method is the same as above, except that it uses `inputLen` bytes of the supplied byte array, starting at `inputOffset`.

public final int update(byte[] input, int inputOffset, int inputLen, byte[] output) throws IllegalStateException, ShortBufferException

> This method works like the previous method. The output, however, is written into the supplied `output` array. If the output array is too small to hold the results of the call to `update()`, a `ShortBufferException` is thrown. This method returns the total number of bytes that were written to the output array.

public final int update(byte[] input, int inputOffset, int inputLen, byte[] output, int outputOffset) throws IllegalStateException, ShortBufferException

> This method is the same as above, except that the output is written to the given `output` array, starting at `outputOffset`. As before, a `ShortBufferException` is thrown if there's not enough space in the output array.

Let's see how `update()` works in practice. In the following examples, assume that we have already obtained a DES key.

```
Cipher cipher = Cipher.getInstance("DES/ECB/PKCS5Padding");
cipher.init(Cipher.ENCRYPT_MODE, key);
byte[] plain5 = "comic".getBytes();
byte[] plain7 = "serious".getBytes();
byte[] step1 = cipher.update(plain5);
byte[] step2 = cipher.update(plain7);
```

The block size of a DES cipher is 8 bytes. In the first call to `update()`, we pass only 5 bytes, which is not enough for a full block. Thus, no data is returned, and the length of the `step1` array is 0. Our next call to `update()` adds 7 more bytes, for a total of 12. This is enough to encrypt and return 1 block of data. The `step2` array is 8 bytes long and contains the first block of ciphertext. What happened to the 4 leftover bytes? The `Cipher` is still keeping track of them. You can encrypt them, if they are the end of the plaintext, with the `doFinal()` methods, which I'll discuss in a moment.

There's an alternate approach to the previous example that may be a little cleaner, depending on what you're trying to do:

```
Cipher cipher = Cipher.getInstance("DES/ECB/PKCS5Padding");
cipher.init(Cipher.ENCRYPT_MODE, key);
byte[] plain5 = "comic".getBytes();
byte[] plain7 = "serious".getBytes();
int outputLength = cipher.getOutputSize(plain5.length + plain7.length);
byte[] ciphertext = new byte[outputLength];
int length1 = cipher.update(plain5, 0, plain5.length,
    ciphertext);
int length2 = cipher.update(plain7, 0, plain7.length,
    ciphertext, length1);
```

First, we ask the `Cipher` how big the output will be for our total input. The total length is the sum of the lengths of the plaintext arrays, or 12 bytes. Because this is a padding cipher, the second incomplete block will be padded. Thus, the `Cipher` calculates an output size of 16 bytes. We create an array of this length, called `ciphertext`. Then we use `update()` to write the output data into the array. The first call to `update()`, as before, writes no data and returns 0. The second call encrypts one block and writes the ciphertext into the supplied array.

You can tell the `Cipher` to finish encrypting or decrypting by calling one of the `doFinal()` methods. There are six varieties of this method, but they all do basically the same thing:

public final byte[] doFinal() throws IllegalStateException, IllegalBlockSizeException, BadPaddingException

This method tells the `Cipher` to finish an encryption or decryption operation. Any leftover data from previous calls to `update()` is processed. The data is padded, if this is a padding cipher. The output is returned as a byte array.

If the Cipher has not been initialized, an IllegalStateException is thrown. When encrypting, an IllegalBlockSizeException is thrown if the length of the input data is not a multiple of the block size and the Cipher does not implement padding. When decrypting, an IllegalBlockSizeException is thrown if the length of the input data is not an integral number of blocks. Finally, a BadPaddingException is thrown by padding Ciphers when the decrypted plaintext does not contain correct padding.

public final int doFinal(byte[] output, int outputOffset) throws IllegalStateException,
IllegalBlockSizeException, ShortBufferException, BadPaddingException

This method is the same as above, except that the output is written to the supplied array, starting at outputOffset. The number of output bytes is returned. A ShortBufferException is thrown if the output array is not long enough.

public final byte[] doFinal(byte[] input) throws IllegalStateException,
IllegalBlockSizeException, BadPaddingException

Use this method to add the supplied input data to the Cipher and then finish an encryption or decryption operation. It is equivalent to calling update(input), followed by doFinal(), except that the output from both steps is returned from this method.

public final byte[] doFinal(byte[] input, int inputOffset, int inputLen) throws
IllegalStateException, IllegalBlockSizeException, BadPaddingException

This method is the same as above, except that it uses inputLen bytes of the supplied array, starting at inputOffset.

public final int doFinal(byte[] input, int inputOffset, int inputLen, byte[] output) throws
IllegalStateException, IllegalBlockSizeException, ShortBufferException,
BadPaddingException

This method is the same as above, except that it writes output data into the supplied array. A ShortBufferException is thrown if the output array is too small.

public final int doFinal(byte[] input, int inputOffset, int inputLen, byte[] output,
int outputOffset) throws IllegalStateException, IllegalBlockSizeException,
ShortBufferException, BadPaddingException

This method is the same as the preceding method, except that the output data is written to the supplied array starting at outputOffset.

To see how this method works, let's extend the last example by adding a call to doFinal() at the end:

```
Cipher cipher = Cipher.getInstance("DES/ECB/PKCS5Padding");
cipher.init(Cipher.ENCRYPT_MODE, key);
byte[] plain5 = "comic".getBytes();
byte[] plain7 = "serious".getBytes();
```

```
int outputLength = cipher.getOutputSize(plain5.length + plain7.length);
byte[] ciphertext = new byte[outputLength];
int length1 = cipher.update(plain5, 0, plain5.length,
    ciphertext);
int length2 = cipher.update(plain7, 0, plain7.length,
    ciphertext, length1);
int length3 = cipher.doFinal(ciphertext, length1 + length2);
```

As before, we add 12 bytes to the `Cipher`, using `update()`. One block is
encrypted, leaving 4 leftover bytes. The call to `doFinal()` causes the `Cipher` to
pad the 4 leftover bytes, creating a full 8-byte block. This block is encrypted and
written into our `ciphertext` array. The value of `length3` is 8, representing the
ciphertext block that was produced in the call to `doFinal()`.

The example is a bit contrived. In many cases, you can encrypt or decrypt data
with a single call to `doFinal()`, like this:

```
Cipher cipher = Cipher.getInstance("DES/ECB/PKCS5Padding");
cipher.init(Cipher.ENCRYPT_MODE, key);
byte[] plaintext = "comicserious".getBytes();
byte[] ciphertext = cipher.doFinal(plaintext);
```

Cipher's Close Relatives

Cipher Streams

If you are able to encrypt or decrypt all of your data in one shot, then a call to
`doFinal()` is all you need. In some cases, however, you need to encrypt data in
pieces. For example, loading a large file into memory to encrypt it would not be
practical.

The JCE offers two classes that worry about the details of encrypting or decrypting a
stream of data. `javax.crypto.CipherInputStream` and `javax.crypto.Cipher-`
`OutputStream` can be used to encrypt and decrypt data without thinking too
hard. They are subclasses of the standard `FilterInputStream` and `FilterOut-`
`putStream` classes, so they work smoothly with the rest of the stream classes in the
`java.io` package. You can construct one of these streams by specifying an underlying stream (as with all filtered streams) and an initialized `Cipher` object.[*]

The following example encrypts or decrypts an entire disk file. Like the `Secret-`
`Writing` application (in Chapter 1), it reads a private key from *SecretKey.ser*. If that
file does not exist, `Cloak` creates a new key and saves it in a newly created file,

---

[*] Don't confuse the cipher stream classes with stream ciphers. `CipherInputStream` and `CipherOut-`
`putStream` are stream classes that can use any cipher, including block ciphers, to encrypt and decrypt
data. They are useful classes because they plug in to the rest of the `java.io` package.

SecretKey.ser. The input file is read using an ordinary `FileInputStream`. The file is encrypted or decrypted using a `CipherOutputStream`.

```java
import java.io.*;
import java.security.*;

import javax.crypto.*;

public class Cloak {
  public static final int kBufferSize = 8192;

  public static void main(String[] args) throws Exception {
    // Check arguments.
    if (args.length < 3) {
      System.out.println("Usage: Cloak -e|-d inputfile outputfile");
      return;
    }

    // Get or create key.
    Key key;
    try {
      ObjectInputStream in = new
          ObjectInputStream(new FileInputStream("SecretKey.ser"));
      key = (Key)in.readObject();
      in.close();
    }
    catch (Exception e) {
      KeyGenerator generator = KeyGenerator.getInstance("DES");
      generator.init(new SecureRandom());
      key = generator.generateKey();
      ObjectOutputStream out = new ObjectOutputStream(
          new FileOutputStream("SecretKey.ser"));
      out.writeObject(key);
      out.close();
    }

    // Get a cipher object.
    Cipher cipher = Cipher.getInstance("DES/ECB/PKCS5Padding");

    // Encrypt or decrypt.
    if (args[0].indexOf("e") != -1)
      cipher.init(Cipher.ENCRYPT_MODE, key);
    else
      cipher.init(Cipher.DECRYPT_MODE, key);

    FileInputStream in = new FileInputStream(args[1]);
    FileOutputStream fileOut = new FileOutputStream(args[2]);
    CipherOutputStream out = new CipherOutputStream(fileOut, cipher);
    byte[] buffer = new byte[kBufferSize];
```

```
        int length;
        while ((length = in.read(buffer)) != -1)
          out.write(buffer, 0, length);
        in.close();
        out.close();
    }
}
```

javax.crypto.SealedObject

JCE 1.2 includes a utility class that uses encryption, `javax.crypto.SealedObject`. Instances of this class act as containers for other objects. The contained object is encrypted to provide confidentiality. You can construct a `SealedObject` to contain any `Serializable` object:

public SealedObject(Serializable object, Cipher c) throws IOException, IllegalBlockSizeException

> This constructor wraps a `SealedObject` around the supplied `Serializable` object. The supplied cipher is used to encrypt (seal) the object. The cipher should already be initialized for encryption. If an error occurs in serializing the object or encrypting it, an exception is thrown.

To retrieve the original, unencrypted object, use `getObject()`:

public final Object getObject(Cipher c) throws IOException, ClassNotFoundException, IllegalBlockSizeException, BadPaddingException

> This method decrypts the contained object using the given `Cipher`. Exceptions are thrown if the `Cipher` is not properly initialized or if there is an error with the padding.

Suppose, for example, that you wanted to serialize an object to send over a network connection. To prevent spies from viewing the contents of the object, or even deserializing it themselves, you can use `SealedObject`. Without any cryptographic protection, your code might look like this:

```
// set up the socket connection
ObjectOutputStream out = new ObjectOutputStream(socket.getOutputStream());
out.writeObject(secretObject);
```

You could send a sealed version of the object instead, like this:

```
// set up the socket connection and obtain the key
ObjectOutputStream out = new ObjectOutputStream(socket.getOutputStream());
Cipher cipher = Cipher.getInstance("DES/ECB/PKCS5Padding");
cipher.init(Cipher.ENCRYPT_MODE, key);
SealedObject so = new SealedObject(secretObject, cipher);
out.writeObject(so);
```

On the other end of the network connection, you need to deserialize the Sealed-Object and retrieve its contents, using getObject():

```
// set up the socket connection and obtain the key
ObjectInputStream in = new ObjectInputStream(socket.getInputStream());
SealedObject so = (SealedObject)in.readObject();
Cipher cipher = Cipher.getInstance("DES/ECB/PKCS5Padding");
cipher.init(Cipher.DECRYPT_MODE, key);
Object secretObject = so.getObject(cipher);
```

Passphrase Encryption

Passphrase encryption is a "quick-and-dirty" method for encrypting data. Instead of having to manage a private key in a file, a passphrase is used to generate a key. A passphrase is something a person can remember and type, which eliminates the need to store a key in a file somewhere. A passphrase is just like a password, except it's usually longer. The key is constructed by calculating a message digest of the passphrase. The digest value is used to construct a key for a symmetric cipher.

The usual caveats about passwords apply to passphrases. People are likely to choose easy-to-remember passphrases, which are also easy to guess. Dictionary attacks are also possible, though a passphrase is usually longer than a password, thereby making dictionary attacks more expensive. People also are likely to keep their passphrases in wallets, stuck to computer monitors, tattooed on their foreheads, or in other obvious places. If you want a simple encryption method that provides moderate security, however, passphrase encryption may be sufficient.

Salt and Vinegar

You can reduce the efficiency of a dictionary attack by using *salt*. Typically, an attacker compiles a list of common or likely passphrases. Then he or she calculates the digest of each passphrase and stores it (this is the dictionary). Now the attacker can construct a key from each digest value to see if a piece of ciphertext decrypts or not.

Salt is additional data concatenated to the passphrase. The passphrase and salt are digested together. This means that the attacker's dictionary now needs to contain many more entries, one for each possible salt value for each probable passphrase. To understand this, consider a very simple attacker's dictionary. It contains three DES key possibilities based on common passphrases. (md5() denotes the operation of digesting using an MD5 message digest.)

```
md5( gandalf )
md5( sex )
md5( secret )
```

When the attacker finds some passphrase-encrypted data, he or she can simply use the three prebuilt keys in the dictionary to decrypt the data and see if anything intelligible is produced. Now let's see how salt makes the attacker's life difficult. We'll just consider a two-bit salt, which I'll represent as a number from 0 to 3. The attacker's dictionary now must include these DES key possiblities:

```
md5(0,  gandalf )
md5(0,  sex )
md5(0,  secret )

md5(1,  gandalf )
md5(1,  sex )
md5(1,  secret )

md5(2,  gandalf )
md5(2,  sex )
md5(2,  secret )

md5(3,  gandalf )
md5(3,  sex )
md5(3,  secret )
```

Adding a 2-bit salt multiplied the size of the dictionary by 4. If you use a 64-bit salt, as described in this section, it multiplies the dictionary size by 2^{64}, which is a big number.

Iterations are another way to foil dictionary attacks. Let's look at the simple dictionary once more:

```
md5( gandalf )
md5( sex )
md5( secret )
```

The iteration count specifies how many times the passphrase should be digested to produce a key. The following dictionary, for example, has entries for one, two, and three iterations:

```
md5( gandalf )
md5( sex )
md5( secret )

md5(md5( gandalf ))
md5(md5( sex ))
md5(md5( secret ))

md5(md5(md5( gandalf )))
md5(md5(md5( sex )))
md5(md5(md5( secret )))
```

Much like salt, the iteration count is designed to make dictionary attacks infeasible.

JCE 1.2 includes an implementation of passphrase encryption, based on PKCS#5, a standard published by RSA Data Security, Inc.[*] No rocket science is involved in PKCS#5 passphrase encryption; it's based on the MD5 message digest and a DES cipher in CBC mode. You could write it yourself, if you wanted. But JCE 1.2 includes an implementation of the algorithm, so there's no point reinventing it.

Test Drive

In this section, we'll develop a simple class, PBE, to demonstrate passphrase encryption. It will accept a passphrase typed on the command line and either encrypt or decrypt a file. It is used as follows:

```
java PBE option passphrase inputfile outputfile
```

The option parameter should be −e for encryption and −d for decryption. The PBE class has a single method, main(), that does all the work. It begins by reading parameters from the command line.

```
import java.io.*;
import java.security.*;
import java.security.spec.*;

import javax.crypto.*;
import javax.crypto.spec.*;

public class PBE {
   public static void main(String[] args) throws Exception {
      String options = args[0];
      String passphrase = args[1];
      File inputFile = new File(args[2]);
      File outputFile = new File(args[3]);
```

The name of the passphrase encryption algorithm in the JCE is PBEWithMD5AndDES. We'll be using this unwieldy name a few times, so we assign it to a local variable. We also create a byte array, salt, and fix the iteration count at 20.

```
String algorithm = "PBEWithMD5AndDES";
byte[] salt = new byte[8];
int iterations = 20;
```

This class either encrypts a file or decrypts it. It sets a local Boolean variable based on what option was entered on the command line:

```
boolean encrypting = (options.indexOf("e") != -1);
```

---

[*] You may remember PKCS#5 from earlier in this chapter, when I talked about cipher padding. The document is mostly concerned with passphrase encryption; padding is discussed along the way.

To create a DES key from a passphrase, you need to use a `SecretKeyFactory`, as described in Chapter 4, *Random Numbers*. First, create a `PBEKeySpec` from the supplied passphrase. Then a `SecretKeyFactory` for the passphrase encryption algorithm is used to create a key:

```
// Create a key from the supplied passphrase.
KeySpec ks = new PBEKeySpec(passphrase.toCharArray());
SecretKeyFactory skf = SecretKeyFactory.getInstance(algorithm);
SecretKey key = skf.generateSecret(ks);
```

Next, the `PBE` class reads the input file. When encrypting, the entire input file is read. When decrypting, we expect to find the salt value at the beginning of the file.

```
// Read the input.
FileInputStream in = new FileInputStream(inputFile);
int length = (int)inputFile.length();
if (!encrypting) in.read(salt);
byte[] input = new byte[length - (encrypting ? 0 : 8)];
in.read(input);
in.close();
```

If `PBE` is encrypting a file, it creates a salt value based on the digest of the passphrase and the input file:

```
if (encrypting) {
  // Create the salt from eight bytes of the digest of P || M.
  MessageDigest md = MessageDigest.getInstance("MD5");
  md.update(passphrase.getBytes());
  md.update(input);
  byte[] digest = md.digest();
  System.arraycopy(digest, 0, salt, 0, 8);
}
```

To initialize the `Cipher` with the salt and iteration count, we need an `Algorithm-ParameterSpec` that encapsulates this information. The JCE supplies such a class, `javax.crypto.spec.PBEParameterSpec`:

```
// Create the algorithm parameters.
AlgorithmParameterSpec aps = new PBEParameterSpec(salt, iterations);
```

The `Cipher` is created and initialized, and the input data is transformed:

```
// Encrypt or decrypt the input.
Cipher cipher = Cipher.getInstance(algorithm);
int mode = encrypting ? Cipher.ENCRYPT_MODE : Cipher.DECRYPT_MODE;
cipher.init(mode, key, aps);
byte[] output = cipher.doFinal(input);
```

We're ready to write to the output file now. If `PBE` has just encrypted a file, the salt is written to the output also:

```
// Write the output.
OutputStream out = new FileOutputStream(outputFile);
```

```
        if (encrypting) out.write(salt);
        out.write(output);
        out.close();
    }
}
```

You can use the -e option to encrypt a file and any other option to decrypt it. For example, a sample session follows. I start with a simple text file, called *plaintext*. PBE is used to encrypt this file; the encrypted filename is *ciphertext*. Then PBE is used to decrypt this file. The results are placed in a file called *decrypted*:

```
C:\ type plaintext
Meet me at midnight down by the old rail yard.


C:\ java PBE -e "This is the passphrase." plaintext ciphertext


C:\ type ciphertext
"_>9-_`>y++-    _    8_PH[  +o+>P&-»p `v \+> _w3l_u_y·`< O+,_+__F_TA=3a+ƒ|+


C:\ java PBE -d "This is the passphrase." ciphertext decrypted


C:\ type decrypted
Meet me at midnight down by the old rail yard.


C:\
```

If you type even one character of the passphrase incorrectly, the ciphertext will not decrypt properly. In a real application, of course, the passphrase should never be visible, as it is here. You would probably use an AWT TextField with the setEchoChar() method to conceal the passphrase.[*]

Inside Cipher

So far, you've looked at different ways you can use the Cipher class. Now, I'll show you how to write your own cipher implementation. First, I'll talk about CipherSpi, the superclass of any cipher implementation. We'll develop a generic BlockCipher class to handle the mundane details of block formatting. Finally, I'll present two cipher "wrapper" classes that implement CBC and CFB mode with any existing block cipher.

SPI

The methods in javax.crypto.CipherSpi mirror methods in Cipher's API. As a matter of fact, the SPI is a little simpler than the API because overloaded API methods like update() and doFinal() call fewer overloaded versions of their SPI counterparts.

---

[*] In the Swing world, you would use a JPasswordField.

Setup

Suppose you want to implement DES in CBC mode with PKCS#5 padding. There are several ways to do this. You might, for example, write a class that supports this exact combination of mode and padding with DES. Alternately, you could write a class that implements DES in CBC mode and could support several different padding schemes. Finally, you might just write a generic DES class that supports multiple modes and padding schemes.

If you write generic classes and set them up properly in a provider (see Chapter 9, *Writing a Provider*), your implementation will be notified what mode and padding scheme it should use. This notification occurs through calls to the following methods:

protected abstract void engineSetMode(String mode) throws NoSuchAlgorithmException
> This method informs the cipher implementation that it should operate in the given mode. If the mode is not supported by the implementation, an exception should be thrown.

protected abstract void engineSetPadding(String padding) throws NoSuchPaddingException
> This method tells the CipherSpi to use the given padding scheme. If it is not supported, an exception should be thrown.

Suppose you write a generic DES implementation. If you set up your provider properly, your class will be instantiated when someone requests "DES/CBC/PKCS5Padding" in a call to Cipher.getInstance(). Your implementation's engineSetMode() will be called with "CBC" and engineSetPadding() will be called with "PKCS5Padding."

Alternately, you might write a generic DES CBC mode implementation. As before, if your provider is properly configured, your class will be instantiated when someone asks for a "DES/CBC/PKCS5Padding" cipher. Then engineSetPadding() will be called to let your implementation know it should use "PKCS5Padding."

Basic information

The getBlockSize(), getOutputSize(), and getIV() methods in Cipher's API all have counterparts in CipherSpi. When the API method is called, the corresponding SPI method will be called in your cipher implementation:

protected abstract int engineGetBlockSize()
> This method returns the block size of the cipher, in bytes.

protected abstract int engineGetOutputSize(int inputLen)
> This method returns the length of the output that will be produced by a call to update() or doFinal() with input data of the given length. This is a

maximum value; the length of the data returned by the next `update()` or `doFinal()` may be shorter than what this method returns.

protected abstract byte[] engineGetIV()

>   If this `CipherSpi` is running in a feedback mode, this method returns the IV.

Initializing

`CipherSpi` contains just two methods for initialization:

protected abstract void engineInit(int opmode, Key key, SecureRandom random) throws InvalidKeyException

>   This method handles algorithm-independent cipher initializiation. `opmode` should be one of `Cipher.ENCRYPT_MODE` or `CIPHER.DECRYPT_MODE`. You should check that the supplied `Key` is the correct type for your cipher algorithm; if not, throw an `InvalidKeyException`. Finally, if your cipher implementation needs random numbers, you should use the supplied `Secure-Random` to generate them.

protected abstract void engineInit(int opmode, Key key, AlgorithmParameterSpec params, SecureRandom random) throws InvalidKeyException, InvalidAlgorithmParameterException

>   This method handles algorithm-specific cipher initialization. The `opmode`, `key`, and `random` parameters have the same meanings as above. An additional object, `params`, contains algorithm-specific parameters. Your `CipherSpi` subclass should attempt to cast this object to a recognized parameter type and extract information from it. If you don't recognize the type of the object, throw an `InvalidAlgorithmParameterException`. For example, a cipher in a feedback mode will expect to receive an `IvParameterSpec` object, from which the IV can be extracted.

Feeding

The `Cipher` class has a bevy of overloaded `update()` and `doFinal()` methods that are used to feed data into the cipher and gather the results. These methods end up calling `engineUpdate()` or `engineDoFinal()` in `CipherSpi`. It's up to the cipher implementation to provide data buffering and make sure the block boundaries come out right.

protected abstract byte[] engineUpdate(byte[] input, int inputOffset, int inputLen)

>   This method is called to add input data to the cipher. `inputLen` bytes of data are added from the supplied `input` array, starting at `inputOffset`. Your implementation can transform (encrypt or decrypt) some or all of the input data and return the result as a byte array.

protected abstract int engineUpdate(byte[] input, int inputOffset, int inputLen,
byte[] output, int outputOffset) throws ShortBufferException

> This method works as above, but it writes the output data into the supplied
> array, starting at `outputOffset`. It returns the number of output bytes
> written. If the output array is not large enough, a `ShortBufferException`
> should be thrown.

protected abstract byte[] engineDoFinal (byte[] input, int inputOffset, int inputLen) throws
IllegalBlockSizeException, BadPaddingException

> This method will be called when an encryption or decryption operation should
> be finished. Your cipher implementation should transform any cached input
> data and the supplied input data. The results are returned in a byte array. If
> your implementation does not implement padding, and if this method is passed
> a partial block, it should throw an `IllegalBlockSizeException`. When
> decrypting, padding ciphers should throw a `BadPaddingException` if the
> padding is missing or malformed.

protected abstract int engineDoFinal (byte[] input, int inputOffset, int inputLen,
byte[] output, int outputOffset) throws ShortBufferException, IllegalBlockSizeException,
BadPaddingException

> This method is similar to the previous method, but it writes its output data
> into the supplied array, starting at `outputOffset`. If the output array is not
> big enough, a `ShortBufferException` is thrown.

BlockCipher

If you implement a subclass of `Cipher`, you'll have to face the issue of *block
handling*. Block handling refers to a cipher's ability to deal with different-sized
chunks of data. A programmer can send any amount of data to your cipher at any
time, via the `update()` and `doFinal()` methods. Your `CipherSpi` subclass must
then contain the logic that breaks down the input data into block-sized chunks for
encrypting or decrypting.

In this section, we'll develop a class that takes care of the buffering and block
handling for a generic block cipher. The class is `oreilly.jonathan.crypto`
`.BlockCipher`; it's a subclass of `CipherSpi`. It defines `CipherSpi`'s `engineUp-`
`date()` and `engineDoFinal()` methods, implementing a simple buffering scheme.
In addition to the rest of `CipherSpi`'s methods, subclasses of `BlockCipher` will
have to implement the following methods:

protected abstract int engineTransformBlock(byte[] input, int inputOffset, int inputLength,
byte[] output, int outputOffset) throws ShortBufferException

> This method is called whenever a full block needs to be encrypted or
> decrypted. The input block is contained in `inputLength` bytes of `input`,

starting at `inputOffset`. The transformed block should be written into
`output` starting at `outputOffset`. The number of bytes written is returned. If
the output array is too small, a `ShortBufferException` should be thrown.

protected abstract int engineTransformBlockFinal(byte[] input, int inputOffset,
int inputLength, byte[] output, int outputOffset) throws ShortBufferException

This method is similar to the method above, except it signifies the end of an
encryption or decryption operation. This method may be passed less than a
full block. When encrypting, padding ciphers should add padding. When
decrypting, padding ciphers should remove padding.

The `BlockCipher` class consists of three sections. In the first section, it declares
the abstract `engineTransformBlock()` and `engineTransformBlockFinal()`
methods. Then there are a handful of methods that manage `BlockCipher`'s
internal data buffering scheme. Finally, `BlockCipher` contains definitions for
`engineUpdate()` and `engineDoFinal()`.

The class begins with definitions of the block transforming methods.

```
package oreilly.jonathan.crypto;

import java.math.BigInteger;
import java.security.*;
import java.security.spec.*;

import javax.crypto.*;

public abstract class BlockCipher
    extends CipherSpi {
  protected abstract int engineTransformBlock(byte[] input,
      int inputOffset, int inputLength, byte[] output, int outputOffset)
      throws ShortBufferException;

  protected abstract int engineTransformBlockFinal(byte[] input,
      int inputOffset, int inputLength, byte[] output, int outputOffset)
      throws ShortBufferException;
```

`BlockCipher` stores extra input data in an internal buffer. The buffered data is
used with input data supplied in subsequent `engineUpdate()` and `engineDo-`
`Final()` calls:

```
    protected byte[] mBufferedData;
    protected int mBufferedLength;
```

The `checkBufferedData()` method checks to see if the buffer exists. If not, or if
it is not the same length as the block size, a new buffer is created:

```
    protected void checkBufferedData() {
      if (mBufferedData == null ||
```

```
            mBufferedData.length != engineGetBlockSize()) {
        mBufferedData = new byte[engineGetBlockSize()];
        mBufferedLength = 0;
    }
}
```

The following method returns the length of the data stored in the buffer. Subclasses may need to call this method to calculate engineGetOutputSize():

```
protected int getBufferedDataLength() {
    checkBufferedData();
    return mBufferedLength;
}
```

To retrieve the buffered data, call getBufferedData(). The data will be copied into the supplied array, and the internal buffer is reset (by setting mBuffered-Length to 0):

```
protected void getBufferedData(byte[] output, int offset) {
    checkBufferedData();
    System.arraycopy(mBufferedData, 0, output, offset, mBufferedLength);
    mBufferedLength = 0;
}
```

The addToBufferedData() method adds the specified data to the internal buffer:

```
protected void addToBufferedData(byte[] input, int offset, int length) {
    checkBufferedData();
    System.arraycopy(input, offset,
        mBufferedData, mBufferedLength, length);
    mBufferedLength += length;
}
```

The first engineUpdate() method in BlockCipher calls the second overloaded version of the same method:

```
protected byte[] engineUpdate(byte[] input, int inputOffset,
    int inputLen) {
    int length = 0;
    byte[] out = new byte[engineGetOutputSize(inputLen)];
    try { length = engineUpdate(input, inputOffset, inputLen, out, 0); }
    catch (ShortBufferException sbe) {}
    if (length < out.length) {
        byte[] shorter = new byte[length];
        System.arraycopy(out, 0, shorter, 0, length);
        out = shorter;
    }
    return out;
}
```

The algorithm in the second `engineUpdate()` method is as follows:

1. Create a single input array from the buffered data and the supplied input data.

2. Calculate the location and length of the last fractional block in the input data.

3. Transform all full blocks in the input data.

4. Save the last fractional block in the internal buffer.

We begin by combining the buffered data and the input data to create a single input array:

```
protected int engineUpdate(byte[] input, int inputOffset, int inputLen,
    byte[] output, int outputOffset) throws ShortBufferException {
// Create a single array of input data.
int bufferedLength = getBufferedDataLength();
byte[] totalInput = new byte[inputLen + bufferedLength];
getBufferedData(totalInput, 0);
System.arraycopy(input, inputOffset,
    totalInput, bufferedLength, inputLen);
```

Next, we calculate the location and size of the last fractional block of input data:

```
// Figure out the location of the last fractional block.
int blockSize = engineGetBlockSize();
int lastBlockSize = totalInput.length % blockSize;
int lastBlockOffset = totalInput.length - lastBlockSize;
```

Then we transform each full block in the input array:

```
// Step through the array.
int outputLength = 0;
for (int i = 0; i < lastBlockOffset; i += blockSize)
  outputLength += engineTransformBlock(totalInput, i, blockSize,
      output, outputOffset + outputLength);
```

Finally, we copy the last fractional block into the internal buffer:

```
// Copy the remainder into mBufferedData.
addToBufferedData(totalInput, lastBlockOffset, lastBlockSize);
return outputLength;
}
```

As with `engineUpdate()`, the first overloaded `engineDoFinal()` method simply calls the second overloaded version of the same method.

```
protected byte[] engineDoFinal(byte[] input, int inputOffset,
    int inputLen) throws IllegalBlockSizeException, BadPaddingException {
int length = 0;
byte[] out = new byte[engineGetOutputSize(inputLen)];
try { length = engineDoFinal(input, inputOffset, inputLen, out, 0); }
catch (ShortBufferException sbe) {}
```

```
                if (length < out.length) {
                  byte[] shorter = new byte[length];
                  System.arraycopy(out, 0, shorter, 0, length);
                  out = shorter;
                }
                return out;
            }
```

The procedure in `engineDoFinal()` is similar to that of `engineUpdate()`, but slightly different:

1. As before, create a single input array from the buffered data and the supplied input data.

2. Find the location and size of the last partial or *full* block. In `engineUpdate()`, we were just interested in the last partial block.

3. Transform each full block in the input array by calling `engineTransformBlock()`.

4. Transform the final partial or full block by calling `engineTransformBlockFinal()`.

```
    protected int engineDoFinal(byte[] input, int inputOffset, int inputLen,
        byte[] output, int outputOffset) throws ShortBufferException,
        IllegalBlockSizeException, BadPaddingException {
      // Create a single array of input data.
      int bufferedLength = getBufferedDataLength();
      byte[] totalInput = new byte[inputLen + bufferedLength];
      getBufferedData(totalInput, 0);
      if (inputLen > 0)
        System.arraycopy(input, inputOffset,
            totalInput, bufferedLength, inputLen);
      // Find the location of the last partial or full block.
      int blockSize = engineGetBlockSize();
      int lastBlockSize = totalInput.length % blockSize;
      if (lastBlockSize == 0 && totalInput.length > 0)
        lastBlockSize = blockSize;
      int lastBlockOffset = totalInput.length - lastBlockSize;
      // Step through the array.
      int outputLength = 0;
      for (int i = 0; i < lastBlockOffset; i += blockSize)
        outputLength += engineTransformBlock(totalInput, i, blockSize,
            output, outputOffset + outputLength);
```

The final partial or full block is transformed using `engineTransformBlockFinal()`. Subclasses should implement padding in this method.

```
      // Transform the final partial or full block.
      outputLength += engineTransformBlockFinal(totalInput, lastBlockOffset,
```

```
            lastBlockSize, output, outputOffset + outputLength);
        return outputLength;
    }
}
```

This might seem like a lot of work, and little to show for it, but `BlockCipher` will come in handy in the next section, when we develop a CBC mode class. You'll see `BlockCipher` again in Chapter 9 when I present an implementation of the ElGamal cipher algorithm.

CBCWrapper

We can implement CBC mode on top of any existing block cipher. We'll write a `CBCWrapper` class that works just like any other cipher but uses an underlying block cipher to do its work. It's analogous to the way a `FilterOutputStream` wraps around an `OutputStream` and adds functionality.

Let's start by making a subclass of `BlockCipher` (presented in the last section) and putting it in the `oreilly.jonathan.crypto` package.

```
package oreilly.jonathan.crypto;

import java.security.*;
import java.security.spec.*;

import javax.crypto.*;
import javax.crypto.spec.*;

public class CBCWrapper
    extends BlockCipher {
```

Member variables are used to keep track of the state of the cipher, the underlying block cipher, and the internal CBC buffer. This buffer is initially filled with the IV.

```
    protected int mState;
    protected Cipher mWrappedCipher;
    protected byte[] mBuffer;
```

The no-argument constructor constructs a `CBCWrapper` with an underlying DES block cipher:

```
    public CBCWrapper()
        throws NoSuchAlgorithmException, NoSuchPaddingException {
        // Default to DES.
        this(Cipher.getInstance("DES/ECB/NoPadding"));
    }

    protected CBCWrapper(Cipher wrapped) { mWrappedCipher = wrapped; }
```

CBCWrapper implements CBC mode and PKCS#5 padding. Any attempt to set a different mode or padding scheme will cause an exception to be thrown:

```
protected void engineSetMode(String mode)
    throws NoSuchAlgorithmException {
  throw new NoSuchAlgorithmException("CBCWrapper supports no modes.");
}

protected void engineSetPadding(String padding)
    throws NoSuchPaddingException {
  throw new NoSuchPaddingException("CBCWrapper supports no padding.");
}
```

The block size of the CBCWrapper is determined by the block size of the underlying cipher:

```
protected int engineGetBlockSize() {
  return mWrappedCipher.getBlockSize();
}
```

The engineGetOutputSize() method calculates the output data size for a given input data size. If the CBCWrapper is encrypting data, for example, this method figures out how long the ciphertext will be for a given plaintext length. Because we are implementing PKCS#5 padding, this method always returns a length that is a multiple of the block size. If we are encrypting data, and the length of the input data happens to be an integral number of blocks, we need to add an entire block of padding. When we decrypt, the decrypted data will always be shorter than the ciphertext, due to the removal of the padding. However, we won't know how much shorter it will be, so our engineOutBufferSize() method returns the input length when the cipher is decrypting. Note that the input length is the sum of the supplied input length and the length of the internally buffered data, returned by calling getBufferedDataLength(). This method is inherited from BlockCipher, CBCWrapper's superclass.

```
protected int engineGetOutputSize(int inLen) {
  int blockSize = mWrappedCipher.getBlockSize();
  int length = inLen + getBufferedDataLength();
  int blocks = (length + blockSize - 1) / blockSize;
  if (mState == Cipher.ENCRYPT_MODE && length % blockSize == 0)
    blocks++;
  return blockSize * blocks;
}
```

getIV() returns a copy of the internal CBC buffer. Note that, strictly speaking, this is not equal to the original IV after some encryption or decryption has been done.

```
protected byte[] engineGetIV() { return (byte[])(mBuffer.clone()); }
```

When a `CBCWrapper` is initialized, it passes the given key to the underlying block cipher. A new internal buffer is created that is the same size as the underlying cipher's block size. It is filled with random data from the supplied `SecureRandom`:

```
protected void engineInit(int opmode, Key key, SecureRandom random)
    throws InvalidKeyException {
  try { engineInit(opmode, key, null, random); }
  catch (InvalidAlgorithmParameterException iape) {}
  mBuffer = new byte[mWrappedCipher.getBlockSize()];
  random.nextBytes(mBuffer);
}
```

If an `IvParameterSpec` object is passed to `init()`, the IV is extracted from it:

```
protected void engineInit(int opmode, Key key,
    AlgorithmParameterSpec params, SecureRandom random)
    throws InvalidKeyException, InvalidAlgorithmParameterException {
  mState = opmode;
  mWrappedCipher.init(opmode, key, random);
  if (params != null) {
    if (params instanceof IvParameterSpec) {
      IvParameterSpec spec = (IvParameterSpec)params;
      mBuffer = (byte[])(spec.getIV().clone());
    }
    else throw new InvalidAlgorithmParameterException();
  }
}
```

To transform a block, we simply check if we're encrypting or decrypting and call the appropriate method. The guts of the CBC algorithm are contained in the `encryptBlock()` and `decryptBlock()` methods, which are presented next:

```
protected int engineTransformBlock(byte[] input,
    int inputOffset, int inputLength, byte[] output, int outputOffset)
    throws ShortBufferException {
  if (mState == Cipher.ENCRYPT_MODE)
    return encryptBlock(input, inputOffset, inputLength,
        output, outputOffset);
  else if (mState == Cipher.DECRYPT_MODE)
    return decryptBlock(input, inputOffset, inputLength,
        output, outputOffset);
  return 0;
}
```

In `engineTransformBlockFinal()`, we need to add padding if we're encrypting or remove padding if we're decrypting. If we're encrypting and the input data is a multiple of the block size, then a full block of padding must be added.

```
protected int engineTransformBlockFinal(byte[] input,
    int inputOffset, int inputLength, byte[] output, int outputOffset)
    throws ShortBufferException {
```

```
          int blockSize = mWrappedCipher.getBlockSize();
      if (mState == Cipher.ENCRYPT_MODE) {
        if (inputLength == blockSize) {
          byte[] result = new byte[blockSize * 2];
          int length = encryptBlock(input, inputOffset, inputLength,
              output, outputOffset);
          byte[] paddingBlock = pad(null, 0, 0);
          length += encryptBlock(paddingBlock, 0, blockSize,
              output, outputOffset + length);
          return length;
        }
```

Otherwise, an incomplete block should be padded and encrypted:

```
          byte[] paddedBlock;
      paddedBlock = pad(input, inputOffset, inputLength);
      return encryptBlock(paddedBlock, 0, blockSize,
          output, outputOffset);
    }
```

To decrypt ciphertext, we simply pass block-sized chunks to the underlying cipher for decryption and XOR the results with the internal buffer. This is accomplished in the decryptBlock() method. Once the data is decrypted, we have to remove the PKCS#5 padding that we added earlier. To do this, we pull off the last byte of decrypted data. This byte should contain the number of padding bytes that were added. We subtract this value from the original data length, yielding the correct length of the decrypted data. This length is returned from engineTransformBlockFinal().

```
      else if (mState == Cipher.DECRYPT_MODE) {
        int length = decryptBlock(input, inputOffset, inputLength,
            output, outputOffset);
        int paddingLength = (int)output[outputOffset + length - 1];
        return length - paddingLength;
      }
      return 0;
    }
```

Now I have some gritty details to explain. First, the pad() method takes an incomplete block and returns a padded block. It implements the padding described in PKCS#5. A call to pad(null, 0, 0) returns a full block of padding (in a 64-bit block, 8 bytes with the value 8).

```
    protected byte[] pad(byte[] in, int inOff, int inLen) {
      int blockSize = mWrappedCipher.getBlockSize();
      byte[] paddedBlock = new byte[blockSize];
      if (in != null)
        System.arraycopy(in, inOff, paddedBlock, 0, inLen);
      for (int i = inLen; i < blockSize; i++)
        paddedBlock[i] = (byte)(blockSize - inLen);
```

```
    return paddedBlock;
}
```

It's in the `encryptBlock()` and `decryptBlock()` that the CBC magic really happens. In `encryptBlock()`, we begin by XORing the plaintext block with the internal buffer. The buffer holds the IV initially and thereafter holds ciphertext to be combined with the next block of plaintext.

```
protected int encryptBlock(byte[] in, int inOff, int inLen,
    byte[] out, int outOff) {
// XOR plaintext with mBuffer
int blockSize = mWrappedCipher.getBlockSize();
byte[] amalgam = new byte[blockSize];
for (int i = 0; i < blockSize; i++)
    amalgam[i] = (byte)(in[inOff + i] ^ mBuffer[i]);
```

Then we encrypt the result of the XOR. The ciphertext is placed in both the output array and the internal buffer, to be used with the next encryption:

```
// encrypt block
byte[] ciphertext = null;
try { ciphertext = mWrappedCipher.doFinal(amalgam); }
catch (IllegalBlockSizeException ibse) {}
catch (BadPaddingException bpe) {}
System.arraycopy(ciphertext, 0, out, outOff, blockSize);
// put ciphertext in mBuffer
System.arraycopy(ciphertext, 0, mBuffer, 0, blockSize);
return blockSize;
}
```

The `decryptBlock()` method works in much the same way, except that it reverses the encryption process. First, we decrypt a block of ciphertext:

```
protected int decryptBlock(byte[] in, int inOff, int inLen,
    byte[] out, int outOff) {
// decrypt block
int blockSize = mWrappedCipher.getBlockSize();
byte[] ciphertext = new byte[blockSize];
System.arraycopy(in, inOff, ciphertext, 0, blockSize);
byte[] amalgam = null;
try { amalgam = mWrappedCipher.doFinal(ciphertext); }
catch (IllegalBlockSizeException ibse) {}
catch (BadPaddingException bpe) {}
```

This done, we XOR the decrypted data with the internal buffer, which produces plaintext. Then the ciphertext block is copied into the internal buffer to be used in the next decryption:

```
// XOR amalgam with mBuffer
for (int i = 0; i < blockSize; i++)
    out[outOff + i] = (byte)(amalgam[i] ^ mBuffer[i]);
```

```
        // put ciphertext in mBuffer
        System.arraycopy(ciphertext, 0, mBuffer, 0, blockSize);
        return blockSize;
    }
}
```

You can't test the CBCWrapper class directly. In Chapter 9, you'll see how to make it part of your own cryptographic provider.

Although CBCWrapper's default constructor creates an underlying DES cipher, you can easily create a subclass of CBCWrapper for any underlying block cipher algorithm. Suppose you had a provider installed that supports the IDEA algorithm. You could create a class that implements IDEA in CBC mode with PKCS#5 padding as follows:

```
package oreilly.jonathan.crypto;

import java.security.*;

import javax.crypto.*;

public class IDEACBCPKCS5
    extends CBCWrapper {
  public IDEACBCPKCS5()
      throws NoSuchAlgorithmException, NoSuchPaddingException {
      super(Cipher.getInstance("IDEA/ECB/NoPadding"));
  }
}
```

Then you could configure your provider to use this class in response to requests for "IDEA/CBC/PKCS5Padding." The IDEACBCPKCS5 class would act like an IDEA cipher in CBC mode, using the IDEA/ECB/NoPadding cipher as the underlying cipher.

CFBWrapper

Like CBC mode, eight-bit CFB mode can be implemented in a class that wraps a regular block cipher. With this in mind, we'll develop the CFBWrapper class. We'll make it a subclass of CipherSpi and put it in the oreilly.jonathan.security package. It looks a lot like the CBCWrapper class from before, but the inner workings are a little different. Any cipher in eight-bit CFB mode encrypts one byte at a time. Although you might be tempted to make this class a child of BlockCipher, it's more efficient to have it descend directly from CipherSpi:

```
package oreilly.jonathan.crypto;

import java.security.*;
import java.security.spec.*;
```

```
import javax.crypto.*;
import javax.crypto.spec.*;

public class CFBWrapper
    extends CipherSpi {
```

Internally, CFB mode uses a block cipher and a block-sized buffer. We'll represent these as member variables. The mState variable keeps track of the cipher's state, either ENCRYPT_MODE or DECRYPT_MODE.

```
protected int mState;
protected Cipher mWrappedCipher;
protected byte[] mBuffer;
```

As before, we provide a no-argument constructor that creates a default CFBWrapper with an underlying DES cipher:

```
public CFBWrapper()
    throws NoSuchAlgorithmException, NoSuchPaddingException {
  // Default to DES.
  this(Cipher.getInstance("DES/ECB/NoPadding"));
}

protected CFBWrapper(Cipher wrapped) { mWrappedCipher = wrapped; }
```

As with CBCWrapper, the CFBWrapper class supports no additional modes or padding schemes:

```
protected void engineSetMode(String mode)
    throws NoSuchAlgorithmException {
  throw new NoSuchAlgorithmException("CFBWrapper supports no modes.");
}

protected void engineSetPadding(String padding)
    throws NoSuchPaddingException {
  throw new NoSuchPaddingException("CFBWrapper supports no padding.");
}
```

The engineGetBlockSize() method returns the block size, in bytes, of this cipher. Because the CFBWrapper class acts like a stream cipher, it encrypts one byte at a time:

```
protected int engineGetBlockSize() { return 1; }
```

For CFBWrapper, the output length of an encryption or decryption is always equal to the input length:

```
protected int engineGetOutputSize(int inLen) { return inLen; }

protected byte[] engineGetIV() { return (byte[])(mBuffer.clone()); }
```

Like `CBCWrapper`, `CFBWrapper` is a cipher wrapper. When you call `init()`, CFB passes the key to the underlying cipher and clears the internal buffer:

```
protected void engineInit(int opmode, Key key, SecureRandom random)
    throws InvalidKeyException {
  try { engineInit(opmode, key, null, random); }
  catch (InvalidAlgorithmParameterException iape) {}
  mBuffer = new byte[mWrappedCipher.getBlockSize()];
  random.nextBytes(mBuffer);
}
```

The underlying block cipher is always initialized for encryption, regardless of whether this `CFBWrapper` will be encrypting or decrypting. As before, we extract an IV if it is passed to us:

```
protected void engineInit(int opmode, Key key,
    AlgorithmParameterSpec params, SecureRandom random)
    throws InvalidKeyException, InvalidAlgorithmParameterException {
  mState = opmode;
  mWrappedCipher.init(Cipher.ENCRYPT_MODE, key);
  if (params != null) {
    if (params instanceof IvParameterSpec) {
      IvParameterSpec spec = (IvParameterSpec)params;
      mBuffer = (byte[])(spec.getIV().clone());
    }
    else throw new InvalidAlgorithmParameterException();
  }
}
```

The first overloaded `engineUpdate()` calls the second version of the method:

```
protected byte[] engineUpdate(byte[] input, int inputOffset,
    int inputLen) {
  byte[] out = new byte[inputLen];
  try { engineUpdate(input, inputOffset, inputLen, out, 0); }
  catch (ShortBufferException sbe) {}
  return out;
}
```

In CFB mode, we have no worries about block buffering or padding. `engineUpdate()`, therefore, calls `engineDoFinal()` directly:

```
protected int engineUpdate(byte[] input, int inputOffset, int inputLen,
    byte[] output, int outputOffset) throws ShortBufferException {
  int length = 0;
  try { length = engineDoFinal(input, inputOffset, inputLen,
      output, outputOffset); }
  catch (IllegalBlockSizeException ibse) {}
  catch (BadPaddingException bpe) {}
  return length;
}
```

As before, the first overloaded `engineDoFinal()` calls the second overloaded version:

```
protected byte[] engineDoFinal(byte[] input, int inputOffset,
    int inputLen) throws IllegalBlockSizeException, BadPaddingException {
  byte[] out = new byte[inputLen];
  try { engineDoFinal(input, inputOffset, inputLen, out, 0); }
  catch (ShortBufferException sbe) {}
  return out;
}
```

In `engineDoFinal()`, we encrypt or decrypt each byte of input, one at a time, using the `encryptByte()` and `decryptByte()` methods:

```
protected int engineDoFinal(byte[] input, int inputOffset, int inputLen,
    byte[] output, int outputOffset) throws ShortBufferException,
    IllegalBlockSizeException, BadPaddingException {
  for (int i = 0; i < inputLen; i++) {
    if (mState == Cipher.ENCRYPT_MODE)
      output[outputOffset + i] = encryptByte(input[inputOffset + i]);
    else
      output[outputOffset + i] = decryptByte(input[inputOffset + i]);
  }
  return inputLen;
}
```

The `encryptByte()` and `decryptByte()` methods implement the meat of the CFB mode algorithm. In `encryptByte()`, we first encrypt the internal buffer:

```
protected byte encryptByte(byte p) {
  int blockSize = mWrappedCipher.getBlockSize();
  byte[] encryptedBlock = null;
  try { encryptedBlock = mWrappedCipher.doFinal(mBuffer); }
  catch (IllegalBlockSizeException ibse) {}
  catch (BadPaddingException bpe) {}
```

Then we XOR the leftmost byte of the buffer with the incoming plaintext byte:

```
byte left = encryptedBlock[0];
byte c = (byte)(p ^ left);
```

Finally, we shift the buffer and return the ciphertext byte:

```
  shiftBuffer(c);
  return c;
}
```

Decryption is much the same, except the plaintext is recovered by XORing the ciphertext and the leftmost byte of the buffer:

```
protected byte decryptByte(byte c) {
  byte[] encryptedBlock = null;
```

```
        try { encryptedBlock = mWrappedCipher.doFinal(mBuffer); }
        catch (IllegalBlockSizeException ibse) {}
        catch (BadPaddingException bpe) {}
        byte left = encryptedBlock[0];
        byte p = (byte)(c ^ left);
        shiftBuffer(c);
        return p;
    }
```

The last method in `CFB`, `shiftBuffer()`, is used to shift the buffer left one byte:

```
    protected void shiftBuffer(byte fill) {
      for (int i = 0; i < mBuffer.length - 1; i++)
        mBuffer[i] = mBuffer[i + 1];
      mBuffer[mBuffer.length - 1] = fill;
    }
  }
```

Hybrid Systems

Hybrid systems combine the strengths of symmetric and asymmetric ciphers. In a hybrid system, an asymmetric cipher is used for authentication and data integrity, and a symmetric cipher is used for confidentiality. Symmetric ciphers are faster than asymmetric ciphers, so it makes sense to use symmetric ciphers for most of a message or conversation. Likewise, asymmetric ciphers are well suited to authentication and session key exchange.

You can "roll your own" hybrid system, as I'll demonstrate in Chapters 10 and 11. Here I'll discuss the most widespread hybrid standards.

PGP

Pretty Good Privacy (PGP) is a piece of software that was designed to bring strong cryptography to the masses. It encrypts messages, using a combination of symmetric and asymmetric ciphers. Encrypted messages can then be safely transported over an insecure network, like the Internet. Another user with PGP can then decrypt the messages. PGP provides authentication, data integrity, and confidentiality.

PGP contains no startling cryptographic innovations; it uses well-known, off-the-shelf cryptographic algorithms. It is important because it is a de facto standard. The last widely distributed version is PGP 2.6.2, which uses RSA for signing and key exchange and IDEA for message encryption. PGP 5.0 is the latest version, released in August 1997; it supports additional algorithms for signing and encryption.

The Cryptix toolkit includes some support for PGP; for more information, see *http://www.systemics.com/software/cryptix-java/*.

S/MIME

Secure/Multipurpose Internet Mail Extensions (S/MIME) is a proposed standard for cryptographically enhanced email. It is a hybrid system that places an encrypted message in a "digital envelope." The message itself is encrypted using a symmetric cipher, while the session key for the symmetric cipher is encrypted using an asymmetric cipher. X.509 certificates are used for authentication. Signatures protect the integrity of the message and its envelope.

S/MIME is the darling of RSA Data Security, Inc., and it is endorsed by an impressive array of vendors, including Netscape and Microsoft. The standard is built on a handful of other standards, including MIME, PKCS#7, PKCS#10, and X.509. You can read more about it at *http://www.rsa.com/smime/*.

SSL

The Secure Sockets Layer (SSL) is a standard developed by Netscape Communications, Inc., to allow for secure communications between network clients and servers.[*] While PGP is oriented around messages, where encryption and transmission are separate steps, SSL is designed for conversations, where encryption and transmission occur simultaneously. SSL support is built into popular web browsers like Netscape's Navigator and Communicator and Microsoft's Internet Explorer. If you've ever visited a page whose URL began with *https* instead of *http*, you've already used SSL; *https* means the HTTP protocol on top of SSL. SSL can authenticate each side of the communication, using public key certificates. SSL communications are confidential as well, through the use of a session key and a symmetric cipher. Finally, SSL ensures data integrity so that an attacker cannot replay part of a conversation or change data in transit.

An SSL conversation has distinct stages, as illustrated in Figure 7-4. Each side of the conversation has the opportunity to authenticate itself to the other side, using X.509 certificates. Then they negotiate a *cipher suite*, which specifies the symmetric and asymmetric algorithms that will be used in the SSL conversation. A public key algorithm is used for session key exchange, and the remainder of the conversation is encrypted using a symmetric cipher. The cipher suite can be changed at any time during the conversation.

Sources

Several pieces of software from Sun support SSL. If you're interested in getting the SSL classes separately, contact Sun directly. Table 7-4 summarizes the packages

---

[*] SSL is documented at *http://home.netscape.com/assist/security/ssl/protocol.html*.

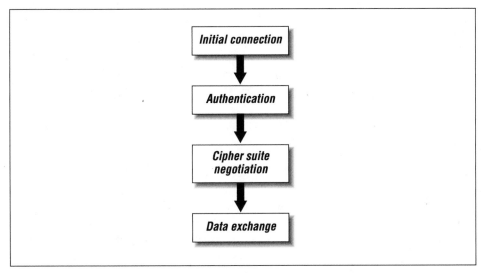

Figure 7-4: SSL conversation

that include SSL support. As this book goes to press, Sun is planning to release the SSL classes as a standard extension library. You can see documentation for these classes at *http://java.sun.com/security/ssl/API_users_guide.html.*

Table 7-4: Sun's SSL Classes

Package	Location
HotJava Browser 1.1	*http://java.sun.com/products/hotjava/1.1/*
Java Server Toolkit	*http://java.sun.com/products/java-server/toolkit/*
Java Electronic Commerce Framework	*http://java.sun.com/products/commerce/*

There are a few third-party Java SSL implementations available as well. These are shown in Table 7-5.

Table 7-5: Third-Party Java SSL Implementations

Package	Location
JCP SSL	*http://www.jcp.co.uk/*
Baltimore Technologies J/SSL	*http://www.baltimore.ie/jssl/*
Phaos Technology SSLava	*http://www.phaos.com/products/sslavafr.htm*
IAIK iSaSiLk	*http://wwwjce.iaik.tu-graz.ac.at/iSaSiLk/isasilk.htm*

Using the browser

Another way to use SSL in Java is from an applet. Basically, you use a java.net.URL object to open an HTTPS URL. This allows you to retrieve web pages and other resources securely, using your browser's HTTPS implementation. Your applet needs to know nothing about SSL except that it opens `https:` URLs instead of `http:` URLs. For example, you might normally write something like this:

```
URL u = new URL("http://www.verisign.com/");
DataInputStream theHTML = new DataInputStream(u.openStream());
```

Instead, you could write this:

```
URL u = new URL("https://www.verisign.com/");
DataInputStream theHTML = new DataInputStream(u.openStream());
```

Although the simplicity of this approach is alluring, it has two serious drawbacks. First, SSL implementations vary from browser to browser. And even if the browser itself supports HTTPS, it may not support this feature in its JVM. Unless you are developing applets for a single type of browser, you shouldn't expect to open `https:` URLs and have them work every time.

Second, the applet sandbox constrains applets to make network connections only to the host they came from. Even if the browser supports SSL from Java, your applet will be able to make an SSL connection only back to its home server.[*]

SET

The Secure Electronic Transaction (SET) protocol was developed by VISA and Mastercard to encourage electronic commerce. In theory, it works like SSL. In implementation, the systems are quite different. For example, SET uses two public key pairs, one for authentication and one for session key exchange. For more information on SET, see *http://www.mastercard.com/set/* or *http://www.visa.com/cgi-bin/vee/nt/ecomm/set/downloads.html?2+0.*

The Java Electronic Commerce Framework (JECF) includes support for SET. Because the JECF is still in early releases, it's very possible that its SET support will change before the first official release. For more information, refer to the JECF web pages at *http://java.sun.com/products/commerce/*.

---

* You could work around this restriction with a signed applet, as I'll discuss in Chapter 8, *Signed Applets*. You'll be fighting an uphill battle, however, against both the platform dependencies of HTTPS and the platform dependencies of signed applets. Another approach might be better for your health and sanity.

8

Signed Applets

Signed applets are a Java 1.1 innovation. A signed applet is a cryptographically signed collection of class files and other supporting files, like graphic or sound files. Signed applets are exciting because they can step outside the restrictive applet sandbox of the Java 1.0 world. This means they can do more interesting and useful work than before, like writing and reading disk files and opening network connections to arbitrary hosts.

In theory, a signed applet works like this:

1. A software developer (let's say Josephine) obtains a certificate from a trusted Certificate Authority (CA), like VeriSign. The CA takes some trouble to verify Josephine's identity before issuing her a certificate.

2. While cruising the Web, you happen to browse to a page that contains an applet Josephine has written. She has cryptographically signed it using her private key. Your browser tells you that the applet is signed by Josephine and asks if the applet should be allowed to step outside the sandbox.

Why should this make you feel safe executing the applet?

* Because the applet is signed, you know it hasn't been modified by a malicious third party.

* Because Josephine's identity is vouched for by a CA, who signed her certificate, you can have some assurance that Josephine is who she says she is.

Currently, signed applets are stubborn and complex beasts. Three popular browsers (Sun's HotJava™, Netscape's Navigator, and Microsoft's Internet Explorer) support signed applets, but each browser has a different applet archive format and different procedures for signing applets. In Netscape Navigator and Microsoft Internet Explorer, the situation is further clouded by interactions with certificate authorities like VeriSign.

Each browser uses a different scheme for signing, mostly because there is no standard certificate database on the client's machine. When a signed applet is downloaded, its signature is verified using the signer's public key. The signer's public key is contained in a certificate that accompanies the applet. Each browser has its own internal certificate database.

Quite apart from incompatible processes and formats, signed applets are hard to use because the technology isn't mature. This is a nice way of saying that there are a lot of bugs left in the development tools.

In this section, I'll describe how to create and run a signed applet for HotJava 1.0 from Javasoft, Netscape Navigator 4.01, and Microsoft Internet Explorer 4.0. I'll concentrate on the details of packaging and signing your applet although I'll also cover browser configuration briefly. I won't spend a lot of time on the details of each vendor's tools and browsers; instead, this chapter serves as a quick start for producing signed applets on these three browser platforms.

I'll begin by introducing a simple applet, Renegade, that attempts to step outside the applet sandbox. Then I'll show how to sign the applet for the three browsers.

Renegade

For all three browsers, we'll use the same applet, called Renegade. Renegade isn't really dangerous, but it does try to find out your name, using System.getProperty("user.name"). This action is not allowed in the applet sandbox, to protect the privacy of the user. In Renegade, we enclose this call in a try block in case a SecurityException is thrown. Save the source code for this class in *Renegade.java*.

```
import java.applet.*;
import java.awt.*;

public class Renegade extends Applet {
  private String mMessage;

  public void init() {
    try {
      mMessage = "Your name is " + System.getProperty("user.name") + ".";
    }
    catch (SecurityException e) {
      mMessage = "Can't get your name, due to a SecurityException.";
    }
  }

  public void paint(Graphics g) {
    g.drawString("Renegade", 25, 25);
    g.drawString(mMessage, 25, 50);
```

```
    }
  }
```

The HTML page that contains this applet, *Renegade.html*, is as follows:

```
<html>
<head>
</head>
<body>
  <applet code = Renegade width = 300 height = 200></applet>
</body>
</html>
```

If you point your browser at this applet, the call to `System.getProperty()` fails, just as we expected. Figure 8-1 shows this applet in Navigator 4.01.

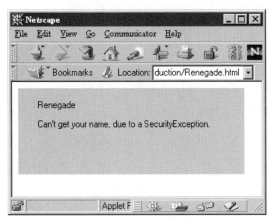

Figure 8-1: The unsigned Renegade applet can't get out of the sandbox

HotJava

The simplest case is for HotJava, just because it was developed by the same people who brought you the Security API. HotJava recognizes applets archived in JAR files. (See Appendix C, *JAR*, for a description of the `jar` tool.) As discussed in Appendix D, *Javakey*, you can use `javakey` to sign a JAR using one of the identities that's defined in the `javakey` database. HotJava recognizes the signed JAR and allows you to define a security policy for the signer.

A security policy is a set of rules for a particular signer. For example, I might have the following security policy defined for applets signed by Josephine:

* Applets can access the `user.name` system property.

* Applets can write files to the local disk in the *c:\temp* directory.

* Applets can make network connections to *www.josephine.com*.

HotJava allows you to define this kind of fine-grained security policy for different signers. We'll take a peek at this feature a little later.

For HotJava, then, creating a signed applet follows three steps:

1. Prepare a signer.

2. Bundle up the applet.

3. Sign the applet.

Prepare a Signer

You can use javakey to create a signer and generate keys for it. Refer to Appendix D if you're not sure how to do this. Marian will be the signer for the Renegade applet. We'll use her self-signed certificate to sign the applet.

If you didn't install Marian as a signer, do it now. First, create Marian in the javakey database:

```
C:\ javakey -cs Marian true
Created identity [Signer]Marian[identitydb.obj][trusted]
```

Generate a set of keys for Marian like this:

```
C:\ javakey -gk Marian DSA 1024
Generated DSA keys for Marian (strength: 1024).
```

Now we need to generate Marian's self-signed certificate. First, create a certificate directive file, *MarianCertificate.directive*, with the following contents:

```
issuer.name=Marian

subject.name=Marian
subject.real.name=Maid Marian
subject.org.unit=Overprotected Daughters
subject.org=Royal Castle
subject.country=England

start.date=06 February 1998
end.date=31 December 1998
serial.number=1001

signature.algorithm=DSA

out.file=Marian.certificate
```

Generate the certificate as follows, using the -gc option:

```
C:\ javakey -gc MarianCertificate.directive
Generated certificate from directive file MarianCertificate.directive.
```

At this point, Marian is a signer with a key pair and a self-signed certificate. In a more realistic scenario, you would have a certificate from a CA, vouching for Marian's identity. Self-signed certificates are not very trustworthy. I use them in this example for demonstration purposes only.

Unfortunately, JDK 1.1 doesn't provide tools to interact with CAs to produce "real" certificates. In JDK 1.2, javakey is replaced by keytool and jarsigner. keytool has a facility for generating certificate requests for a CA, as described in Chapter 5, *Key Management*.

NOTE   In JDK 1.2, javakey no longer exists. A new tool, jarsigner, is used to sign JARs using key information from a keystore. The keystore can be managed with keytool. As of JDK 1.2 beta2, however, the signed JARs produced by jarsigner don't work with HotJava 1.0 or HotJava 1.1; the browser simply treats the JAR like a regular, unsigned archive.

Bundle the Applet

HotJava recognizes JAR files, which are created using the jar tool. Our applet contains only one file, so we can create the JAR using the following command:

```
jar -cf Renegade.jar Renegade.class
```

This takes *Renegade.class* and puts it in a new JAR called *Renegade.jar*.

Sign the Applet

We'll use the javakey tool to sign the JAR, as described in Appendix D. The directive file should look like this:

```
signer=Marian
cert=1
chain=0
signature.file=MARIANSG
out.file=hjRenegade.jar
```

Save this in a file called *MarianSign.directive*. Then you can sign the JAR using the following command:

```
javakey -gs MarianSign.directive Renegade.jar
```

The JAR is signed with Marian's private key, and the resulting signed JAR is *hjRenegade.jar*.

Test the Applet

To run the applet, we need an HTML page that references the signed JAR we just created. This file, *hjRenegade.html*, is shown here.

```html
<html>
<head>
</head>
<body>
  <applet code = Renegade.class archive = hjRenegade.jar
      width = 400 height = 200></applet>
</body>
</html>
```

If *Renegade.class* and *hjRenegade.jar* are both present in the directory with this HTML file, HotJava will use *Renegade.class*, the unsigned version of the applet class. To avoid this, remove *Renegade.class* from the directory containing the HTML and JAR files.

Now run HotJava and point it at the *hjRenegade.html* page. HotJava asks for permission, on the applet's behalf, to access the user.name property. This is shown in Figure 8-2.

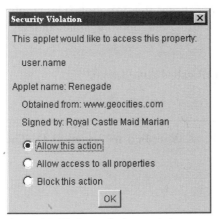

Figure 8-2: HotJava asks for permission

If you allow the action, the applet is then displayed in all of its glory.[*] HotJava remembers that you have granted this permission for the remainder of your session.

---

[*] If you are using Windows 95, the user.name property may return "unknown," depending on how Windows 95 is set up. Nevertheless, it demonstrates that the applet was permitted to call System.getProperty()—and no SecurityException was thrown.

Set Up the Browser

There is a way to make permissions more permanent in HotJava. In particular, we can grant a specific set of permissions to a signer. Any signed applets that HotJava encounters will automatically be given the permissions of the signer.

To enable this, proceed to **Edit → Preferences → Applet Security** in the HotJava menu. Then choose the link to the Advanced Security Settings page. Marian's certificate should show up in the list box. To apply specific permissions to Marian, you'll first need to verify her certificate. Click on the **Verify** button to do this. Then click OK. Below the list box area, you'll now be able to choose specific permissions for Marian. Figure 8-3 shows the Advanced Security Settings after Marian's certificate has been verified.[*]

Applets signed by Marian get default permissions. To assign specific permissions, first uncheck **Use default permissions for this site or certificate**. For example, for Marian you might check **Applet may access all properties** instead. Next time you run HotJava and the signed Renegade applet, you won't be prompted with a permission question.

We glossed over verifying the certificate signature, blithely stating that the certificate was verified and you should go ahead and mark it as such. HotJava is reluctant to accept a self-signed certificate, so it asks you to perform additional verification. The idea is that you will talk to the certificate owner, in person, and verify that the certificate signature is correct by reading the numbers off. Note that this applies only to a self-signed certificate. Having verified Marian's certificate, any other certificates signed by Marian are automatically verified.

In a more perfect world, Marian's signed applet would be accompanied by a "real" certificate, issued by a CA, instead of Marian's self-signed certificate. In JDK 1.1, however, there are no tools for generating real certificates. In JDK 1.2, keytool includes facilities for requesting a certificate from a CA. The signed archives produced by jarsigner, however, do not yet work with HotJava.

Navigator

The steps involved in creating a signed applet are similar for other browsers. It's the details of each step that differ severely. Netscape Navigator also recognizes JAR files, but it can't recognize signatures produced by javakey. Similarly, HotJava is unable to recognize signatures intended for Navigator.

---

[*] There's a peculiar bug in HotJava 1.0. If you've already visited the security settings pages of HotJava, before viewing the signed applet, then Marian's certificate won't show up in the Advanced Security Settings page, even after you view the page with the signed applet. The sequence of events that works is (a) start HotJava, (b) view the signed applet page, and (c) view the certificate in the Advanced Security Settings page.

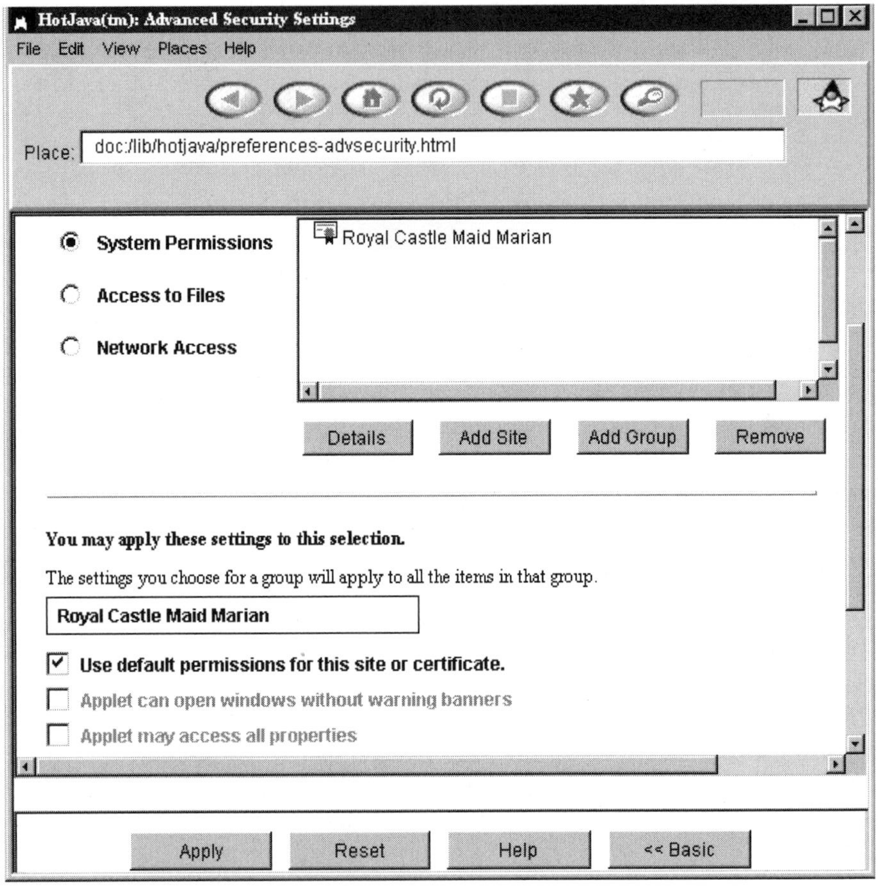

Figure 8-3: HotJava Advanced Security Settings

Prepare a Signer

To sign an applet for Navigator, you must have an appropriate signing certificate in Navigator's database. You can purchase such a certificate from a Certificate Authority (CA). I bought a "Class 2 Digital ID" from VeriSign (see *http://www.veri-sign.com/*) for $19.95. I can use this certificate to sign code; it lasts for one year. You should be aware that VeriSign isn't the only game in town. There are plenty of CAs in the world. I just used VeriSign because they've made it convenient to buy certificates on the Web. VeriSign has streamlined the process of getting a certificate; it's fairly easy to give them your 20 bucks and get a certificate in return. Behind this simple process is a lot of legal documentation. If you're serious about using your certificate, you should read all of it.

VeriSign offers two classes of certificates for code signing:

- Class 2 certificates, for individual software developers, cost $20 per year. VeriSign does some quick automated checks on the information you give them and can issue a certificate within five minutes of receiving your information.

- Class 3 certificates, for software development companies, cost $400 per year. VeriSign requires more information and checks more carefully for these types of certificates.

To sign code for Navigator, I bought a Class 2 certificate. To do this yourself, start at the VeriSign home page, *http://www.verisign.com/*. Follow the instructions about how to enroll for a certificate. When I followed this process, Navigator generated a key pair for me and sent the public key to VeriSign. After a few minutes, VeriSign sent me email, giving me a URL to use to pick up my certificate. The certificate was downloaded to Navigator, which stored it in a private certificate database along with my private key from before. Netscape's signing tool, zigbert, is able to access this certificate database to sign code. I'd like to detail the process, but VeriSign changes it frequently enough that anything I told you would probably be out of date by the time this book is printed.

There is a way to test signed applets in Navigator without paying for a certificate, using something Netscape calls *codebase trust*. You can read more about this at *http://developer.netscape.com/library/technote/security/sectn2.html.*

Ask for Permission

HotJava was able to run the Renegade applet without modification. It's a different story in Netscape Navigator. Even if your applet is signed, Navigator won't let you perform security-sensitive operations without asking permission first. Before stepping outside the sandbox, your applet needs to ask if it's allowed. Netscape calls this system the *Capabilities API*. It works like this:

1. Your signed applet uses the Capabilities API to ask Navigator for permission to do something potentially dangerous. For example, your applet might ask for the privilege of writing to a local file.

2. Navigator checks its privileges database to see if the action is allowed for the applet's signer. If no entry in the database exists, it prompts the user with a dialog box. The user chooses whether the action is allowed or denied; this decision can be saved in the privileges database for future reference.

This is all well and good, but it means that we must modify our original Renegade applet. Furthermore, by adding support for the Capabilities API, we are making an applet that will run only in a Netscape browser. This is contrary to Java's original "write once, run everywhere" mantra. It's true that each browser recognizes signed applets in a different format, which already torpedoes your ability to create a single signed applet and have it run everywhere. By adding support for the Capabilities API, however, you have to actually modify the applet class itself, which is more of a problem than simply packaging up the applet in different ways.

Nevertheless, if you are willing to change the applet itself, here is the way to do it. In the Renegade applet, we just add a static call to `netscape.security.PrivilegeManager`, asking permission to read a system property:

```java
import java.applet.*;
import java.awt.*;

import netscape.security.PrivilegeManager;

public class PrivilegedRenegade extends Applet {
  private String mMessage;

  public void init() {
    try {
      PrivilegeManager.enablePrivilege("UniversalPropertyRead");
      mMessage = "Your name is " + System.getProperty("user.name") + ".";
    }
    catch (netscape.security.ForbiddenTargetException e) {
      mMessage = "Can't get your name, due to a ForbiddenTargetException.";
    }
    catch (SecurityException e) {
      mMessage = "Can't get your name, due to a SecurityException.";
    }
  }

  public void paint(Graphics g) {
    g.drawString("PrivilegedRenegade", 25, 25);
    g.drawString(mMessage, 25, 50);
  }
}
```

To compile this class, you need to have the Netscape Java classes in your CLASS-PATH. On my machine, this meant adding the following path:

```
c:\Program Files\Netscape\Communicator\Program\Java\Classes\java40.jar
```

You can read more about the Capabilities API at *http://developer.netscape.com/library/ documentation/signedobj/capsapi.html.*

Sign the Applet

Netscape's signing tool is called `zigbert`. You can find information about `zibgert` at *http://developer.netscape.com/library/documentation/signedobj/zigbert/.* `zigbert` signs directories, not archives, so you'll actually have to perform the signing operation before you create a JAR.

In our case, we have just one file to sign, *PrivilegedRenegade.class.* Move this file into its own directory, called *signdir.* To sign this directory, you have to tell zigbert where to find your keys and certificates and which certificate should be used for signing. On my Win95 machine, Netscape's keys and certificates are in the *c:\Program Files\Netscape\users\jonathan* directory. I'll use the one that I got from VeriSign:

```
C:\ zigbert -d"c:\Program Files\Netscape\users\jonathan" -k"Jonathan B
Knudsen VeriSign Trust Network ID" signdir
using key "Jonathan B Knudsen VeriSign Trust Network ID"
using certificate directory: c:\Program Files\Netscape\users\jonathan
Generating signdir/META-INF/manifest.mf file..
--> PrivilegedRenegade.class
Generating zigbert.sf file..
using key database: c:\Program Files\Netscape\users\jonathan/key3.db
tree "signdir" signed successfully

C:\
```

zigbert creates the signature files and the manifest file in the new *META-INF* directory.

Use Version 0.6, Not Version 0.6a

As of this writing, Netscape provides two versions of zigbert. Version 0.6 requires a system file, *msvcrtd.dll,* to be present on your system. If you don't have this file, you might be tempted to use version 0.6a, which doesn't require the file. Don't do it! Version 0.6a of zigbert does not work. Any signed archives you produce with zigbert 0.6a will not work correctly. In fact, zigbert itself can't even verify them.

To use version 0.6, the correctly working version, you'll need *msvcrtd.dll.* Don't worry; you probably already have *msvcrt.dll* on your system (in *c:\windows\system,* most likely). To get zigbert 0.6 to run, just make a copy of *msvcrt.dll* and name the copy *msvcrtd.dll.*

Bundle the Applet

Now that you've used zigbert to create the signing information, we need to bundle the *PrivilegedRenegade.class* file and the signing information into a JAR. When you downloaded zigbert, you should also have received a tool called zip, which can be used to create a JAR.[*] You just need to tell it the name of the JAR

---

[*] Although you should be able to use Sun's tool, jar, to bundle up the applet, I don't recommend it. Even though JARs should be standard, browsers tend to be finicky. It's safest to use Netscape's tool to create JARs for Netscape's browser.

and the files you want to add to it. To create an archive for our `PrivilegedRene`-gade class, run the following command in the signdir directory:

```
C:\ zip -r ..\nsRenegade.jar *
  adding: PrivilegedRenegade.class (deflated 44%)
  adding: META-INF/manifest.mf (deflated 14%)
  adding: META-INF/zigbert.sf (deflated 27%)
  adding: META-INF/zigbert.rsa (deflated 40%)

C:\
```

That's all there is to it. You can verify that the archive is correctly signed, using `zigbert`:

```
C:\ zigbert -d"c:\Program Files\Netscape\users\jonathan" -v nsRenegade.jar
using certificate directory: c:\Program Files\Netscape\users\jonathan
archive "nsRenegade.jar" has passed crypto verification.

        status    path
      ------------  --------------------
        verified   PrivilegedRenegade.class

C:\
```

Test the Applet

We need a slightly altered HTML page for our Netscape-oriented applet. The class name is now `PrivilegedRenegade`, and the signed archive that contains it is *nsRenegade.jar*. Here is the modified HTML page, *nsRenegade.html*:

```
<html>
<head>
</head>
<body>
  <applet code = PrivilegedRenegade.class archive = nsRenegade.jar
      width = 400 height = 200></applet>
</body>
</html>
```

Note that if both *PrivilegedRenegade.class* and *nsRenegade.jar* are present in the directory with *nsRenegade.html*, the browser will use the class file and ignore the signed archive. This can be confusing; the applet will still run, but it will not be signed. To avoid this, remove *PrivilegedRenegade.class* to force the browser to look in the archive for the class.

Point Navigator at *nsRenegade.html*. As with our HotJava example, Navigator determines that the applet is asking to play outside the sandbox. Having no precedent for this, Navigator asks the user if it's allowed, as shown in Figure 8-4.

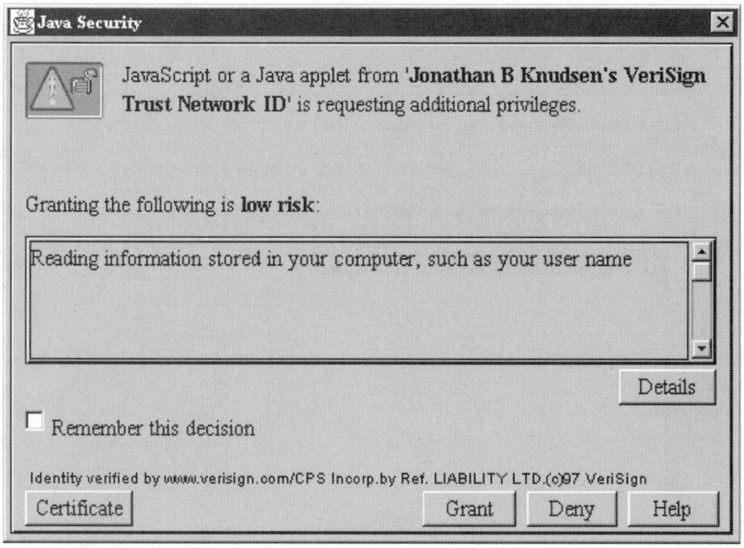

Figure 8-4: Navigator asks for permission

You can grant or deny the privilege and optionally make the decision "stick," using the **Remember this decision** checkbox.

Set Up the Browser

You can now examine (but not configure!) the privileges for this applet signer in detail. Choose the **Security Info** item from the Communicator menu. Then choose the Java/JavaScript option. You should see the name of your signer in the list, as in Figure 8-5.

Although this window contains a button labeled **Edit Privileges**, clicking on the button gives you only a summary of the privilege decisions you've made for this signer. Fine-grained editing capabilities will presumably come along later.

Internet Explorer

Microsoft, as usual, has come up with entirely new solutions to the problem of code signing. It uses its own archive format and a set of code-signing tools based around the Microsoft CryptoAPI.

Recipe

You'll have to install two pieces of software to sign code for Internet Explorer. First, you'll need the browser, Internet Explorer 4.0, available from *http://www*

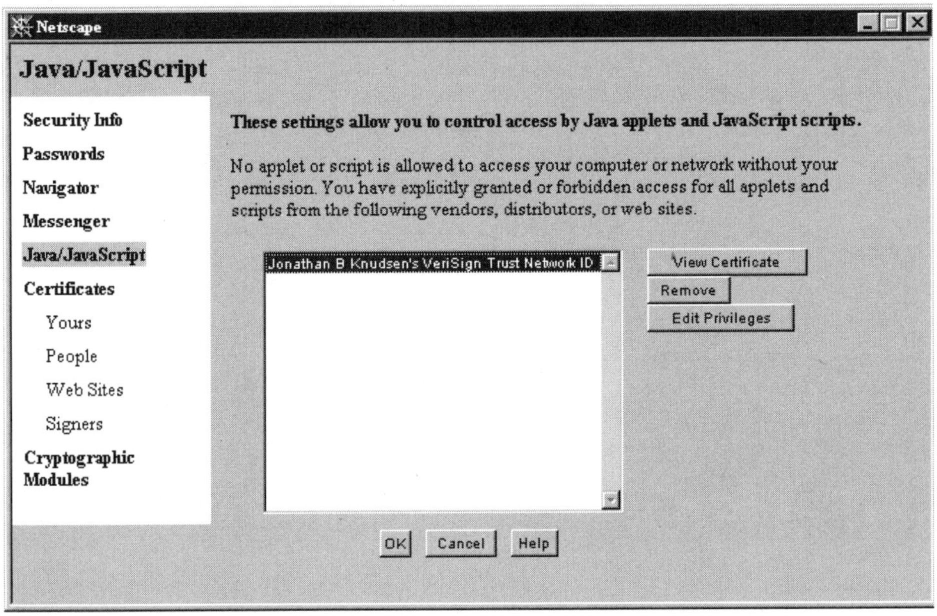

Figure 8-5: Navigator's code signers

.microsoft.com/ie/ie40/. For the archive and code-signing tools, you'll need the SDK for Java 2.0, available from *http://www.microsoft.com/java/*.

Prepare a Signer

Microsoft's tools allow you to create a *test* certificate that you can use for signing. This means you can experiment with signed applets without shelling out $20 for a real certificate. If you want to sign code with a real certificate, you can buy one from VeriSign (*http://www.verisign.com/*).

To create a test certificate, you can use tools that are installed as part of the SDK for Java, in the *SDK-Java.20\Bin\PackSign* directory:

```
MakeCert -sk JonathanKey -n CN=JonathanCompany Jonathan.cert
```

This creates a certificate file called *Jonathan.cert*. It uses the secret key called JonathanKey. If there is no such key, MakeCert creates one. This key is stored in a private key management database and can be accessed later. The -n option is used to specify what name is placed on the newly created certificate. You need a Software Publisher Certificate (SPC) to sign code. The SDK for Java has a handy utility that converts a certificate into an SPC:

```
Cert2SPC Jonathan.cert Jonathan.spc
```

This is all you need to do to create a test signer. You have an SPC file and a private key, which are sufficient to sign code.

If you buy a certificate from VeriSign, it comes to you in the form of a private key file and an SPC file. Save both of these files in safe places. Be especially careful with the private key. On Windows 95 systems, this means putting the files on a floppy disk or some other removable media that you can keep physically secure. On Windows NT systems, the concepts of file ownership and permissions can give your files some protection, so you might decide that leaving your private key file on the hard disk is an acceptable risk.

Bundle the Applet

Microsoft applets are bundled into *cabinet files,* which have a *.cab* extension. You can use the `cabarc` tool to manipulate cabinet files. In our case, we simply want to create a new cabinet file that contains *Renegade.class.* We'll use the n option to create a new cabinet file:

```
C:\ cabarc n ieRenegade.cab Renegade.class

Microsoft (R) Cabinet Tool - Version 1.00.0601 (03/18/97)
Copyright (c) Microsoft Corp 1996-1997. All rights reserved.

Creating new cabinet 'ieRenegade.cab' with compression 'MSZIP':
  -- adding Renegade.class

Completed successfully

C:\
```

Sign the Applet

The tool that is used for signing is called `SignCode`. If you created a test signer, then you can sign your cabinet file as follows:

```
SignCode -spc Jonathan.spc -k JonathanKey ieRenegade.cab
```

This uses the `JonathanKey` private key to sign the given cabinet file and attaches the *Jonathan.spc* certificate to the file.

If you have a real certificate from a CA, you should have received an SPC file and a private key file. When I bought a certificate from VeriSign, I received these files and saved them as *Jonathan.spc* and *Jonathan.pvk.* The command I used to sign the `Renegade` applet looks like this:

```
SignCode -spc Jonathan.spc -v Jonathan.pvk ieRenegade.cab
```

You can check to see if a cabinet file has been signed using ChkTrust, as follows:

```
ChkTrust ieRenegade.cab
```

This command will bring up a window that describes the signature on the cabinet file. You can view the certificate associated with the signed cabinet file, if you wish.

Test the Applet

Again, we need a new HTML file to run the applet. Here is the Internet Explorer version of the HTML page, *ieRenegade.html*:

```
<html>
<head>
</head>
<body>
  <applet code = Renegade width = 300 height = 200>
  <param name = cabbase value = ieRenegade.cab>
  </applet>
</body>
</html>
```

As with the other browsers, you should remove *Renegade.class* from the directory containing the HTML page. This will force Internet Explorer to look inside the archive file for the Renegade class.

Run Internet Explorer and point it at the *ieRenegade.html* file. As before, the browser recognizes the signed archive and displays a message, asking you if the applet should be allowed to run. This is shown in Figure 8-6.

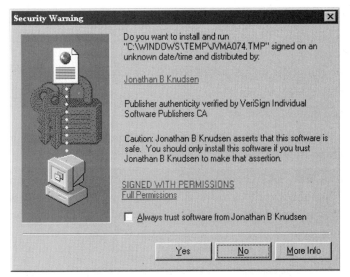

Figure 8-6: Internet Explorer asks if it can run a signed applet

Note that Internet Explorer gives you an all-or-nothing decision. You can either run the applet, allowing it full access outside the sandbox, or prevent it from running. HotJava, you'll recall, would ask permission each time the applet tried to do something outside the sandbox. Microsoft's approach probably reflects its real interest, ActiveX, which cannot be controlled with fine-grained policies the way Java applets can.

Microsoft has a system, somewhat like Netscape's Capabilities API, that can be used to ask for specific permissions. It is described at *http://www.microsoft.com/java/security/*.

Summary

Currently, signed applets are hard to work with for two reasons:

* Each of the large browser vendors uses a different format for signed applets.

* Code signing tools are buggy.

You can compensate for the first problem, on the server side, by detecting the type of client browser and returning a page containing a browser-specific applet. (Yuck!) You can compensate for the second problem by sweating a lot and tearing your hair out. If your application design relies on signed applets, you should think long and hard before proceeding. Chapter 12, *Outside the Box*, discusses some popular application architectures and the pros and cons of using an applet as a client. If you are developing an application in a partly closed environment, where you know that only one brand of browser will be used, then signed applets may be practical.

As this book goes to press, an interesting alternative technology is emerging: Sun's Java Activator. This is a Java Runtime Environment (JRE) that runs as a plug-in or extension with Netscape Navigator and Internet Explorer. Basically, it enables applets to use Sun's JVM instead of Netscape's, or Microsoft's. Signed applets are supported in Activator, but the exact technique is evolving. Check the documentation for details.

Furthermore, it's not clear what will happen to Navigator vis-a-vis Java, now that Navigator is free and the source code will be published. Netscape has stated that it will no longer produce a JVM, instead making the browser accept any JVM developed by Sun or Microsoft or anyone else. How this will affect signed applets remains to be seen.

9

Writing a Provider

If you can't find a cryptographic provider that implements the algorithms you want to use, it may be worth your while to write your own provider. A cryptographic provider is just a collection of classes that implement cryptographic algorithms—signatures, ciphers, or message digests. One of the classes, which will be a subclass of java.security.Provider, maps algorithm names to class names. The Provider subclass represents the provider as a whole. When you give an algorithm name to a getInstance() method, it is this class that figures out what type of object will be returned.

In this chapter, we'll develop a provider and several classes that implement the ElGamal cipher and signature algorithms. First, we'll look at a very simple crypto-graphic provider. Next, I'll introduce the ElGamal algorithms and show how the provider can accommodate them. In the remainder of the chapter, I'll show the code for the ElGamal key pair generation, signatures, and ciphers. If you're inter-ested only in learning how to create your own provider, just read the beginning of this chapter.

Getting Started

Algorithm Names and Implementations

A cryptographic provider is a set of classes that implement cryptographic algorithms. A Provider subclass keeps track of how the algorithm names and classes are related. Basically, it's a list of algorithm names and their corresponding implementations. For example, in Chapter 7, *Encryption*, we developed the CBCWrapper class, which (by default) supports DES in CBC mode with PKCS#5 padding. We also developed the CFBWrapper class, which supports DES in eight-bit CFB mode with no padding. A simple provider then might map algorithm names to class names like this:

```
DES/CBC/PKCS5Padding : oreilly.jonathan.crypto.CBCWrapper
DES/CFB/NoPadding : oreilly.jonathan.crypto.CFBWrapper
```

Remember, though, that a cryptographic provider can include several different kinds of algorithms: key pair generation, signatures, ciphers, and others. How does the provider know which is which? The algorithm name is actually made up of a type and a name, as follows:

```
Cipher.DES/CBC/PKCS5Padding : oreilly.jonathan.crypto.CBCWrapper
Cipher.DES/CFB/NoPadding : oreilly.jonathan.crypto.CFBWrapper
```

The type corresponds to a cryptographic concept class, like `Cipher` or `Signature`. The implementation class is the corresponding SPI class, like `javax.crypto.CipherSpi` or `java.security.SignatureSpi`. Later, for example, we'll develop a class that implements the ElGamal signature algorithm. It's a subclass of `SignatureSpi`. To associate the algorithm name and the implementation class, our provider will have the following mapping:

```
Signature.ElGamal : oreilly.jonathan.crypto.ElGamalSignature
```

A Simple Provider

Let's stick with the simple case, just to get started. We'll create a `Provider` subclass that includes the mappings for the `CBCWrapper` and `CFBWrapper` classes. Our provider is represented by `oreilly.jonathan.security.Provider`, a subclass of `java.security.Provider`.

`Provider` is a subclass of `java.util.Hashtable`; it maintains the mappings between algorithm names and implementations as a list of string mappings. You can add a mapping using `put()`.

Our first provider subclass is very short:

```
package oreilly.jonathan.crypto;

import java.security.*;

public class Provider
    extends java.security.Provider {
  public Provider() {
    super ("Jonathan",
        1.2,
        "Jonathan's Cryptography Provider");

    put("Cipher.DES/CBC/PKCS5Padding",
        "oreilly.jonathan.crypto.CBCWrapper");
    put("Cipher.DES/CFB/NoPadding", "oreilly.jonathan.crypto.CFBWrapper");
  }
}
```

The call to super() specifies the provider's short name, version, and long name. The short name is used in the getInstance() methods that accept a provider name. For example, you could explicitly request the DSA key generator from the SunJCE provider as follows:

```
kpg = KeyPairGenerator.getInstance("DSA", "SunJCE");
```

Our provider is imaginatively named "Jonathan."

An Algorithm by Any Other Name

Sometimes you may want to return the same implementation for different algorithm names. In the default SUN provider, for example, you'll get the same message digest implementation in both of the following lines of code:

```
MessageDigest one = MessageDigest.getInstance("SHA-1");
MessageDigest two = MessageDigest.getInstance("SHA");
```

We might, for example, want "DES/CFB8/NoPadding" to also map to CFBWrapper because that class implements eight-bit CFB mode. We can accomplish this in our provider by defining an algorithm alias, as follows:

```
put("Alg.Alias.Cipher.DES/CFB8/NoPadding", "DES/CFB/NoPadding");
```

With this additional information in our provider, the following lines will be equivalent:

```
Cipher one = Cipher.getInstance("DES/CFB8/NoPadding");
Cipher two = Cipher.getInstance("DES/CFB/NoPadding");
```

Installing the Provider

As we saw in Chapter 3, *Architecture,* there are two ways to install the Jonathan provider on your system. To statically add the Jonathan provider, edit the *java.security* file found in the *lib/security* directory underneath the JDK installation directory. You'll need to add a line for the Jonathan provider like the following:

```
security.provider.n=oreilly.jonathan.crypto.Provider
```

In this case, n is the preference position for the provider. For example, this is how providers are configured on my system:

```
security.provider.1=sun.security.provider.Sun
security.provider.2=com.sun.crypto.provider.SunJCE
security.provider.3=oreilly.jonathan.crypto.Provider
security.provider.4=cryptix.security.Cryptix
security.provider.5=iaik.security.provider.IAIK
```

In my case, the Jonathan provider is always the third provider queried for algorithms.

What if you write an application that uses the Jonathan provider, but you don't want your users to have to mess around with the *java.security* file? Your application can add the Jonathan provider at runtime using the following code:

```
java.security.Provider p = new oreilly.jonathan.crypto.Provider();
Security.addProvider(p);
```

This adds the Jonathan provider to the end of the preference list; to place it in a particular spot, use `insertProviderAt()`.

Adding the ElGamal Classes

In this chapter, we'll develop a full suite of classes to support ElGamal signatures and ciphers. The Jonathan provider will need to know about some of the implementation classes, namely:

```
oreilly.jonathan.crypto.ElGamalKeyPairGenerator
oreilly.jonathan.crypto.ElGamalSignature
oreilly.jonathan.crypto.ElGamalCipher
```

Thus, we just need to add the correct associations to our simple provider class. It's a piece of cake:

```
package oreilly.jonathan.crypto;

import java.security.*;

public class Provider
    extends java.security.Provider {
  public Provider() {
    super ("Jonathan",
        1.2,
        "Jonathan's Cryptography Provider");

    put("KeyPairGenerator.ElGamal",
        "oreilly.jonathan.crypto.ElGamalKeyPairGenerator");
    put("Cipher.ElGamal", "oreilly.jonathan.crypto.ElGamalCipher");
    put("Signature.ElGamal", "oreilly.jonathan.crypto.ElGamalSignature");

    put("Cipher.DES/CBC/PKCS5Padding",
        "oreilly.jonathan.crypto.CBCWrapper");
    put("Cipher.DES/CFB/NoPadding", "oreilly.jonathan.crypto.CFBWrapper");

    put("Alg.Alias.Cipher.DES/CFB8/NoPadding", "DES/CFB/NoPadding");
  }
}
```

The hard part is actually implementing the algorithms. We'll spend the rest of the chapter doing just that.

ElGamal

ElGamal is named after its creator, Taher ElGamal. Although it was not patented directly, a patent covering Diffie-Hellman key exchange was considered to cover ElGamal as well. Lucky for us, the patent expired as I wrote this book. ElGamal is now free.

I won't try to explain the math or demonstrate why it's a secure set of algorithms. The equations themselves are not too hard to understand.

Key Pair Generation

Here's the recipe for generating a key pair:

1. Create a random prime number, p. This number is called the *modulus*. The size of p is the same as the key size, so a 2048-bit key has a p that is 2048 bits.

2. Choose two other random numbers, g and x, both less than p. The private key is x.

3. Calculate $y = g^x$ mod p. The public key is p, g, and y.

Signature

To generate a signature using the private key, follow these steps:

1. Choose a random number, k, that is *relatively prime* to p − 1. Relatively prime means that k and p − 1 have no factors in common (except 1).

2. Calculate $a = g^k$ mod p and $b = \dfrac{m - xa}{k}$ mod (p − 1),

   where m is the message. The signature is the numbers a and b.

To verify such a signature, you just have to check that $y^a a^b$ mod p = g^m mod p.

Cipher

ElGamal encryption consists of two steps:

1. Choose a random number, k, that is relatively prime to p − 1.

2. Calculate $a = g^k$ mod p and $b = y^k m$ mod p, where m is the plaintext message. The ciphertext is the numbers a and b. It is twice as large as the modulus, p.

To decrypt, calculate $m = \dfrac{b}{a^x}$ mod p. This works because:

$$\frac{b}{a^x} \bmod p = \frac{y^k m}{g^{kx}} \bmod p = \frac{g^{kx} m}{g^{kx}} \bmod p = m \bmod p.$$

All of this math can be accomplished using `java.math.BigInteger`. Implementing the algorithm in a `Cipher`, however, can be tricky. The reason has to do with the size of the numbers involved.

Take another look at the equation used for decryption. The message, m, will always be less than the modulus, p. If you want to encrypt a message that is larger than the modulus value, the message will have to be split into manageable pieces. Specifically, the message should be split into pieces that are less than the bit length of p.

The size of the ciphertext also depends on the size of the modulus. The ciphertext values, a and b, range from 0 to p – 1. The size of the ciphertext, then, is twice the number of bits as in p.

For example, a 512-bit key has a 512-bit p. Any incoming messages will have to be split into pieces that are 511 bits or smaller. Because `Cipher` deals only with bytes, not bits, the incoming block size will be (512 – 1) / 8 = 63 bytes. The ciphertext, on the other hand, will be twice the modulus length, or 128 bytes (1024 bits). As you read the code for `ElGamalCipher`, you'll see how these lengths are calculated.[*]

Generating Keys

Key Classes

As shown earlier, an ElGamal public key consists of p, g, and y. The matching private key is x. We'll need classes to encapsulate these values.

If you look back at the algorithm for verifying a signature, you'll notice it uses not only x, but p and g as well. Thus, we'll make our private key class contain p, g, and x. The public and private key classes then both descend from `ElGamalKey`, which is simply a container for p and g.

```
package oreilly.jonathan.crypto;

import java.math.BigInteger;
import java.security.*;

public class ElGamalKey
    implements Key {
  private BigInteger mP, mG;
```

---

[*] Schneier, in the second edition of *Applied Cryptography*, incorrectly states that the ciphertext is twice the length of the plaintext. The ciphertext is twice the length of the modulus, and the plaintext should be slightly shorter than the modulus. Thus, the ciphertext is a little more than twice the length of the plaintext.

```
    protected ElGamalKey(BigInteger g, BigInteger p) {
      mG = g;
      mP = p;
    }

    protected BigInteger getG() { return mG; }
    protected BigInteger getP() { return mP; }

    public String getAlgorithm() { return "ElGamal"; }
    public String getFormat() { return "NONE"; }
    public byte[] getEncoded() { return null; }
  }
```

The ElGamal public key consists of p, g, and y. Because p and g are already contained in ElGamalKey, the public key class has to contain just y:

```
package oreilly.jonathan.crypto;

import java.math.BigInteger;
import java.security.*;

public class ElGamalPublicKey
    extends ElGamalKey
    implements PublicKey {
  private BigInteger mY;

    protected ElGamalPublicKey(BigInteger y, BigInteger g, BigInteger p) {
      super(g, p);
      mY = y;
    }

    protected BigInteger getY() { return mY; }
  }
```

And ElGamalPrivateKey simply holds x:

```
package oreilly.jonathan.crypto;

import java.math.BigInteger;
import java.security.*;

public class ElGamalPrivateKey
    extends ElGamalKey
    implements PrivateKey {
  private BigInteger mX;

    protected ElGamalPrivateKey(BigInteger x, BigInteger g, BigInteger p) {
      super(g, p);
      mX = x;
    }
```

```
      protected BigInteger getX() { return mX; }
}
```

ElGamalKeyPairGenerator

The key pair generation procedure was outlined previously. The `BigInteger` class makes it possible to translate this procedure almost effortlessly into code:

```
package oreilly.jonathan.crypto;

import java.math.BigInteger;
import java.security.*;

public class ElGamalKeyPairGenerator
    extends KeyPairGeneratorSpi {
  private int mStrength = 0;
  private SecureRandom mSecureRandom = null;

  // Strength is interpreted as the bit length of p.
  public void initialize(int strength, SecureRandom random) {
    mStrength = strength;
    mSecureRandom = random;
  }

  public KeyPair generateKeyPair() {
    if (mSecureRandom == null) {
      mStrength = 1024;
      mSecureRandom = new SecureRandom();
    }
    BigInteger p = new BigInteger(mStrength, 16, mSecureRandom);
    BigInteger g = new BigInteger(mStrength - 1, mSecureRandom);
    BigInteger x = new BigInteger(mStrength - 1, mSecureRandom);
    BigInteger y = g.modPow(x, p);

    ElGamalPublicKey publicKey = new ElGamalPublicKey(y, g, p);
    ElGamalPrivateKey privateKey = new ElGamalPrivateKey(x, g, p);
    return new KeyPair(publicKey, privateKey);
  }
}
```

The key pair generator is initialized with a measure of strength and a `Secure-Random`, which are stored in member variables. In `generateKeyPair()`, we set a default value for the strength in case `initialize()` has not been called. Then we're ready to begin creating the ElGamal key pair. First, we create a random prime number, p. The key pair generator's strength determines the length of this number, in bits (commonly known as the "key length"). In the `BigInteger` constructor, the number 16 determines the probability that the returned number is really a prime. The probability of its being prime is $1 - .5^n$ for a given "certainty" value, n. So our certainty of 16 means that p has a probability of .99998474 of being prime. You can increase this value to be more certain that you have a prime number, but it will take longer to calculate. For more information about the BigInteger constructors used for p, g, and x, see Appendix A, *BigInteger*. Once we've created p, g and x are created as random numbers smaller than p. Then y is calculated from g, x, and p. This done, we simply create the appropriate public and private keys, package them in a KeyPair, and return the result.

Signature

To implement an ElGamal signature class, we'll have to implement the Service Provider Interface (SPI) of Signature, which is contained in SignatureSpi. I talked briefly about the SPI in Chapter 3; SignatureSpi contains all the methods you need to define to implement a signature algorithm:

```
package oreilly.jonathan.crypto;

import java.io.ByteArrayOutputStream;
import java.math.BigInteger;
import java.security.*;

public class ElGamalSignature
    extends SignatureSpi {
```

A Signature is intialized with a key, which is used later to either generate or verify a signature value. We'll save the intialization key in a member variable until we need it:

```
protected ElGamalKey mKey;
```

As data is added to our ElGamalSignature with the update() method, we'll accumulate it in a ByteArrayOutputStream. When the time comes to generate or verify the signature value, we'll use the data from this stream:

```
protected ByteArrayOutputStream mOut;
```

In the signature calculations, later, we'll frequently make use of the number 1 as a BigInteger. Here, I use a static member variable to hold this special value:

```
protected static BigInteger kOne = BigInteger.valueOf(1);
```

When the initVerify() method of Signature is called, it eventually calls the SPI method engineInitVerify(). In our implementation, we first check to make sure we've received an ElGamalPublicKey because a public key is always used to verify a signature. Then we save the key and create a new ByteArrayOutputStream to hold the data that will be used to verify the signature:

```
protected void engineInitVerify(PublicKey key)
    throws InvalidKeyException {
```

```
    if (!(key instanceof ElGamalPublicKey))
      throw new InvalidKeyException("I didn't get an ElGamalPublicKey.");
    mKey = (ElGamalKey)key;
    mOut = new ByteArrayOutputStream();
  }
```

Likewise, the SPI method `engineInitSign()` gets called when `Signature`'s `initSign()` method is called. As before, we check to make sure we have the right kind of key (a private key this time). Then we save the key in a member variable and create a new `ByteArrayOutputStream` for the message data:

```
  protected void engineInitSign(PrivateKey key) throws InvalidKeyException {
    if (!(key instanceof ElGamalPrivateKey))
      throw new InvalidKeyException("I didn't get an ElGamalPrivateKey.");
    mKey = (ElGamalKey)key;
    mOut = new ByteArrayOutputStream();
  }
```

`Signature`'s `update()` methods end up calling the corresponding `engineUp-date()` SPI methods. Our implementations of `engineUpdate()` write the input data to the internal `ByteArrayOutputStream`. This means that the `ElGamalSig-nature` class accumulates all the data you feed it. If you want to calculate the signature on a 20-MB file, this is probably not a good approach. For small pieces of data, like certificates, it works just fine.

```
  protected void engineUpdate(byte b) throws SignatureException {
    mOut.write(b);
  }

  protected void engineUpdate(byte[] b, int off, int len)
      throws SignatureException {
    mOut.write(b, off, len);
  }
```

`engineSign()` is the SPI equivalent of `sign()` in the `Signature` API. It will not be called unless your `SignatureSpi` has been correctly initialized for signing. In `ElGa-malSignature`, `engineSign()` contains the implementation of the math described earlier. First, we extract some parameters from the stored private key that was originally passed to `initSign()`. For convenience, we also calculate the value $p - 1$.

```
  protected byte[] engineSign() throws SignatureException {
    BigInteger x = ((ElGamalPrivateKey)mKey).getX();
    BigInteger g = mKey.getG();
    BigInteger p = mKey.getP();
    BigInteger pminusone = p.subtract(kOne);
```

Next, `engineSign()` randomly picks k, such that it is relatively prime to $p - 1$:

```
    BigInteger k;
    do {
```

```
        k = new BigInteger(p.bitLength() - 1, new SecureRandom());
    } while (k.gcd(pminusone).equals(kOne) == false);
```

All the bytes of message that were accumulated in the `ByteArrayOutputStream` are converted to a `BigInteger` called m:

```
    BigInteger m = new BigInteger(1, mOut.toByteArray());
```

The signature is represented by the values a and b, where a = g^k mod p and b = $\frac{m - xa}{k}$ mod (p − 1). The variable `top` is used as an intermediate result, to simplify the calculation:

```
    BigInteger a = g.modPow(k, p);
    BigInteger top = m.subtract(x.multiply(a)).mod(pminusone);
    BigInteger b = top.multiply(
        k.modPow(kOne.negate(), pminusone)).mod(pminusone);
```

We've calculated the signature, but we need to return the a and b values as a byte array. We create an array that is twice the key's modulus length and write bytes representing a and b into this array. The helper function, `getBytes()`, is presented later.

```
    int modulusLength = (p.bitLength() + 7) / 8;
    byte[] signature = new byte[modulusLength * 2];
    byte[] aBytes = getBytes(a);
    int aLength = aBytes.length;
    byte[] bBytes = getBytes(b);
    int bLength = bBytes.length;
    System.arraycopy(aBytes, 0,
        signature, modulusLength - aLength, aLength);
    System.arraycopy(bBytes, 0,
        signature, modulusLength * 2 - bLength, bLength);
    return signature;
}
```

To verify a signature, you call `verify()` in `Signature`'s API. This calls the corresponding SPI method, `engineVerify()`. The first thing this method does is extract some parameters from the stored public key:

```
    protected boolean engineVerify(byte[] sigBytes)
        throws SignatureException {
    BigInteger y = ((ElGamalPublicKey)mKey).getY();
    BigInteger g = mKey.getG();
    BigInteger p = mKey.getP();
```

Next, we need to extract the signature values, a and b, from the supplied byte array. To do this, we create a `BigInteger` from each half of the signature byte array:

```
    int modulusLength = (p.bitLength() + 7) / 8;
    byte[] aBytes = new byte[modulusLength];
```

```
byte[] bBytes = new byte[modulusLength];
System.arraycopy(sigBytes, 0, aBytes, 0, modulusLength);
System.arraycopy(sigBytes, modulusLength, bBytes, 0, modulusLength);
BigInteger a = new BigInteger(1, aBytes);
BigInteger b = new BigInteger(1, bBytes);
```

Now it's a matter of calculating $y^a a^b$ mod p and g^m mod p and checking to see if they're equal:

```
BigInteger first = y.modPow(a, p).multiply(a.modPow(b, p)).mod(p);

BigInteger m = new BigInteger(1, mOut.toByteArray());
BigInteger second = g.modPow(m,p);

return first.equals(second);
}
```

The next method in `ElGamalSignature` is `getBytes()`, which returns an array of bytes representing a `BigInteger` value. Although `BigInteger` has such a method, it uses an extra bit to indicate the sign of the number. In `ElGamalSignature`'s calculations, all the numbers are positive; we have no interest in a sign bit. This helper method, `getBytes()`, returns an array of bytes that is only as long as it needs to be, ignoring the sign of the number:

```
protected byte[] getBytes(BigInteger big) {
  byte[] bigBytes = big.toByteArray();
  if ((big.bitLength() % 8) != 0) {
    return bigBytes;
  }
  else {
    byte[] smallerBytes = new byte[big.bitLength() / 8];
    System.arraycopy(bigBytes, 1, smallerBytes, 0, smallerBytes.length);
    return smallerBytes;
  }
}
```

Finally, we need to implement the SPI methods `engineSetParameter()` and `engineGetParameter()`. These methods provide a general way to set and retrieve algorithm-specific parameters. `ElGamalSignature` has no use for parameters, so these methods are empty. In JDK 1.2, these methods are deprecated, and the compiler will warn you about this. You can't, however, create a concrete `SignatureSpi` subclass without defining them:

```
protected void engineSetParameter(String param, Object value)
    throws InvalidParameterException {}
protected Object engineGetParameter(String param)
    throws InvalidParameterException { return null; }
}
```

Cipher

The `ElGamalCipher` class contains the magic of the ElGamal cipher algorithm. This class indirectly extends `javax.crypto.CipherSpi`; it lives in the `oreilly.jonathan.crypto` package along with the rest of the ElGamal classes. Just as the signature classes implemented the methods of `SignatureSpi`, `ElGamalCipher` needs to implement the methods of `CipherSpi`.

To simplify the implementation of the ElGamal cipher, this class is a subclass of `BlockCipher`, which was presented in Chapter 7. `BlockCipher` provides buffering and block handling and saves some trouble in implementing the ElGamal algorithm:

```
package oreilly.jonathan.crypto;

import java.math.BigInteger;
import java.security.*;
import java.security.spec.*;

import javax.crypto.*;

public class ElGamalCipher
    extends BlockCipher {
```

The block sizes of the cipher depend on the size of its key, as discussed earlier. When the cipher is initialized for encryption or decryption, we calculate the size of a plaintext block and the size of a ciphertext block. The key itself and the block sizes are stored in member variables. We also store the state of the cipher (either `Cipher.ENCRYPT_MODE` or `Cipher.DECRYPT_MODE`) and whatever `SecureRandom` is passed to our `ElGamalCipher` when it is initialized:

```
protected int mState;
protected Key mKey;
protected SecureRandom mSecureRandom;
protected int mPlainBlockSize;
protected int mCipherBlockSize;
```

This class supports no modes or padding, so `engineSetMode()` and `engineSetPadding()` both throw exceptions when called:

```
protected void engineSetMode(String mode)
    throws NoSuchAlgorithmException {
  throw new NoSuchAlgorithmException("ElGamalCipher supports no modes.");
}

protected void engineSetPadding(String padding)
    throws NoSuchPaddingException {
  throw new NoSuchPaddingException("ElGamalCipher supports no padding.");
}
```

There's a bit of a lie here. ElGamalCipher doesn't actually implement a padding scheme, but it can accept data that is not exactly block-sized. When encrypting, ElGamalCipher will fill up an incomplete block with zeros, but it is unable to remove them when decrypting, which makes it fall short of a true padding scheme. Thus, the length of decrypted data will always be a multiple of the block size. If the length of the original plaintext was not a multiple of the block size, then the decrypted data will have extra zero bytes on the end of it. Figure 9-1 shows what happens, for an 8-byte block size and 13 bytes of plaintext.

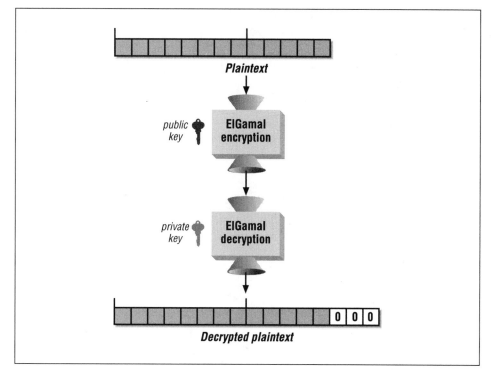

Figure 9-1: Block handling in ElGamalCipher

Although ElGamalCipher could implement PKCS#5-style padding, it's not a satisfactory solution. Consider, for example, a 1024-bit (or larger) ElGamal key. The ciphertext block size for this key will be (1024) / 8 * 2 = 256 bytes. Suppose we had to add a whole block of padding; it would be 256 bytes, each with a value of 256. But a byte holds values only from 0 to 255. Thus, some other method of padding is needed. Note that this is not specific to ElGamal; any cipher with a ciphertext block size greater than 255 bytes will not be able to use PKCS#5 padding. Therefore, keep ElGamalCipher relatively simple, no padding is implemented. As it stands now, it's a very useful class; you just need to be careful about trailing zeros in the decrypted plaintext.

The plaintext and ciphertext block sizes are calculated later. Here, `engineGet-BlockSize()` just returns the appropriate size, based on the state of the cipher:

```
protected int engineGetBlockSize() {
  if (mState == Cipher.DECRYPT_MODE)
    return mCipherBlockSize;
  else
    return mPlainBlockSize;
}
```

Calculating an output buffer size is a bit tricky. Based on the state of the cipher, we figure out how many input blocks are represented by `inLen`. Then the number of output bytes needed can be calculated. Note that we need to be careful to include the length of any data that has been buffered by our parent class, `BlockCipher`. Calls to `getBufferedDataLength()` return the length of the buffered data.

```
protected int engineGetOutputSize(int inLen) {
  int inBlocks;
  int outLength;

  if (mState == Cipher.ENCRYPT_MODE) {
    inBlocks = (inLen + getBufferedDataLength() + mPlainBlockSize - 1) /
        mPlainBlockSize;
    outLength = inBlocks * mCipherBlockSize;
  }
  else {
    inBlocks = (inLen + getBufferedDataLength() + mCipherBlockSize - 1) /
        mCipherBlockSize;
    outLength = inBlocks * mPlainBlockSize;
  }
  return outLength;
}
```

In cipher implementations that implement a feedback mode, the `getIV()` method returns the initialization vector. Our implementation of ElGamal runs just in ECB mode, so this method returns `null`:

```
protected byte[] engineGetIV() { return null; }
```

When the cipher is initialized for encryption or decryption, we calculate the plaintext and ciphertext block sizes, based on the size of the key. `engineInit()` uses another method, `calculateBlockSizes()`, to figure out the block sizes. First we check that the correct kind of key has been used to initialize the cipher. The supplied key is saved in the `mKey` member variable; it will be used later when the cipher encrypts or decrypts data. We also save the cipher's state and the supplied `SecureRandom` before calculating the block sizes.

```
protected void engineInit(int opmode, Key key, SecureRandom random)
    throws InvalidKeyException {
```

```
    if (opmode == Cipher.ENCRYPT_MODE)
      if (!(key instanceof ElGamalPublicKey))
        throw new InvalidKeyException("I didn't get an ElGamalPublicKey.");
    else if (opmode == Cipher.DECRYPT_MODE)
      if (!(key instanceof ElGamalPrivateKey))
        throw new InvalidKeyException("I didn't get an ElGamalPrivateKey.");
    else throw new IllegalArgumentException("Bad mode: " + opmode);

    mState = opmode;
    mKey = key;
    mSecureRandom = random;
    calculateBlockSizes(key);
  }
```

ElGamalCipher doesn't recognize any algorithm-specific initializations, so the
algorithm-specific engineInit() just calls the previous overloaded version of
engineInit():

```
  protected void engineInit(int opmode, Key key,
      AlgorithmParameterSpec params, SecureRandom random)
      throws InvalidKeyException, InvalidAlgorithmParameterException {
    engineInit(opmode, key, random);
  }
```

The following methods simply calculate the size of a plaintext block and a ciphertext block, based on the size of the key used to initialize the cipher:

```
  protected void calculateBlockSizes(Key key) {
    int modulusLength = ((ElGamalKey)key).getP().bitLength();
    mPlainBlockSize = (modulusLength - 1) / 8;
    mCipherBlockSize = ((modulusLength + 7) / 8) * 2;
  }
```

BlockCipher, ElGamalCipher's parent class, handles the details of input buffering and block handling. Our class needs to define just two methods from
BlockCipher, namely engineTransformBlock() and engineTransformBlock-
Final(). Because ElGamalCipher implements no padding, these methods
perform the same function. The second method simply calls the first.

In engineTransformBlock(), we call either encryptBlock() or decrypt-
Block(), based on the state of the cipher:

```
  protected int engineTransformBlock(byte[] input,
      int inputOffset, int inputLength, byte[] output, int outputOffset)
      throws ShortBufferException {
    if (mState == Cipher.ENCRYPT_MODE)
      return encryptBlock(input, inputOffset, inputLength,
          output, outputOffset);
    else if (mState == Cipher.DECRYPT_MODE)
      return decryptBlock(input, inputOffset, inputLength,
```

```
        output, outputOffset);
    return 0;
}

protected int engineTransformBlockFinal(byte[] input,
      int inputOffset, int inputLength, byte[] output, int outputOffset)
      throws ShortBufferException {
    if (inputLength == 0) return 0;
    return engineTransformBlock(input, inputOffset, inputLength,
        output, outputOffset);
}
```

In encryptBlock(), we first build the message value from the input bytes. Note that the messageBytes buffer is block-sized. Even if the plaintext input is shorter, we encrypt a full plaintext block. The remainder of the block will be zeros.

```
    protected int encryptBlock(byte[] in, int inOff, int inLen,
        byte[] out, int outOff) {
    byte[] messageBytes = new byte[mPlainBlockSize];
    int inputLength = Math.min(mPlainBlockSize, inLen);
    System.arraycopy(in, inOff, messageBytes, 0, inputLength);
    BigInteger m = new BigInteger(1, messageBytes);
```

Next, encryptBlock() creates the random number, k. We have to turn some cartwheels to calculate p − 1 in the BigInteger world:

```
    ElGamalPublicKey key = (ElGamalPublicKey)mKey;
    BigInteger p = key.getP();
    BigInteger one = BigInteger.valueOf(1);
    BigInteger pminusone = p.subtract(one);
    BigInteger k;
    do {
      k = new BigInteger(p.bitLength() - 1, mSecureRandom);
    } while (k.gcd(pminusone).equals(one) == false);
```

Then a and b are calculated, using the message value, the key, and k:

```
    BigInteger a = key.getG().modPow(k, p);
    BigInteger b = key.getY().modPow(k, p).multiply(m).mod(p);
```

Finally, a and b are copied into the output buffer. Because the length of a and b might be less than half the ciphertext block size, the values are right-justified:

```
    byte[] aBytes = getBytes(a);
    byte[] bBytes = getBytes(b);
    System.arraycopy(aBytes, 0,
        out, outOff + mCipherBlockSize / 2 - aBytes.length, aBytes.length);
    System.arraycopy(bBytes, 0,
        out, outOff + mCipherBlockSize - bBytes.length,
        bBytes.length);
```

encryptBlock() returns the number of ciphertext bytes written. Because it always processes a block of plaintext, it always generates one block of ciphertext:

```
        return mCipherBlockSize;
    }
```

Decryption is a similar process. First a and b are extracted from the ciphertext input:

```
    protected int decryptBlock(byte[] in, int inOff, int inLen,
            byte[] out, int outOff) {
        // Pull out our key.
        ElGamalPrivateKey key = (ElGamalPrivateKey)mKey;
        BigInteger p = key.getP();

        // Extract a and b.
        byte[] aBytes = new byte[mCipherBlockSize / 2];
        System.arraycopy(in, inOff, aBytes, 0, mCipherBlockSize / 2);
        byte[] bBytes = new byte[mCipherBlockSize / 2];
        System.arraycopy(in, inOff + mCipherBlockSize / 2, bBytes, 0,
            mCipherBlockSize / 2);
        BigInteger a = new BigInteger(1, aBytes);
        BigInteger b = new BigInteger(1, bBytes);
```

Then the message value can be calculated using $m = \dfrac{b}{a^x} \bmod p$:

```
        BigInteger m = b.multiply(a.modPow(key.getX().negate(), p)).mod(p);
```

To finish, the bytes of the message value are copied into the output buffer. We return the number of bytes decrypted, which should always be one plaintext block. Interestingly, the decrypted message m may actually be larger than one plaintext block if the wrong key is used for decryption. The gatedLength variable is used below to avoid throwing ArrayIndexOutOfBoundsExceptions in this case:

```
        byte[] messageBytes = getBytes(m);
        int gatedLength = Math.min(messageBytes.length, mPlainBlockSize);
        System.arraycopy(messageBytes, 0,
            out, outOff + mPlainBlockSize - gatedLength,
            gatedLength);
        return mPlainBlockSize;
    }
```

We use the same getBytes() helper method that you saw in ElGamalSignature:

```
    protected byte[] getBytes(BigInteger big) {
        byte[] bigBytes = big.toByteArray();
        if ((big.bitLength() % 8) != 0) {
            return bigBytes;
        }
        else {
            byte[] smallerBytes = new byte[big.bitLength() / 8];
            System.arraycopy(bigBytes, 1, smallerBytes, 0, smallerBytes.length);
```

```
        return smallerBytes;
      }
    }
  }
```

And that's the whole ElGamalCipher class. There are several enhancements you might want to make, if you're feeling adventurous:

- Implement a padding scheme so that decrypted plaintext will be the same length as the original plaintext.

- Improve exception handling, particularly in the encryptBlock() and decryptBlock() methods.

If you want to test out ElGamalCipher, read on. It's used in the next two chapters.

10

SafeTalk

SafeTalk is a Java application based on the `talk` utility of Unix. `talk` allows two users on different computers to type messages to each other, in real time, over a network. It's not hard to eavesdrop on `talk` because its data is sent in plaintext over the network. SafeTalk adds cryptography to this application, providing authentication for each end of the conversation and encryption for the conversation itself.

SafeTalk builds on work that we've done elsewhere in this book:

- The `KeyManager` class, from Chapter 5, *Key Management,* is used to contain all the keys that SafeTalk uses. This class is used instead of a `KeyStore` derivative to keep the application reasonably simple. If we used a `KeyStore` implementation, we'd have had to implement certificate generation and handling as well.

- SafeTalk exchanges a DES session key using ElGamal encryption. We need the ElGamal classes from Chapter 9, *Writing a Provider,* (with the exception of `ElGamalSignature`) and the Jonathan provider.

SafeTalk, in essence, is a hybrid system, combining both symmetric and asymmetric ciphers (see Chapter 7, *Encryption,* for more on hybrid systems). It uses an ElGamal (asymmetric) cipher to exchange a session key between the two ends of the conversation. The remainder of the conversation is encrypted using a DES (symmetric) cipher and the session key.

Using SafeTalk

The SafeTalk window is shown in Figure 10-1. The top part of the window is split between two text areas. You can type in the top text area. Whatever you type is transmitted to the person on the other end of your conversation. The lower text area displays the text that is received from the other end of the conversation.

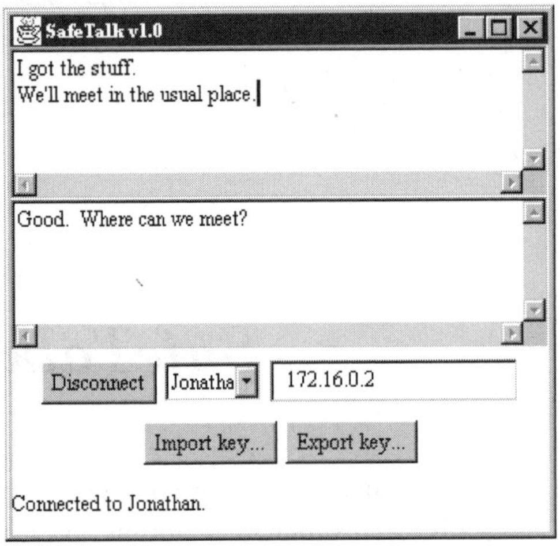

Figure 10-1: The SafeTalk window

First-Time Setup

To use SafeTalk, you'll first have to generate a key file. This involves picking a name for yourself and generating a key pair. SafeTalk will use this key pair to authenticate you and exchange a session key. SafeTalk expects ElGamal keys of any size in a key file called *Keys.ser*. You should create this file in the same directory as the SafeTalk classes. Because we are using the KeyManager class from Chapter 5, you can use KeyManager's command-line interface to create a new key file. For example, I use the following line to create a key file for "Jonathan" with 512-bit keys:

```
C:\ java oreilly.jonathan.security.KeyManager -c Keys.ser Jonathan ElGamal 512
Initializing the KeyPairGenerator...
Generating the key pair...
Done.
```

If you need to review KeyManager or its command-line options, see Chapter 5.

This done, you can run SafeTalk by entering java SafeTalk. The SafeTalk window will pop up and will greet you by name.

Exporting a Key

Once you've generated a key file, you'll need to export your public key and distribute it to everyone with whom you want to converse. To do this, select your own name in the combo box next to the **Connect** button. Then press the **Export key...**

button. Choose a file to hold the exported key. You can distribute this file to other `SafeTalk` users. You can export other people's public keys in the same manner.

Importing a Key

You need to import a public key for anyone with whom you wish to converse. You can import a public key by pressing the **Import key...** button. Choose the file that contains the key. The name corresponding to the public key will appear in the combo box next to the **Connect** button. `SafeTalk` can import only keys that were exported using `SafeTalk`.

Starting a Conversation

To start a conversation, you need to select a recipient from the combo box next to the **Connect** button. In Figure 10-1, Jonathan is selected as the recipient. You also need to indicate the IP address in the text field next to the combo box. When these fields are filled in, press **Connect** to start the conversation. (The text of this button switches between **Connect** and **Disconnect**.) There will be a short pause while `SafeTalk` starts up the conversation.

Receiving a Conversation

To receive a conversation, simply leave `SafeTalk` running. It listens for incoming calls. When a call is received, it is automatically accepted. `SafeTalk` is both a client and a server. You can use it as a client, to start a conversation, and it acts as a server, accepting incoming conversations.

Loopback Testing

You can test `SafeTalk` by using two instances running on the same computer. This presents two hurdles:

- Each `SafeTalk` instance needs a different `KeyManager` file. You'll have to create two distinct key files, each representing a different identity.

- By default, `SafeTalk` listens for conversations on port 7999 and initiates conversations on the same port. If two or more `SafeTalk` instances are running on the same machine, this won't work right.

Fortunately, you can use command-line arguments to tell `SafeTalk` what key file and port numbers to use. The syntax is as follows:

```
java SafeTalk [keyfile listenport connectport] [...]
```

You can create as many `SafeTalk` instances as you want by specifying a key file and port numbers for each instance. Suppose you create key files in *Keys.ser* and

Keys2.ser. You can create two `SafeTalk` instances that talk to each other with the following line:

```
C:\  java SafeTalk Keys.ser 7999 8001 Keys2.ser 8001 7999
```

One `SafeTalk` instance reads its keys from *Keys.ser*, listens on port 7999, and connects on port 8001. The other instance will read keys from *Keys2.ser*, listen on port 8001, and connect on port 7999. Of course, before you can start a conversation, you'll have to export and import the appropriate public keys.

Under the Hood

Now that you know how to use `SafeTalk`, I'll explain how it works, starting with an overview of `SafeTalk`'s architecture. After that, I'll walk you through the code for each class.

Architecture

The `SafeTalk` application has five major components. The `Session` class is the center of this universe; it manages the connection with a remote `SafeTalk` application. The other four classes orbit around `Session`, each with a specific job:

- `SessionServer` listens for incoming socket connections and notifies `Session` if a connection is received. It exists primarily to isolate the action of listening for connections into a thread that's separate from the main application thread.

- `Receiver` is used while a conversation is in progress. It lives in its own thread, listening for incoming data and notifying the `Session`. `Session`, in turn, notifies `SafeTalk`, and the incoming data is shown in the lower text area of the `SafeTalk` window.

- The `SafeTalk` class itself is the GUI. It's a subclass of `Frame`.

- `KeyManager` manages the user's key pair as well as the public keys of recipients. `Session` uses `KeyManager` when it exchanges a session key at the beginning of a conversation. `SafeTalk` uses `KeyManager` to import and export keys. This class is presented in Chapter 5.

Figure 10-2 shows the relationships of the `SafeTalk` classes.

Session

The `Session` class manages the niggly details of socket connections and session key exchange. Because it's a lengthy class, I'll briefly describe `Session`'s methods before I get to the code itself. The following methods are used for connection management:

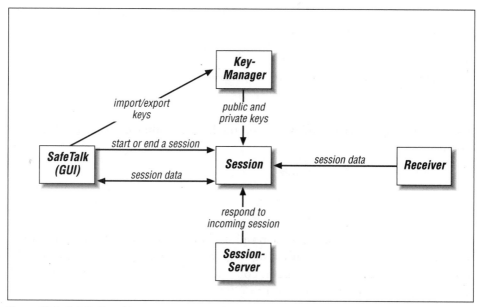

Figure 10-2: SafeTalk architecture

- The connect() method starts a conversation.

- The disconnect() method stops a conversation.

- The isConnected() method indicates if a conversation is in progress.

Two methods are used to exchange data during a conversation:

- send() is used to send data to the other end of the conversation.

- A Receiver object receives data from the other end of the conversation. It calls Session's receiverData() callback method with any received data.

The remainder of Session's methods are concerned with session key exchange:

- initiateConnection() handles the key exchange aspects of starting a conversation with another SafeTalk instance. It is called by connect().

- When a connection is received by the SessionServer, Session's respondToConnection() is called.

- The concatenate() and setupCipherStreams() methods are used by both initiateConnection() and respondToConnection().

As mentioned before, we use the KeyManager class from Chapter 5:

```
import java.io.*;
import java.net.*;
import java.security.*;
```

```
import java.security.spec.*;

import javax.crypto.*;
import javax.crypto.spec.*;

import oreilly.jonathan.security.KeyManager;

public class Session {
```

`Session` uses member variables to keep track of the other parts of the `SafeTalk` application:

```
protected SafeTalk mSafeTalk;
protected KeyManager mKeyManager;
protected SessionServer mServer;
protected Receiver mReceiver = null;
```

You can specify which ports `Session` will use for connections. `Session` listens on port `mListenPort` and initiates outgoing calls on `mConnectPort`. You can set these port numbers in the `Session` constructor. By default, `SafeTalk` creates a `Session` with both of these ports set to 7999:

```
protected int mListenPort;
protected int mConnectPort;
```

Finally, `Session` uses the `mSocket` member variable to keep track of a `Socket` that represents its connection. A related member variable, `mOut`, is an `Output-Stream` that writes data to `mSocket`:

```
protected Socket mSocket = null;
protected Writer mOut = null;
```

When a `Session` is first created, it stores references to a `SafeTalk` and a `KeyManager`, for future reference. It also creates a `SessionServer` that listens for incoming connections:

```
public Session(SafeTalk s, KeyManager keyManager,
    int listenPort, int connectPort) {
  mSafeTalk = s;
  mKeyManager = keyManager;
  mListenPort = listenPort;
  mConnectPort = connectPort;

  mServer = new SessionServer(mListenPort, this);
}
```

The `connect()` method attempts to start a conversation with a user at a remote IP address. First it tries to convert the IP address string to an `InetAddress`. Then `connect()` creates a socket connection to the given address. If this is successful, `connect()` calls `initiateConnection()` to begin the session key exchange:

```
public void connect(String user, String addressName)
    throws Exception {
  InetAddress address = InetAddress.getByName(addressName);
  Socket client = new Socket(address, mConnectPort);
  initiateConnection(client, user);
}
```

The disconnect() method stops a conversation in progress. It attempts to notify the remote end of the conversation by sending a zero byte.[*] disconnect() also notifies the GUI about the disconnection by calling sessionDisconnect() on the SafeTalk object:

```
public synchronized void disconnect() {
  try {
    if (mSocket != null) {
      mOut.write(0);
      mOut.flush();
      mSocket.close();
    }
    mSocket = null;
    mOut = null;
  }
  catch (IOException ioe) {}

  mSafeTalk.sessionDisconnect();
}
```

The isConnected() method is self-explanatory:

```
public boolean isConnected() { return mSocket != null; }
```

When you type text in the SafeTalk window, SafeTalk uses the send() method of Session to transmit the keystrokes to the other end of the conversation:

```
public void send(char c) {
  try { mOut.write(c); mOut.flush(); }
  catch (IOException ioe) {}
}
```

Similarly, when the other end of the conversation sends data to us, Receiver calls the receiverData() method of Session. Session just passes this data on to the GUI, represented by mSafeTalk:

```
public void receiverData(String message) {
  mSafeTalk.sessionData(message);
}
```

---

* The zero, like every other byte in the conversation, is encrypted and sent over the network and will most likely not be transmitted as a zero. The other end of the conversation must be correctly decrypting data in order to recognize the zero byte as the end of a conversation.

The client side of `SafeTalk`'s session key exchange is implemented in `initiate-Connection()`. We'll call the side that initiates the conversation the client and the side that responds to the conversation the server. The key exchange works like this:

1. The client randomly creates half of a DES session key and an IV to be used for the session cipher.

2. The client encrypts both the key half and the IV using the public key of the server (the recipient). Only someone with the recipient's private key can decrypt this information.

3. The client sends its name and the encrypted data from Step 2 to the server.

4. The server decrypts this data using its private key.

5. The server randomly creates the second half of the session key.

6. The server encrypts the second key half and the IV using the client's public key. As possessor of the matching private key, only the client can decrypt this data.

7. The server sends the encrypted data from Step 6 to the client.

8. The client decrypts this data using its private key.

At the end of the exchange, both the client and server have both halves of the key. They assemble them and use the result as a session key. Both the client and server have been authenticated by their use of private keys to decrypt session key information.[*]

On the client side, `Session` begins by creating the first half of the session key and an IV, using a `SecureRandom`:

```
public void initiateConnection(Socket s, String remoteName)
    throws Exception {
  mSocket = s;

  byte[] firstHalf = new byte[4];
  SecureRandom sr = new SecureRandom();
  sr.nextBytes(firstHalf);
  byte[] iv = new byte[8];
  sr.nextBytes(iv);
```

Then this data is encrypted with the server's public key, which comes from the `KeyManager`. The `concatenate()` method simply glues two byte arrays together and returns the result:

---

[*] Note that an attacker can still change or corrupt the data sent over the network connection. Message Authentication Codes (MACs) could be used to detect this kind of attack by ensuring the integrity of each piece of network data. SSL uses this approach.

```
Cipher cipher = Cipher.getInstance("ElGamal");
cipher.init(Cipher.ENCRYPT_MODE, mKeyManager.getPublicKey(remoteName));
byte[] ciphertext = cipher.doFinal(concatenate(firstHalf, iv));
```

Next, our name and the encrypted data is sent to the server:

```
DataOutputStream out = new DataOutputStream(mSocket.getOutputStream());
out.writeUTF(mKeyManager.getName());
out.writeInt(ciphertext.length);
out.write(ciphertext);
```

At this point, the server decrypts the session key half and IV. The server then generates the second half of the session key and encrypts it and the IV with the client's public key. The encrypted data is sent back to the client. We receive it and decrypt it using our private key, which again comes from the KeyManager. Then we extract the second half of the session key, which is just the first four bytes of the decrypted data:

```
DataInputStream in = new DataInputStream(mSocket.getInputStream());
byte[] remoteEncrypted = new byte[in.readInt()];
in.read(remoteEncrypted);

cipher.init(Cipher.DECRYPT_MODE, mKeyManager.getPrivateKey());
byte[] decrypted = cipher.doFinal(remoteEncrypted);
byte[] secondHalf = new byte[4];
System.arraycopy(decrypted, 0, secondHalf, 0, secondHalf.length);
```

Now we have both key halves and we're ready to start up the conversation. The setupCipherStream() method creates a DES key from the key halves and sets up the DES CFB ciphers that are used to encrypt and decrypt the conversation. After the streams are set up, the GUI is notified, via a call to sessionConnect(), that the conversation has started:

```
setupCipherStreams(firstHalf, secondHalf, iv);
mSafeTalk.sessionConnect(remoteName);
}
```

Every Session has an associated SessionServer. The SessionServer's purpose in life is to listen for incoming connections. If one comes in, SessionServer calls respondToConnection(). This method is the mirror image of initiateConnection(); in it, the Session acts as the server in the key-exchange process.

If a conversation is already in progress, the incoming connection is ignored:

```
public void respondToConnection(Socket s)
    throws Exception {
// If we're already connected, dump the incoming call.
if (isConnected()) {
  s.close();
  return;
```

```
    }
    mSocket = s;
```

The first thing received from the client is the client's name. Next, the server gets a chunk of data, encrypted with its public key:

```
    DataInputStream in = new DataInputStream(mSocket.getInputStream());
    String remoteName = in.readUTF();
    byte[] remoteEncrypted = new byte[in.readInt()];
    in.readFully(remoteEncrypted);
```

The data is decrypted using the server's private key:

```
    Cipher cipher = Cipher.getInstance("ElGamal");
    cipher.init(Cipher.DECRYPT_MODE, mKeyManager.getPrivateKey());
    byte[] decrypted = cipher.doFinal(remoteEncrypted);
```

The server pulls out the first half of the session key and the IV from this data:

```
    byte[] firstHalf = new byte[4];
    System.arraycopy(decrypted, 0, firstHalf, 0, 4);
    byte[] iv = new byte[8];
    System.arraycopy(decrypted, 4, iv, 0, 8);
```

Then the second half of the session key is randomly generated. This half, plus the IV, is encrypted with the client's public key, which comes from our KeyManager:

```
    byte[] secondHalf = new byte[4];
    new SecureRandom().nextBytes(secondHalf);

    cipher.init(Cipher.ENCRYPT_MODE, mKeyManager.getPublicKey(remoteName));
    byte[] ciphertext = cipher.doFinal(concatenate(secondHalf, iv));
```

The server sends the ciphertext back to the client:

```
    DataOutputStream out = new DataOutputStream(mSocket.getOutputStream());
    out.writeInt(ciphertext.length);
    out.write(ciphertext);
```

Now we have possession of both halves of the session key, and we're ready to start talking. The GUI is notified of the new conversation with a call to sessionRespond():

```
    setupCipherStreams(firstHalf, secondHalf, iv);
    mSafeTalk.sessionRespond(remoteName);
    }
```

As mentioned earlier, the concatenate() method simply mashes two byte arrays into one larger array:

```
    protected byte[] concatenate(byte[] a, byte[] b) {
        byte[] r = new byte[a.length + b.length];
        System.arraycopy(a, 0, r, 0, a.length);
```

```
        System.arraycopy(b, 0, r, a.length, b.length);
        return r;
    }
```

The last method in `Session`, `setupCipherStreams()`, is called by both `initi-ateConnection()` and `respondToConnection()`. When the client and server have both halves of the session key, they call this method to set up the rest of the conversation.

First, this method creates a key from the supplied key halves, using a `SecretKeyFactory`:

```
    protected void setupCipherStreams(byte[] firstHalf, byte[] secondHalf,
        byte[] iv) throws Exception {
    byte[] keyBytes = concatenate(firstHalf, secondHalf);
    SecretKeyFactory skf = SecretKeyFactory.getInstance("DES");
    DESKeySpec desSpec = new DESKeySpec(keyBytes);
    SecretKey sessionKey = skf.generateSecret(desSpec);
```

Our goal in this method is to create encrypted input and output streams. We'll use the `CipherInputStream` and `CipherOutputStream` classes for this. Additionally, because every keystroke in `SafeTalk` should be transmitted as it is typed, we need a stream cipher instead of a block cipher. To this end, we use DES in CFB mode. Actually, two cipher streams are needed, one to encrypt outgoing data and one to decrypt incoming data.

```
    IvParameterSpec spec = new IvParameterSpec(iv);
    Cipher encrypter = Cipher.getInstance("DES/CFB8/NoPadding");
    encrypter.init(Cipher.ENCRYPT_MODE, sessionKey, spec);
    Cipher decrypter = Cipher.getInstance("DES/CFB8/NoPadding");
    decrypter.init(Cipher.DECRYPT_MODE, sessionKey, spec);
```

Once the ciphers are created, it's a simple matter to create streams around them:

```
    CipherOutputStream out = new CipherOutputStream(
        mSocket.getOutputStream(), encrypter);
    CipherInputStream in = new CipherInputStream(
        mSocket.getInputStream(), decrypter);
```

Then an `OutputStream` is wrapped around the output stream. `Session` uses this `OutputStream` to send data to the far end of the conversation. We wrap a `Receiver` around the input stream. The `Receiver` just listens to the socket for incoming data.

```
    mOut = new OutputStreamWriter(out, "UTF8");
    mReceiver = new Receiver(in, this);
    }
}
```

SessionServer

SessionServer listens on a certain port for incoming connections. If it receives one, it tells its associated Session object to respond to the connection.

SessionServer is constructed with a port number and a reference to a Session object. It listens on the given port; if it receives a connection it notifies the given Session:

```java
import java.io.*;
import java.net.*;

public class SessionServer
    implements Runnable {
  protected int mListenPort;
  protected Session mSession;
  protected SafeTalk mSafeTalk;
  protected ServerSocket mServer;

  public SessionServer(int listenPort, Session s) {
    mListenPort = listenPort;
    mSession = s;

    Thread t = new Thread(this);
    t.start();
  }

  public void run() {
    try {
      mServer = new ServerSocket(mListenPort);
      while (true) {
        Socket client = mServer.accept();
        mSession.respondToConnection(client);
      }
    }
    catch (Exception e) {
      System.out.println("SessionServer.run: " + e.toString());
    }
  }
}
```

Receiver

Receiver is just as single-minded as SessionServer. Once a connection is established, it listens for input and notifies the Session when it receives any.

A Receiver is constructed with an InputStream and a Session. Any data received from the InputStream will be relayed to the Session. The main point of the `Receiver` class is to move the data listening functionality into its own thread, separate from the rest of the application.

`Receiver` expects to receive a single character at a time. If it receives a character with a value of 0, this is the signal for the end of the conversation. The conversation will also be ended if a –1 is received, signifying the end of the stream.

```java
import java.io.*;

public class Receiver
    implements Runnable {
  protected Reader mIn;
  protected Session mSession;

  public Receiver(InputStream in, Session session)
      throws UnsupportedEncodingException {
    mIn = new InputStreamReader(in, "UTF8");
    mSession = session;

    Thread t = new Thread(this);
    t.start();
  }

  public void run() {
    try {
      boolean trucking = true;
      while (trucking) {
        int i = mIn.read();
        if (i == -1 || i == 0)
          trucking = false;
        else {
          char c = (char)i;
          mSession.receiverData(new String(new char[] { c }));
        }
      }
    }
    catch (IOException e) {}
    mSession.disconnect();
  }
}
```

SafeTalk

The `SafeTalk` class is the GUI for the entire application. `SafeTalk` is a `Frame`. It uses member variables to keep track of its buttons and text areas:

```java
import java.awt.*;
import java.awt.event.*;
import java.awt.swing.JScrollPane;
```

```
import java.awt.swing.JTextArea;
import java.io.*;
import java.net.*;
import java.security.*;
import java.util.Enumeration;

import oreilly.jonathan.security.KeyManager;

public class SafeTalk
    extends Frame
    implements ActionListener, KeyListener {
  protected JTextArea mSendArea, mReceiveArea;
  protected Button mConnectButton;
  protected Choice mUserChoice;
  protected TextField mAddressField;
  protected Button mImportButton, mExportButton;
  protected Label mStatusLabel;
```

SafeTalk also keeps references to a Session and a KeyManager as member variables:

```
protected KeyManager mKeyManager;
protected Session mSession;
```

kEOL holds the local platform's newline character, and kBanner is part of a welcome message that's displayed when the SafeTalk window first appears:

```
protected static final String kEOL = System.getProperty("line.separator");
protected static final String kBanner = "SafeTalk v1.0";
```

SafeTalk has two constructors, but the first ends up calling the second with default port values:

```
public SafeTalk(KeyManager km) { this(km, 7999, 7999); }
```

The second constructor accepts a KeyManager and port numbers for incoming and outgoing calls. This constructor attempts to load the Jonathan provider (presented in Chapter 9):

```
public SafeTalk(KeyManager km, int listenPort, int connectPort) {
  super(kBanner);

  java.security.Provider p = new oreilly.jonathan.crypto.Provider();
  Security.addProvider(p);
```

SafeTalk then configures its own display, using setupWindow() and wireEvents():

```
setupWindow();
wireEvents();
show();
```

Finally, SafeTalk's constructor creates a KeyManager from the given filename and a Session from the given incoming and outgoing ports. The populateUsers() method fills the combo box with the names of users for which the KeyManager has public keys:

```
setStatus("Loading keys...");
mKeyManager = km;
populateUsers();
mSession = new Session(this, mKeyManager, listenPort, connectPort);
```

The setStatus() method displays informational messages in the SafeTalk window. Here, users are welcomed by name:

```
setStatus("Welcome to " + kBanner + ", " + mKeyManager.getName() + ".");
}
```

Most of the work that SafeTalk does is triggered when a button is pressed. The **Connect** button serves two functions: If no conversation is in progress, it starts one. If a conversation is running, the **Connect** button terminates it. The text of the button switches to reflect its function. Thus, when the **Connect** button is pressed, either a new conversation is started or an existing conversation is stopped. Calls to setStatus() let the user know what is going on.

```
public void actionPerformed(ActionEvent ae) {
  if (ae.getSource() == mConnectButton ||
      ae.getSource() == mAddressField) {
    if (mSession.isConnected() == false) {
      String user = mUserChoice.getSelectedItem();
      String addressName = mAddressField.getText();
      try {
        mConnectButton.setEnabled(false);
        setStatus("Connecting to " + user + " at " +
            addressName + "...");
        mSession.connect(user, addressName);
        mConnectButton.setLabel("Disconnect");
      }
      catch (Exception e) {
        setStatus(e.toString());
      }
      finally {
        mConnectButton.setEnabled(true);
      }
    }
    else
      mSession.disconnect();
  }
}
```

If the **Import key...** button is pressed, a FileDialog pops up. The user chooses a file that should contain a serialized name and public key. If the file is read successfully, the key gets added to the `KeyManager` and the `KeyManager` is saved. The `populateUsers()` method adds the names from the public key list into the drop-down box in the `SafeTalk` window:

```
else if (ae.getSource() == mImportButton) {
  setStatus("Importing...");
  FileDialog d = new FileDialog(this);
  d.show();
  String file = d.getFile();
  if (file == null) {
    setStatus("Import canceled.");
    return;
  }
  String name;
  PublicKey key;
  try {
    ObjectInputStream in = new ObjectInputStream(
        new FileInputStream(file));
    name = (String)in.readObject();
    key = (PublicKey)in.readObject();
    in.close();
    mKeyManager.addIdentity(name, key);
    mKeyManager.save();
    populateUsers();
    setStatus("Imported " + name + "'s public key.");
  }
  catch (Exception e) {
    setStatus(e.toString());
  }
}
```

If the **Export key...** button is pressed, the public key of the person whose name is selected in the drop-down box is exported. Again, we pop up a `FileDialog` so the user can choose the destination file.

```
else if (ae.getSource() == mExportButton) {
  String name = mUserChoice.getSelectedItem();
  setStatus("Exporting " + name + "'s public key...");
  FileDialog d = new FileDialog(this);
  d.show();
  String file = d.getFile();
  if (file == null) {
    setStatus("Export canceled.");
    return;
  }
  try {
    ObjectOutputStream out = new ObjectOutputStream(
        new FileOutputStream(file));
    out.writeObject(name);
    out.writeObject(mKeyManager.getPublicKey(name));
```

```
            out.close();
            setStatus("Exported " + name + "'s public key to " + file + ".");
          }
          catch (Exception e) {
            setStatus(e.toString());
          }
        }
      }
```

SafeTalk receives key events from its top text area. When a key is typed, SafeTalk gives it to its Session to send to the other end of the conversation:

```
      public void keyPressed(KeyEvent ke) {}
      public void keyReleased(KeyEvent ke) {}
      public void keyTyped(KeyEvent ke) {
        if (mSession.isConnected())
          mSession.send(ke.getKeyChar());
      }
```

sessionConnect(), sessionRespond(), and sessionDisconnect() are called by Session when a call is initiated, received, or ended. All we need to do is notify the user, using setStatus(), and set the label of the **Connect** button appropriately:

```
      public void sessionConnect(String caller) {
        setStatus("Connected to " + caller + ".");
        mConnectButton.setLabel("Disconnect");
      }

      public void sessionRespond(String caller) {
        setStatus("Received connection from " + caller + ".");
        mConnectButton.setLabel("Disconnect");
      }

      public void sessionDisconnect() {
        setStatus("Disconnected.");
        mConnectButton.setLabel("Connect");
      }
```

When Receiver receives data from the other end of the conversation, it is passed to Session, which in turn calls SafeTalk's sessionData() method. Basically, the received character is appended to the lower text area. There are a couple of special cases, however, for newlines and backspaces.

```
      public void sessionData(String message) {
        if (message.equals("\n") || message.equals("\r") ||
            message.equals("\r\n"))
          message = kEOL;
        if (message.equals("\b")) {
          String full = mReceiveArea.getText();
```

```
      int length = full.length();
      if (length > 0) {
        int toRemove = 1;
        if (full.endsWith(kEOL))
          toRemove = kEOL.length();
        mReceiveArea.setText(full.substring(0, length - toRemove));
      }
      return;
    }
    mReceiveArea.append(message);
  }
```

The setStatus() method is used to change the status line in the SafeTalk window. It is the main method that can be used to let the user know what's going on in the application.

```
protected void setStatus(String message) {
  mStatusLabel.setText(message);
}
```

The setupWindow() method creates all the window's components and places them appropriately:

```
protected void setupWindow() {
  setFont(new Font("TimesRoman", Font.PLAIN, 12));
  setSize(320, 300);
  setLocation(100, 100);

  setLayout(new BorderLayout());

  Panel p;
  p = new Panel(new GridLayout(2, 1));
  p.add(new JScrollPane(mSendArea = new JTextArea(40, 12)));
  p.add(new JScrollPane(mReceiveArea = new JTextArea(40, 12)));
  mReceiveArea.setEditable(false);
  add(p, BorderLayout.CENTER);

  p = new Panel(new GridLayout(3, 1));
  Panel p1 = new Panel(new FlowLayout());
  p1.add(mConnectButton = new Button("Connect to"));
  p1.add(mUserChoice = new Choice());
  mUserChoice.add("Users");
  p1.add(mAddressField = new TextField(20));
  p.add(p1);
  p1 = new Panel(new FlowLayout());
  p1.add(mImportButton = new Button("Import key..."));
  p1.add(mExportButton = new Button("Export key..."));
  p.add(p1);
  p.add(mStatusLabel = new Label("[Status text]"));
```

```
    add(p, BorderLayout.SOUTH);
  }
```

The wireEvents() method sets up the event listeners for the window's components. The SafeTalk window actually ends up receiving most of the events; the
event handlers for the buttons and the text area have already been presented.

```
protected void wireEvents() {
  addWindowListener(new WindowAdapter() {
    public void windowClosing(WindowEvent e) {
      dispose();
      System.exit(0);
    }
  });

  mConnectButton.addActionListener(this);
  mAddressField.addActionListener(this);
  mSendArea.addKeyListener(this);

  mImportButton.addActionListener(this);
  mExportButton.addActionListener(this);
}
```

The populateUsers() method reads names from the KeyManager's list of public
keys. It then puts the names in the drop-down box in the SafeTalk window:

```
protected void populateUsers() {
  mUserChoice.removeAll();
  Enumeration e = mKeyManager.identities();
  while (e.hasMoreElements())
    mUserChoice.add(((Identity)e.nextElement()).getName());
  mUserChoice.add(mKeyManager.getName());
}
```

The hard work is finished. All main() has to do is create a SafeTalk():

```
public static void main(String[] args) throws Exception {
  if (args.length == 0) {
    new SafeTalk(KeyManager.getInstance("Keys.ser"));
  }
```

If you include command-line arguments when running SafeTalk, they will be
interpreted in clusters of threes. Each cluster contains a key filename, a listening
port number, and a connecting port number. This is useful for running more than
one SafeTalk instance on one machine, as described in the section on loopback
testing.

```
  else {
    for (int i = 0; i < args.length; i += 3) {
      String keyfile = args[i];
      int listenport = Integer.parseInt(args[i + 1]);
```

```
            int connectport = Integer.parseInt(args[i + 2]);
            new SafeTalk(KeyManager.getInstance(keyfile),
                listenport, connectport);
        }
      }
    }
}
```

11

CipherMail

CipherMail is a cryptographically enabled email client. It can send and receive encrypted, authenticated messages over the Internet. Like SafeTalk, Cipher-Mail uses classes presented elsewhere in this book.

- The KeyManager class, from Chapter 5, *Key Management*, is used to keep track of all of CipherMail's keys.

- The ElGamal cipher and signature classes, presented in Chapter 9, *Writing a Provider*, are used to encrypt a session key and to provide authentication. You'll also need the Jonathan cryptographic provider, oreilly.jonathan.security.Provider.

- The base64 classes, BASE64Encoder and BASE64Decoder, are used to create ASCII mail messages from binary data. These classes are presented in Appendix B, *Base64*, as part of the oreilly.jonathan.util package. Alternately, if you wish, you can use the base64 classes with the same names from the sun.misc package, shipped as part of the JDK.

CipherMail uses its own cryptographic message format in conjunction with standard Internet email transport protocols. CipherMail's use of standard email protocols makes it a tool that is widely useful. This approach, however, has some shortcomings. Specifically, CipherMail encrypts only the body of messages, not their headers. Even if you use CipherMail to encrypt your messages, other people can still find out quite a bit of information simply by examining the messages you send and receive. They'll know whom you're writing to, who writes to you, when you send and receive messages, and the subject lines of the messages. To do something more devious, like concealing the existence of the messages themselves, you'll have to create your own email protocol and a more elaborate set of software. As it stands now, CipherMail strikes a balance between the security of authenticated, confidential email messages and the convenience of standard Internet email protocols and infrastructure.

Using CipherMail

CipherMail's main window represents an in-box. The left part of the window contains a list of received messages, while the right part can display one of them at a time. As messages are selected in the left list, they are displayed in the right panel. Figure 11-1 shows the main window, with the fourth message selected and displayed.

Figure 11-1: The CipherMail window

The **Get** button retrieves mail messages from a mail server. The **Compose...** button pops up a second window where a new, outgoing message can be created. A text label at the bottom of the CipherMail window displays informative status messages.

Figure 11-2 shows how a CipherMail message looks in a conventional mail application.[*] Except for the "CipherMail:" identifier, the remainder of the message is a mess of base64 encoded data. The contents of your message are protected from eavesdroppers and spies. Note, however, that the existence of the message is not concealed, nor are the headers, including the subject line.

First-Time Setup

Like any mail client, CipherMail needs to know some information about you and your mail servers. CipherMail retrieves mail from a POP3 server and sends mail using an SMTP server. Outgoing mail is encrypted using a random session key and

---

* Eudora Light 3.0 is shown here. See *http://www.eudora.com/*.

Figure 11-2: An encrypted CipherMail message in an ordinary mail client

signed using your private key. Before running `CipherMail` for the first time, you'll need a *preferences* file and a key file.

Preferences

`CipherMail` is configured through the use of a text file, called *preferences*. This file tells `CipherMail` about your mail servers and your identity. Here is a *preferences* file I use:[*]

```
POP3=m5.sprynet.com
User=jknudsen
Password=buendia
SMTP=m5.sprynet.com
Email=jknudsen@sprynet.com
KeyManager=Keys.ser
```

The `POP3` and `SMTP` entries identify mail servers. The `User` and `Password` entries are used to log in to the POP3 server. The `Email` entry is used as the return address on outgoing mail. Finally, the `KeyManager` entry is a key file, as described in the next section.

If you wish to use a different file to configure `CipherMail`, you can specify it on the command line. In the following example, `CipherMail` will read its configuration from *prefsKristen*:

```
C:\ java CipherMail prefsKristen
```

---

* Well, not exactly. I changed my POP3 password.

Keys

You can create a key file using KeyManager's command-line interface, as described in Chapter 5. This is exactly the same technique we used in Chapter 10, *SafeTalk*, in the SafeTalk application. CipherMail loads a key file based on the KeyManager entry in your *preferences* file. It should contain your own ElGamal key pair. Furthermore, it should contain public keys for anyone who might send you mail or anyone who will receive your mail.

If you don't have the public key of someone who sends you mail, you can still decrypt the message. You just won't be able to verify the sender's signature. CipherMail will decrypt and display the message as usual. It will complain about not being able to verify the message's signature by printing a warning message in CipherMail's status line.

You can create a key file using KeyManager's -c option. The following line creates a new key file, *Keys.ser*, and populates it with a 512-bit ElGamal key pair. The signer's name is Jonathan.

```
C:\ java oreilly.jonathan.security.KeyManager -c Keys.ser Jonathan ElGamal 512
Initializing the KeyPairGenerator...
Generating the key pair...
Done.
```

To export a key from your key file, use the -e option. The following example exports Jonathan's public key to a file called *JonathanKey.ser*:

```
C:\ java oreilly.jonathan.security.KeyManager -e Keys.ser Jonathan
    JonathanKey.ser
Done.
```

You should distribute this file to anyone interested in sending you mail and anyone who will receive mail from you. Make sure you distribute this file securely: Put it on a floppy disk and hand the disk to your correspondents, or transmit the file over an SSL connection. When you receive exported key files from other people, you can import them as follows:

```
C:\ java oreilly.jonathan.security.KeyManager -i Keys.ser KristenKey.ser
Done.
```

Getting and Reading Mail

To get mail, press the **Get** button. CipherMail will connect to your POP3 server and retrieve your mail. (CipherMail retrieves the messages without deleting them from the server.) The subject line of each message is displayed in the left part of CipherMail's main window. To view a particular message, click on its subject; the text of the message will be displayed in the right part of the window. Normal messages are shown directly. Encrypted messages will be decrypted and displayed. If you receive encrypted messages, you must have the sender's public key in your key file. Otherwise, the message's signature cannot be verified.

Sending Mail

To create a new message, press the **Compose...** button. This pops up the composition window, shown in Figure 11-3. It contains fields for entering the recipient's email address and the subject of the email. The third field, labeled **Key**, is used to choose the key name of the intended recipient. CipherMail will use this name to find a public key in your key file. When the message is done, clicking the **Send** button causes CipherMail to encrypt the message body and send the message to its destination.

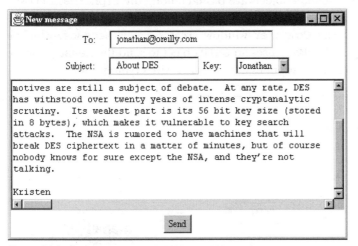

Figure 11-3: Creating a new message

Under the Hood

Architecture

The nucleus of CipherMail is the Message class, which encapsulates an email message. The other four classes of the CipherMail application use the Message class as follows:

- POP3 manages a connection to a POP3 mail server. It receives email messages from the server and converts them to Message instances.

- SMTP manages a connection to an SMTP mail server. It can take a Message instance and convert it into an outgoing email message.

- Composer is a window that is used to create new Messages.

- CipherMail, the main application window, keeps a list of Messages (the inbox) and can display the contents of messages.

Of these classes, CipherMail is the only one that knows anything about cryptography. Message only encapsulates message data, not caring whether its contents are encrypted. POP3 and SMTP understand how to exchange Messages with mail servers. And Composer creates a new, unencrypted Message. It is CipherMail that encrypts the contents of messages before they are sent out and decrypts their contents before they are displayed.

Like SafeTalk, CipherMail uses a KeyManager to keep track of cryptographic keys. The KeyManager class is presented in Chapter 5.

Figure 11-4 shows how Message objects are passed among the CipherMail classes. The POP3 class, for example, retrieves Messages from the Internet and passes them to CipherMail. The Composer window creates a new Message, which it gives to CipherMail; CipherMail uses an SMTP object to send the Message out to the Internet. The KeyManager supplies CipherMail with cryptographic keys.

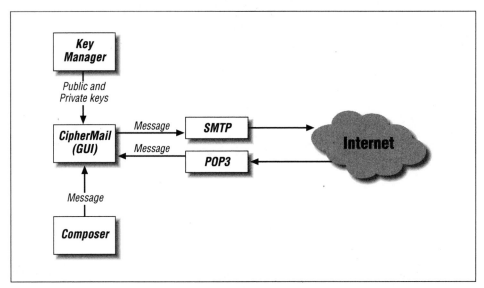

Figure 11-4: CipherMail architecture

Message Format

The Message class encapsulates standard email messages, as described by RFC 822 (*ftp://ds.internic.net/rfc/rfc822.txt*). However, the body of an encrypted message is encoded in a format that is specific to the CipherMail application.

At the top level, the message body contains the string "CipherMail:" followed by an arbitrary-length string of base64 (see Figure 11-2). The body is base64 encoded to ensure safe delivery through the Internet. (Some of the mail servers between you and your recipient may transmit only seven bits of data per byte of message body. The encryption algorithms we use produce arrays of eight-bit bytes. Encoding this "raw" data in base64 ensures that no bits will be lost.)

Inside the base64 string are these items:

- The sender's name
- The session cipher IV
- An encrypted session key
- The signature of the decrypted body
- The encrypted body

Let's say Kristen wants to send a message to Jonathan. Kristen already has a key pair for ElGamal encryption and signatures. She also must know Jonathan's public key. Kristen's `CipherMail` goes through the following procedure to create an outgoing message:

1. First, a signature for the message body is generated, using Kristen's private key.

2. Next, a random session key is generated.

3. The session key is used with a symmetric cipher (DES in CBC mode) to encrypt the message body.

4. The session key is encrypted using an asymmetric cipher (ElGamal) and Jonathan's (the recipient's) public key. Only Jonathan's private key can be used to decrypt the session key.

5. Kristen's name, the IV, the encrypted session key, the body signature, and the encrypted body are all mashed into a byte array and encoded as base64. The string "CipherMail:" is prepended to the base64 string, and the whole thing makes up the body of the email message.

Jonathan, likewise, has an ElGamal key pair and knows Kristen's public key. When he receives the message, his `CipherMail` follows these steps to decrypt the incoming message:

1. If the body of the message begins with "CipherMail:", the message is assumed to be encrypted. The remainder of the message is a base64 string.

2. The base64 string is decoded to a byte array.

3. The byte array is parsed into the sender's name (Kristen), the IV, the encrypted session key, the body signature, and the encrypted body.

4. The session key is decrypted using Jonathan's private key.

5. The body is decrypted using the decrypted session key and the supplied IV.

6. The body signature is verified using Kristen's public key.

Message

The `Message` class encapsulates an email message. A `Message` consists of headers and a body. Each header has a name and a value, separated by a colon. Each header takes one or more lines of the message. A blank line separates the headers from the body of the message. Here is a typical, unencrypted message:

```
From: kknudsen@geocities.com
Date: Tue, 16 Dec 1997 13:36:28 -0500
To: jonathan@oreilly.com
Subject: Chapter 11
Status:

Hi Jonathan,

I've marked up the changes to Chapter 11.  I'll leave the
manuscript in the hollow oak tree by the river.

Kristen
```

In the `Message` class, we keep track of the headers using a `Hashtable`. The header names are the `Hashtable` keys, and the header values are the `Hashtable` values. A `String` member variable holds the message body.

```
import java.io.*;
import java.util.Enumeration;
import java.util.Hashtable;

public class Message {
  protected Hashtable mHeaders = new Hashtable();
  protected String mBody;
```

A class variable, `kEOL`, holds the value of a newline:

```
public static final String kEOL = "\r\n";
```

`Message`'s first constructor accepts no arguments. It is used when `CipherMail` creates new outgoing messages:

```
public Message() {}
```

The second constructor reads the message headers and body from the supplied `BufferedReader`. First, we read and parse the headers. Lines that start with whitespace are continuations of the previous line's header. All other lines are parsed by finding the colon that separates the header name and value.

```
public Message(BufferedReader in) throws IOException {
  // Read headers.
  String line;
  String key = null;
  while ((line = in.readLine()).equals("") == false) {
    if (line.startsWith("\t") || line.startsWith(" ")) {
      if (key != null) {
        // Add to previous key.
        String value = (String)mHeaders.get(key);
        value += kEOL + line;
        mHeaders.put(key, value);
      }
    }
    else {
      int colon = line.indexOf(": ");
      if (colon != -1) {
        key = line.substring(0, colon);
        String value = line.substring(colon + 2);
        mHeaders.put(key, value);
      }
    }
  }
```

A blank line separates the headers from the body. Once this blank line is read, the body can be read. When we read a message from a POP3 mail server, a line with a single period on it signifies the end of the body:

```
  // Read body.
  StringBuffer body = new StringBuffer();
  while ((line = in.readLine()).equals(".") == false)
    body.append(line + kEOL);
  mBody = body.toString();
}
```

You can find out the value of a particular header using getHeader(). This method simply asks the Hashtable for the value corresponding to the header name:

```
public String getHeader(String key) {
  return (String)mHeaders.get(key);
}
```

You can set the value of a header field with setHeader(). Composer uses this method when it creates new messages.

```
public void setHeader(String key, String value) {
  mHeaders.put(key, value);
}
```

The getBody() and setBody() methods are self-explanatory:

```
public String getBody() { return mBody; }
public void setBody(String body) { mBody = body; }
```

The getHeaders() method returns a String containing all the correctly formatted message headers. It simply dumps out all the key and value pairs from the internal Hashtable, printing each with a colon between the header name and value:

```
public String getHeaders() {
  StringBuffer sb = new StringBuffer();
  Enumeration e = mHeaders.keys();
  while (e.hasMoreElements()) {
    String key = (String)e.nextElement();
    String value = (String)mHeaders.get(key);
    sb.append(key + ": " + value + kEOL);
  }
  return sb.toString();
}
```

getFull() returns the same thing as getHeaders(), except with the message body appended:

```
public String getFull() {
  StringBuffer sb = new StringBuffer();
  sb.append(getHeaders());
  sb.append(kEOL);
  sb.append(getBody());
  return sb.toString();
}
```

POP3

The POP3 class manages a connection to a POP3 server, used for retrieving email. It implements only the subset of POP3 commands that we need for CipherMail. If you want to read more about POP3, refer to RFC 1725, available at *ftp://ds.internic.net/rfc/rfc1725.txt.*

The POP3 class uses member variables to keep track of the connection to the POP3 server and its associated input and output streams:

```
import java.io.*;
import java.net.*;
import java.text.*;
import java.util.StringTokenizer;

public class POP3 {
  Socket mSocket = null;
  PrintWriter mOut;
  BufferedReader mIn;
```

Upon construction, the POP3 establishes a connection to the POP3 server and sets up the input and output streams. It then checks for a welcoming message using the getOK() method, which we'll look at later.

```
public POP3(String host) throws IOException {
  mSocket = new Socket(host, 110);
  mOut = new PrintWriter(mSocket.getOutputStream(), true);
  mIn = new BufferedReader(
      new InputStreamReader(mSocket.getInputStream()));

  getOK();
}
```

POP3 servers accept a username and password for login. Note that this is not secure, as the password is transmitted in cleartext over the network. This is a well-known weakness of several popular Internet protocols, including telnet and FTP. The POP3 standard offers a stronger method of authentication; to find out more, read RFC 1725. Interestingly, CipherMail compensates for this deficiency. For example, someone might snoop on your POP3 username and password; this would enable him or her to retrieve your mail from the POP3 server. He or she can even delete messages from your server so that you never receive them. If the mail is encrypted using CipherMail, however, the attacker will not be able to read the messages without your private key. And even though it is easy to forge mail using SMTP, no one can create a CipherMail message that appears to be from you without possessing your private key.

```
public void login(String user, String password)
    throws IOException {
  mOut.println("USER " + user);
  getOK();
  mOut.println("PASS " + password);
  getOK();
}
```

The size() method queries the POP3 server to find out how many messages are waiting:

```
public int size() throws IOException {
  mOut.println("STAT");
  String line = getOK();

  int size = -1;
  try {
    StringTokenizer st = new StringTokenizer(line, " \t\r\n");
    st.nextToken(); // Skip status message.
    NumberFormat nf = NumberFormat.getInstance();
    size = nf.parse(st.nextToken()).intValue();
  }
  catch (ParseException e) {}
  return size;
}
```

You can retrieve messages by calling `retrieve()`. The message is returned as a Message object:

```
public Message retrieve(int index) throws IOException {
  mOut.println("RETR " + index);
  getOK();

  return new Message(mIn);
}
```

When the POP3 session is finished, use the `quit()` method to sever the connection to the server:

```
public void quit() throws IOException {
  mOut.println("QUIT");
  try { getOK(); }
  catch (IOException ioe) {}
  mSocket.close();
  mIn.close();
  mOut.close();
}
```

The `getOK()` method checks for the OK message from the POP3 server. Any other response causes an `IOException` to be thrown.

```
protected String getOK() throws IOException {
  String line = mIn.readLine();
  if (line.substring(0, 3).equals("+OK") == false) {
    throw new IOException(line);
  }
  return line;
}
}
```

SMTP

The `SMTP` class manages a connection to an SMTP server, used for sending email. Like the `POP3` class, `SMTP` implements only the subset of SMTP that `CipherMail` needs. If you'd like to read more about SMTP, it's described in RFC 821, available from *ftp://ds.internic.net/rfc/rfc821.txt*.

Like the `POP3` class, `SMTP` uses member variables to keep track of the socket connection to the SMTP server and its associated streams:

```
import java.io.*;
import java.net.*;
import java.text.*;
import java.util.StringTokenizer;

public class SMTP {
```

```
Socket mSocket = null;
PrintWriter mOut;
BufferedReader mIn;
```

When an SMTP is constructed, it opens a connection to the specified host and sets up the associated input and output streams. It looks for a welcome message using the getResponse() method, which is presented later in this section.

```
public SMTP(String host) throws IOException {
  mSocket = new Socket(host, 25);
  mOut = new PrintWriter(mSocket.getOutputStream(), true);
  mIn = new BufferedReader(
      new InputStreamReader(mSocket.getInputStream()));

  getResponse();
}
```

To log in to the SMTP server, you just have to provide your IP address:

```
public void login() throws IOException {
  String address = mSocket.getInetAddress().getHostAddress();
  mOut.println("HELO " + address);
  getResponse();
}
```

To send a piece of email, we send the MAIL FROM, RCPT TO, and DATA commands, followed by the full text of the message:

```
public void send(String sender, Message m) throws IOException {
  mOut.println("MAIL FROM: " + sender);
  getResponse();
  mOut.println("RCPT TO: " + m.getHeader("To"));
  getResponse();
  mOut.println("DATA");
  getResponse();

  mOut.write(m.getFull());
  mOut.println();
  mOut.println(".");
  mOut.flush();

  getResponse();
}
```

The quit() method closes our connection with the SMTP server:

```
public void quit() throws IOException {
  mOut.println("QUIT");
  try { getResponse(); }
  catch (IOException ioe) {}
  mSocket.close();
  mIn.close();
```

```
    mOut.close();
  }
```

Finally, the getResponse() method is used to check for a good response from the server. All SMTP server responses have a response code associated with them. Anything below 400 indicates success. If we receive a code of 400 or greater, an IOException is thrown, indicating an error was returned from the SMTP server:

```
protected String getResponse() throws IOException {
  String line;
  do line = mIn.readLine();
  while (mIn.ready());

  try {
    NumberFormat nf = NumberFormat.getInstance();
    String codeString = line.substring(0, 3);
    int code = nf.parse(codeString).intValue();
    if (code >= 400)
      throw new IOException(line);
  }
  catch (ParseException pe) {
    throw new IOException("No response code: " + line);
  }
  return line;
  }
}
```

Composer

Composer is the window that is used to create new messages. It is a subclass of Frame and contains member variables representing each of its controls:

```
import java.awt.*;
import java.awt.event.*;
import java.io.*;
import java.security.Identity;
import java.util.Properties;
import java.util.Enumeration;

import oreilly.jonathan.security.KeyManager;

public class Composer
    extends Frame
    implements ActionListener {
  protected TextField mToField, mSubjectField;
  protected Choice mKeyChoice;
  protected TextArea mMessageArea;
  protected Button mSendButton;
```

The `Composer` class also contains a reference back to the `CipherMail` instance that created it. When the new message is finished, `Composer` will ask `CipherMail` to send the message:

```
protected CipherMail mCipherMail;
```

When a `Composer` is created, it simply sets up its GUI and event handling using `setupWindow()` and `wireEvents()`, which I'll get to later. `populateKeys()` is called to fill the combo box labeled **Key** with all the keys from the `KeyManager`:

```
public Composer(CipherMail cm, KeyManager km) {
    super("New message");
    mCipherMail = cm;

    setupWindow();
    populateKeys(km);
    wireEvents();
    show();
}
```

There's only one button on the `Composer` window, the **Send** button. If it is pressed, `Composer` constructs a new `Message` and tells the `CipherMail` object to send it. Then the `Composer` window dismisses itself by calling `dispose()`.

```
public void actionPerformed(ActionEvent ae) {
    // Construct message.
    Message m = new Message();
    m.setHeader("To", mToField.getText());
    m.setHeader("Subject", mSubjectField.getText());
    m.setBody(mMessageArea.getText());
    // Hide ourselves.
    setVisible(false);
    // Ask CipherMail to send it.
    mCipherMail.sendMessage(m, mKeyChoice.getSelectedItem());
    // Clean up.
    dispose();
}
```

The `setupWindow()` method simply places the `Composer`'s components on the window:

```
protected void setupWindow() {
    setFont(new Font("TimesRoman", Font.PLAIN, 12));
    setSize(450, 300);
    setLocation(200, 200);

    setLayout(new BorderLayout());

    Panel p = new Panel(new GridLayout(2, 1));
    Panel pi = new Panel(new FlowLayout());
    pi.add(new Label("To:"));
```

```
          pi.add(mToField = new TextField(32));
          p.add(pi);
          pi = new Panel(new FlowLayout());
          pi.add(new Label("Subject:"));
          pi.add(mSubjectField = new TextField(16));
          pi.add(new Label("Key:"));
          pi.add(mKeyChoice = new Choice());
          p.add(pi);
          add(p, BorderLayout.NORTH);

          add(mMessageArea = new TextArea(40, 12), BorderLayout.CENTER);
          mMessageArea.setFont(new Font("Courier", Font.PLAIN, 12));

          p = new Panel(new FlowLayout());
          p.add(mSendButton = new Button("Send"));
          add(p, BorderLayout.SOUTH);
      }
```

The wireEvents() method sets up Composer's event handling. First, it creates an inner class that will close the window when the **Close** button is pressed. Second, it sets up the Composer to receive ActionEvents when the **Send** button is pressed.

```
      protected void wireEvents() {
        addWindowListener(new WindowAdapter() {
          public void windowClosing(WindowEvent e) {
            dispose();
          }
        });

        mSendButton.addActionListener(this);
      }
```

Finally, populateKeys() reads all the key names from the supplied KeyManager and puts them in the **Key** combo box:

```
      protected void populateKeys(KeyManager km) {
        mKeyChoice.removeAll();
        Enumeration e = km.identities();
        while (e.hasMoreElements())
          mKeyChoice.add(((Identity)e.nextElement()).getName());
        mKeyChoice.add(km.getName());
      }
    }
```

CipherMail

The CipherMail class contains both the main GUI for the application as well as all the logic for encrypting and decrypting messages. As we walk through the class, I'll skim over the GUI implementations and spend more time on the cryptography.

```
import java.awt.*;
import java.awt.event.*;
import java.io.*;
import java.security.*;
import java.util.Properties;

import javax.crypto.*;
import javax.crypto.spec.*;

import oreilly.jonathan.security.KeyManager;

public class CipherMail
    extends Frame
    implements ActionListener, ItemListener {
  protected List mMessageList;
  protected TextArea mMessageArea;
  protected Button mGetButton, mComposeButton;
  protected Label mStatusLabel;

  protected Properties mPreferences;
  protected Message[] mMessages;
  protected KeyManager mKeyManager;

  protected static final String kBanner = "CipherMail v1.0";
```

CipherMail's constructor sets up the GUI for the window and loads the indicated preferences file:

```
public CipherMail(String preferencesFile) throws Exception {
  super(kBanner);

  setupWindow();
  wireEvents();
  setVisible(true);

  loadPreferences(preferencesFile);

  setStatus("Welcome to " + kBanner + ", " + mKeyManager.getName() + ".");
}
```

The CipherMail window has just two buttons. If you press the **Get** button, the getMessages() method is called to retrieve messages from the POP3 server. If you press the **Compose...** button, a new Composer window is created.

```
public void actionPerformed(ActionEvent ae) {
  if (ae.getSource() == mGetButton)
    getMessages();
  else if (ae.getSource() == mComposeButton)
    new Composer(this, mKeyManager);
}
```

`ItemEvents` are delivered to this class when different items are selected in the message list on the left side of the `CipherMail` window. Whenever you select an item, we show the matching message by calling `selectMessage()`:

```
public void itemStateChanged(ItemEvent e) {
  if (e.getStateChange() == ItemEvent.SELECTED) {
    selectMessage(mMessageList.getSelectedIndex());
  }
}
```

The `selectMessage()` method shows the headers and body of the specified message in the right text area in `CipherMail`'s main window. It attempts to decrypt the body of the message with `decrypt()`. If the message body was not encrypted, `decrypt()` returns it unchanged. `selectMessage()` also sets the title bar of the `CipherMail` window with the subject and sender of the message.

```
protected void selectMessage(int index) {
  Message m = mMessages[index];
  try { mMessageArea.setText(m.getHeaders() +
      "\r\n" + decrypt(m.getBody())); }
  catch (Exception e) { mMessageArea.setText(e.toString()); }
  String d = m.getHeader("Subject") +
      "[" + m.getHeader("From") + "]";
  setTitle(d);
}
```

When the **Get** button is pressed, `getMessages()` is called to retrieve messages from the POP3 server. A POP3 object is used to manage the server connection. The server name, username, and password are pulled out of the user's *preferences* file. As messages are retrieved, they are added to `CipherMail`'s internal message list (`mMessages`) and added to the message list on the left side of the `CipherMail` window. The first message received is displayed immediately.

```
protected void getMessages() {
  try {
    String host = mPreferences.getProperty("POP3");
    String user = mPreferences.getProperty("User");
    String password = mPreferences.getProperty("Password");
    // Clean out current messages.
    mMessageList.removeAll();
    setTitle(kBanner);
    mMessageArea.setText("");
    // Open POP3 connection.
    setStatus("Connecting to " + host + "...");
    POP3 pop3 = new POP3(host);
    // Login.
    setStatus("Logging in as " + user);
    pop3.login(user, password);
    // Get messages.
```

```
      setStatus("Checking message list size...");
      int size = pop3.size();
      mMessages = new Message[size];
      for (int i = 1; i <= size; i++) {
        setStatus("Retrieving message " + i + " of " + size + "...");
        Message m = pop3.retrieve(i);
        mMessages[i - 1] = m;
        String d = m.getHeader("Subject") +
            "[" + m.getHeader("From") + "]";
        mMessageList.add(d);
        // Display the first one right away.
        if (i == 1) {
          mMessageList.select(0);
          selectMessage(0);
        }
      }

      // Clean up.
      setStatus("Cleaning up...");
      pop3.quit();
      setStatus("Done.");
    }
    catch (IOException ioe) {
      setStatus(ioe.toString());
    }
  }
```

When a message is created in a Composer window, it is sent using CipherMail's sendMessage() method. This method uses an SMTP object to handle the details of communicating with the SMTP host. The SMTP server and return email address are pulled from the user's *preferences* file. The original body of the message is encrypted. The encrypted body is substituted for the original message body before it is sent to the SMTP server.

```
public void sendMessage(Message m, String remoteName) {
  try {
    String host = mPreferences.getProperty("SMTP");
    String email = mPreferences.getProperty("Email");
    // Encrypt the message body.
    String body = m.getBody();
    try { m.setBody(encrypt(body, remoteName)); }
    catch (Exception e) {
      System.out.println("encrypt: " + e.toString());
      setStatus("Sorry, that message couldn't be sent: " + e.toString());
      return;
    }
    // Send the message.
    setStatus("Connecting to " + host + "...");
    SMTP smtp = new SMTP(host);
    smtp.login();
```

```
          setStatus("Sending message...");
          smtp.send(email, m);
          setStatus("Cleaning up...");
          smtp.quit();
          setStatus("Done.");
        }
        catch (IOException ioe) {
          setStatus(ioe.toString());
        }
      }
```

The encrypt() method encrypts a message body, as described in the section on the CipherMail message format. First, encrypt() gathers your name, your private key, and the recipient's public key using the KeyManager:

```
    protected String encrypt(String body, String theirName) throws Exception {
      setStatus("Gathering keys...");
      String ourName = mKeyManager.getName();
      PrivateKey ourPrivateKey = mKeyManager.getPrivateKey();
      PublicKey theirPublicKey = mKeyManager.getPublicKey(theirName);
```

Next, a session key is created. The session key will be used to encrypt the body of the message:

```
    // Create a session key.
    setStatus("Creating a session key...");
    KeyGenerator kg = KeyGenerator.getInstance("DES");
    kg.init(new SecureRandom());
    Key sessionKey = kg.generateKey();
    // Encrypt message body.
    setStatus("Encrypting the message...");
    byte[] bodyPlaintext = body.getBytes();
    Cipher cipher = Cipher.getInstance("DES/CBC/PKCS5Padding");
    cipher.init(Cipher.ENCRYPT_MODE, sessionKey);
    byte[] iv = cipher.getIV();
    byte[] bodyCiphertext = cipher.doFinal(bodyPlaintext);
```

The session key itself is encrypted, using the public key of the recipient. Only someone with the recipient's private key can decrypt the session key. This gives us some assurance that only the intended recipient of the message will be able to read it.

```
    // Encrypt session key.
    setStatus("Encrypting the session key...");
    cipher = Cipher.getInstance("ElGamal");
    cipher.init(Cipher.ENCRYPT_MODE, theirPublicKey);
    byte[] sessionKeyCiphertext = cipher.doFinal(sessionKey.getEncoded());
```

We also create a signature for the body plaintext. This gives the recipient a chance to authenticate us, the sender.

```
    // Sign message body.
    setStatus("Signing the message...");
```

```
Signature s = Signature.getInstance("ElGamal");
s.initSign(ourPrivateKey);
s.update(bodyPlaintext);
byte[] bodySignature = s.sign();
```

Now we need to cram our name, the encrypted session key, the body signature, and the encrypted body into a base64 string. This string will be the new message body. We accomplish this in two steps. First, we convert all the data into a byte array, using a `ByteArrayOutputStream`. Second, we take the data in the `ByteArrayOutputStream` and convert it to base64.

```
// Embed everything in the new body.
setStatus("Constructing the encrypted message...");
ByteArrayOutputStream byteStream = new ByteArrayOutputStream();
DataOutputStream out = new DataOutputStream(byteStream);
// Send our name.
out.writeUTF(ourName);
// Send the session IV.
out.writeInt(iv.length);
out.write(iv);
// Send the encrypted session key.
out.writeInt(sessionKeyCiphertext.length);
out.write(sessionKeyCiphertext);
// Send the message signature.
out.writeInt(bodySignature.length);
out.write(bodySignature);
// Send the encrypted message.
out.writeInt(bodyCiphertext.length);
out.write(bodyCiphertext);

byte[] plaintext = byteStream.toByteArray();
```

To make encrypted messages easily recognizable, the "CipherMail:" string is added in front of the base64 data. When the data is converted to base64, it is one long string. We break up this string every 40 characters and insert a newline:

```
// Convert to base64.
setStatus("Converting to base64...");
oreilly.jonathan.util.BASE64Encoder base64 =
    new oreilly.jonathan.util.BASE64Encoder();
String unbroken = "CipherMail:" + base64.encode(plaintext);
StringBuffer broken = new StringBuffer();
int length = unbroken.length();
int lineLength = 40;
for (int i = 0; i < length; i += lineLength) {
  int last = Math.min(i + lineLength, length);
  broken.append(unbroken.substring(i, last));
  broken.append("\r\n");
}
setStatus("Done encrypting.");
```

```
    return broken.toString();
  }
```

The `decrypt()` method reverses the message encryption process. If the message body doesn't start with "CipherMail:", we know the body is not encrypted and return it verbatim.

```
protected String decrypt(String body) throws Exception {
  if (body.startsWith("CipherMail:") == false)
    return body;
```

Otherwise, we remove all the newlines in the message, leaving one long base64 string.

```
setStatus("Removing newlines...");
String broken = body.substring(11);
StringBuffer unbroken = new StringBuffer();
int last = 0;
int index = 0;
do {
  index = broken.indexOf("\r\n", last);
  if (index == -1)
    unbroken.append(broken.substring(last));
  else
    unbroken.append(broken.substring(last, index));
  last = index + 2;
} while (index != -1 && last < broken.length());
```

The base64 string can be decoded into a byte array. We use a `DataInputStream` wrapped around a `ByteArrayInputStream` to extract data from this array. As you'll recall, it contains the sender's name, an encrypted session key, a signature, and an encrypted message body.

```
setStatus("Translating from base64...");
oreilly.jonathan.util.BASE64Decoder base64 =
    new oreilly.jonathan.util.BASE64Decoder();
byte[] ciphertext = base64.decodeBuffer(unbroken.toString());
DataInputStream in = new DataInputStream(
    new ByteArrayInputStream(ciphertext));
setStatus("Reading sender's name...");
String theirName = in.readUTF();
setStatus("Reading the IV...");
byte[] iv = new byte[in.readInt()];
in.read(iv);
setStatus("Reading encrypted session key...");
byte[] sessionKeyCiphertext = new byte[in.readInt()];
in.read(sessionKeyCiphertext);
setStatus("Reading signature...");
byte[] bodySignature = new byte[in.readInt()];
in.read(bodySignature);
```

```
setStatus("Reading encrypted message...");
byte[] bodyCiphertext = new byte[in.readInt()];
in.read(bodyCiphertext);
```

`CipherMail`'s `KeyManager` retrieves your name and your private key. The session key is decrypted using your private key:

```
// Decrypt the session key.
setStatus("Decrypting the session key...");
String ourName = mKeyManager.getName();
PrivateKey ourPrivateKey = mKeyManager.getPrivateKey();
Cipher cipher = Cipher.getInstance("ElGamal");
cipher.init(Cipher.DECRYPT_MODE, ourPrivateKey);
byte[] sessionKeyPlaintext = cipher.doFinal(sessionKeyCiphertext);
SecretKeyFactory skf = SecretKeyFactory.getInstance("DES");
DESKeySpec desSpec = new DESKeySpec(sessionKeyPlaintext, 0);
SecretKey sessionKey = skf.generateSecret(desSpec);
```

Once the session key is decrypted, the message body can be decrypted using the session key:

```
// Decrypt the body.
setStatus("Decrypting the body...");
cipher = Cipher.getInstance("DES/CBC/PKCS5Padding");
IvParameterSpec spec = new IvParameterSpec(iv);
cipher.init(Cipher.DECRYPT_MODE, sessionKey, spec);
byte[] plaintext = cipher.doFinal(bodyCiphertext);
```

We can't authenticate the sender unless we verify his or her signature. `Cipher-Mail` shows a message in the status line of the `CipherMail` window that indicates if the message signature was verified. If the sender's public key cannot be found in our `KeyManager`, we display an appropriate message:

```
// Verify the signature.
setStatus("Verifying the signature...");
PublicKey theirPublicKey;
try { theirPublicKey = mKeyManager.getPublicKey(theirName); }
catch (NullPointerException npe) {
  setStatus("***** Unable to verify " +
      theirName + "'s signature: I don't have a key! *****");
  return new String(plaintext);
}
Signature s = Signature.getInstance("ElGamal");
s.initVerify(theirPublicKey);
s.update(plaintext);
if (s.verify(bodySignature))
  setStatus(theirName + "'s signature verified.");
else
  setStatus("***** Signature didn't verify! *****");
```

```
                return new String(plaintext);
            }
```

The `loadPreferences()` method loads the named preferences file into a member variable, `mPreferences`. It also loads the `KeyManager` file specified in the preferences file:

```
    protected void loadPreferences(String preferencesFile) throws Exception {
        mPreferences = new Properties();
        FileInputStream in = new FileInputStream(preferencesFile);
        mPreferences.load(in);
        mKeyManager = KeyManager.getInstance(
            mPreferences.getProperty("KeyManager"));
    }
```

`CipherMail`'s status text line, at the bottom of the window, displays informative text for the user. The `setStatus()` method displays these status messages:

```
    public void setStatus(String message) {
        mStatusLabel.setText(message);
    }
```

`setupWindow()` constructs the `CipherMail` GUI:

```
    protected void setupWindow() {
        setFont(new Font("TimesRoman", Font.PLAIN, 12));
        setSize(500, 300);
        setLocation(100, 100);

        setLayout(new BorderLayout());

        Panel p;
        p = new Panel(new BorderLayout());
        p.add(mMessageList = new List(), BorderLayout.WEST);
        p.add(mMessageArea = new TextArea(40, 12),
            BorderLayout.CENTER);
        mMessageArea.setEditable(false);
        mMessageArea.setFont(new Font("Courier", Font.PLAIN, 12));
        add(p, BorderLayout.CENTER);

        p = new Panel(new GridLayout(2, 1));
        Panel p1 = new Panel(new FlowLayout());
        p1.add(mGetButton = new Button("Get"));
        p1.add(mComposeButton = new Button("Compose..."));
        p.add(p1);
        p.add(mStatusLabel = new Label("[Status text]"));
        add(p, BorderLayout.SOUTH);
    }
```

The `wireEvents()` method is used to set up the event handling for `CipherMail`. It creates an inner class, for closing `CipherMail` itself. The **Get** and **Compose...**

buttons are configured to send `ActionEvents` to `CipherMail`. The message list will send `ItemEvents` to `CipherMail` as different message headers are selected.

```
protected void wireEvents() {
  addWindowListener(new WindowAdapter() {
    public void windowClosing(WindowEvent e) {
      dispose();
      System.exit(0);
    }
  });

  mGetButton.addActionListener(this);
  mComposeButton.addActionListener(this);

  mMessageList.addItemListener(this);
}
```

`CipherMail`'s `main()` method simply instantiates a `CipherMail`. `CipherMail` will attempt to load its configuration information from the given preferences file, which by default is named *preferences*.

```
public static void main(String[] args) throws Exception {
  String preferencesFile = "preferences";
  if (args.length > 0) preferencesFile = args[0];
  new CipherMail(preferencesFile);
}
}
```

12

Outside the Box

Cryptography is a powerful tool, but it is only part of the application programmer's repertoire. To create a secure application, the programmer needs to see the entire system, analyze its weaknesses, and plug up the holes. The first 11 chapters of this book cover cryptographic programming in Java; in this chapter I'll point out some other noteworthy areas of security programming, with a specific focus on Java. If you're new to secure systems design, this chapter should open your eyes to secure systems design issues. A lot of things can go wrong with a secure system; I'll try to hit the high points in this chapter.

Application Design

The structure of your application affects the kind of attacks that can be made against it. In this section, I'll discuss security considerations in standalone applications as well as traditional client/server architectures. The section ends with a discussion of the pros and cons of using a web browser as your application's client platform.

Self-Contained

A self-contained application has all of its logic in one place. In Java, this means that all of the *.class* files it uses are on one machine.

A self-contained application that does not make network connections has limited security requirements. The only threat in this type of application is that someone will steal its data. There are two ways this can happen, excluding more exotic surveillance techniques:

- Someone will gain physical control of your computer and use it to steal your application's data.

- Someone will gain virtual control of your computer and use it to steal your application's data.

If you are concerned about data theft, you can encrypt your data before storing it on disk. This way, even if someone steals the data files, it will be hard to get any useful information out of them without your encryption key. The encryption key should not be stored on the computer, unless it is protected in some way. The PBE class, presented in Chapter 7, *Encryption*, allows you to protect an encryption key with a passphrase. If you are lucky enough to have smart cards in your system, the smart card is a good place to store a key. If you are not so lucky, a floppy disk can serve as a poor man's smart card.

Other self-contained applications do make network connections, like email clients and web browsers. Their security requirements are more complicated. These applications often require confidentiality and authentication. In an Internet-based credit card purchase, for example, both the buyer and the seller need proof of each other's identity (authentication). The buyer also wants to have his or her credit card number remain a secret (confidentiality). These things are possible, of course. Certificates and ciphers provide authentication and confidentiality services.

But before you rush off to write a self-contained network application, make sure you know how the application will manage keys. The application needs to be able to access and verify certificates whenever it makes a remote connection. Where do the certificates come from? Who issues them? What happens when they expire? You can use the existing structure of Certificate Authorities and X.509 certificates or you can create your own, as best suits your application. Regardless, be aware that key management will probably be the hardest part of the application.

Demonstration Software

Another interesting application of cryptography is in "demo" software. Software vendors often distribute demonstration versions of software, that is, an application that has all but a few key features working. This allows people to try out the software before buying it. When somebody does decide to pay, the vendor gives the buyer a password that "unlocks" the rest of the application. This scheme is attractive to software vendors because it's akin to giving away free samples of drugs; someone's bound to get hooked and buy more. It's attractive to buyers, too, because they get to try a product before coughing up the money for it. Furthermore, when they do pay, there's instant gratification when the password is entered. The whole application is already there; nothing more need be downloaded.

Legions of 14-year-olds will "crack" the demo faster than you can say "Don't you have anything better to do?" Typically, they'll disassemble the code, a process of reverse engineering, and hardwire the demo to believe that it's a fully functioning version. This process is easier in Java than in other languages. (See the discussion, later in this chapter, on disassemblers and code obfuscators.)

If you design your application properly, however, you could encrypt a few key *.class* files, leaving only the demo functionality unencrypted. When somebody buys the software, you could give the buyer a cryptographic key (based on the software's serial number) that would decrypt the rest of the application. This keeps your application safe from cracking. Of course, it doesn't stop someone who bought a copy from making copies for someone else, but that's always a problem, even with software that comes in a box.

This scheme will make your distribution hairy. In particular, you would want each copy of your software to have a different decryption key, which means each copy needs to be encrypted separately. When a buyer calls up to buy the software, you need to figure out which key to send him or her. Each copy of the software should have a serial number. A master list would map serial numbers to decryption keys. You could simplify this by encrypting every 100, or 1000, copies of your software with the same key, but it's still a headache.[*]

Alternately, you could encrypt each copy of the software with the same key and distribute part of the key with each copy. If the key value is k, you might distribute a random value r_n with each copy. Each copy would have a complementary value such that $r_n \oplus u_n = k$. When someone paid for the full version of your software, you would simply send them u_n, which could be combined with r_n to produce the key, k. Then the rest of the software could be decrypted using k. This way, you only need to keep a list of partial keys, u_n, correlated to serial numbers. The weakness in this scheme is that all the copies of the software are encrypted with the same key. If someone figures out what the key is (possibly by buying a copy of the software), he or she can write a demo-cracker program that will work with every copy of your demo software.

Client/Server

Client/server architecture is typically two-tier or three-tier. In the two-tier architecture, many clients connect to a single server. In the three-tier version, there's an additional layer between the client and server, typically called the transaction layer or business layer.

The client and server are really pieces of the same application, but they reside on different machines. The server typically contains a database that holds all the application's data. The client shows data to the user and will ask the server to make changes on the user's behalf.

---

[*] Cranial pain, figurative or literal, seems to be a popular currency when paying for security.

Client/server applications have the same authentication and confidentiality requirements as discussed for self-contained network applications. The server needs to be paranoid. Because the client is widely (and possibly freely) distributed, the server must assume that there will be mischievous users who will try to use the client to do things they're not supposed to do. More devious attacks may be launched by custom-built applications *pretending* to be clients. Thus, the authentication from client to server must be carefully designed and implemented. Authentication in the other direction is just as important. Clients need to know that they are connecting to the real server and not an imposter.

Client/server applications also need to deal with *access control*. Once users are authenticated, their access to the server's resources is limited. The server needs to ensure that no clients are allowed to overstep their bounds. Note that this logic must be on the server. If it's on the client, someone could reprogram the client to perform illegal actions.

Three-tier client/server applications are an extension of the two-tier architecture. They provide an attacker with more places to subvert the application: at the client, the middle tier, or the server. Authentication between the middle tier and the server is just as important as between the client and the middle tier.

Client Applets

When developing a Java client/server application, a web browser seems like an attractive platform for the client. Making the client side of your application an applet means that anyone with a browser will be able to run the client. If you're trying to reach a wide audience, this is particularly compelling. Furthermore, the client applet is loaded from a web server, automatically. No client installation is required.

On the other hand, applets have their share of problems. Netscape and Microsoft were slow to incorporate Java 1.1 into their browsers. You may have to develop your applet using an older version of Java, just to be sure it runs on the majority of browsers. Sun created something called the Porting and Tuning Center, which is supposed to keep browsers more synchronized with Java versions, but it's too early to tell if it'll work.

Another possible snag is that different browsers all have their own Java implementations. Virtual machine and API bugs or inconsistencies may cause your applet trouble on some platforms. To overcome this hurdle, rigorous testing on the major platforms is necessary.

And then there's that sandbox thing. By default, applets are limited in what they can do, which may cause trouble in your client/server paradise. If you can't work around the limitations of the sandbox, you'll need to resort to signed applets, as described in Chapter 8, *Signed Applets*. But that's a big, nasty can of worms. It might just be easier to develop a standalone client application than to make it a signed applet.

Access Control

A secure application controls access to its resources. Consider an application that runs a business. Typically, such an application presents a number of interfaces to a central database. One window lets the people who answer the phones enter orders into the database. Other windows might allow accountants to track sales and expenses. Businesses are secretive about their financial figures, so the order entry people probably can't access the financial windows. And probably the accountants shouldn't be allowed in any part of the application except the financial windows.

An *access control list* (ACL) can implement these types of policy decisions. An ACL is simply a list of identities and the permissions they are allowed. In JDK 1.1, abstractions for implementing ACLs are provided in the `java.security.acl` package. In JDK 1.2, the problem of access control is better addressed. For a full description, see O'Reilly's *Java Security*.

Decompilers and Bytecode Obfuscation

On the Internet, protecting intellectual property has always been something of a joke, but not a very funny joke. Computers make it easy to copy information one time or a thousand times, and networked computers make it easy to distribute information. For people worried about royalties or per-use fees, the Internet is an ungodly nightmare.

You, as a developer, may also be worried about protecting your intellectual property, your Java programs. What can other people find out from the class files of your programs? They can find out quite a lot, using something called a *decompiler*. Just as a compiler takes source code and creates class files, a decompiler takes class files and creates source code. A good decompiler produces source code that can be immediately recompiled. Decompiling is not a new technique; it can be applied to the binary executables of any operating system. Java's class file structure, however, makes it particularly easy to reproduce readable source code from executable class files.

A popular decompiler is Hanpeter van Vliet's Mocha. Mocha is free, but you get what you pay for; it does have bugs, and it chokes on some Java 1.1 classes.[*] You can download Mocha from *http://www.brouhaha.com/~eric/computers/mocha.html*. A

---

[*] Hanpeter passed away in 1996, so Mocha is unsupported software. Borland seems to have incorporated Mocha into its JBuilder product, so presumably it now handles updates to Mocha. Borland has also made some claims to Mocha's licensing. Read the fine print carefully if you download this software.

newcomer in the free decompiler arena is JAD, available at *http://web.unicom .com.cy/%7Ekpd/jad.html*. If you're willing to pay for a decompiler, try WingDis (*http://www.wingsoft.com/wingdis.shtml*) or SourceAgain (*http://www.ahpah.com/*). Finally, the JDK itself has a tool, `javap`, that lets you examine the contents of a class file. Its output looks more like assembly code than Java. If you know how to read it, it's a clear explanation of how the class operates.

How can you prevent your programs from being decompiled or disassembled? You can't, although you can slow down the process. To do this, you need a tool called a *bytecode obfuscator*. An obfuscator removes as much information as it can from your class files without rendering them inoperable. You can still run a decompiler on an obfuscated class file, but the resulting source code is less readable. Two free obfuscators are Hashjava and Jobe, available at *http://www.sbktech.org/hashjava.html* and *http://www.primenet.com/~ej/index.html*, respectively. Jshrink is a commercial obfuscator, available at *http://www.e-t.com/jshrink.html*.

Another approach to foiling decompilation is to encrypt the class files of an application. The classes are decrypted as they are used, usually by a `ClassLoader`. In fact, this is a relatively simple thing to do, using a subclass of `ClassLoader` and a `CipherInputStream`. The hard part in this approach is figuring out where to keep the encryption key. If you keep it with the rest of the application, then it's pretty easy for a cracker to find the key and use it to decrypt your class files, which can then be decompiled. Suppose, instead, that you require the user to enter the key every time the application is run. This is inconvenient, at best, and offers no better protection–an attacker can pose as a legitimate user in order to receive the decryption key. The bottom line is that a scheme that encrypts class files offers little protection from decompilation.

Given the ease of examining a program's innards, you can see why it's important to use strong cryptographic algorithms rather than relying on "secret" algorithms. Sooner or later, someone will figure out how your program works. When designing a secure system, assume from the start that your attackers have the entire source code of your program.

Endpoint Security

Most of cryptography is concerned with securing communications between two parties. This requires two elements: cryptography for authentication and session encryption, and trusted executable code at each endpoint. It's the "trusted executable code" that concerns us here.

Think back to the `SafeTalk` application in Chapter 10, *SafeTalk*. How could it be compromised by messing around with class files?

- You could modify the `javax.crypto.CipherOutputStream` class to send plaintext to another IP address, unbeknownst to the user.

- You could modify the `Session` class to always choose the same key for encryption. Intercepted communications could then be easily decrypted.

And how would these class files be modified? A virus could do the work, or a rogue ActiveX control. If the class files come from a file server, they might be modified in transit from the server to your computer.

An interesting paper describes how a Netscape exectuable was modified in transit from server to client, available at *http://http.cs.berkeley.edu/~gauthier/endpoint-security.html*. The technique of NFS spoofing described in the paper could easily be used to modify class files instead of binary executables.

How can you prevent this kind of attack? Inside your application, there's nothing you can do because it's the class files of your application that get modified in this attack. Outside your application, you can take the following measures:

- Don't use an insecure file transfer protocol to obtain executables. In the paper mentioned above, executable files obtained using NFS were modified in transit.

- Scan for viruses, and scan frequently.

- Don't run insecure downloadable content. Unsigned Java applets are contained in the applet sandbox, and they should be safe (browser bugs notwithstanding). JavaScript^{TM} is also constrained, although browser bugs can open up security holes. Unsigned ActiveX controls are just plain scary; they can control any aspect of your computer. Signed ActiveX controls are only slightly better; you can make an all-or-nothing security decision based on whether you trust the control's signer. Note, however, that once you let an ActiveX control go, it has free rein on your system; there's no way to constrain it with fine-grained policies, as you can with signed Java applets.

File Security

The files on a local disk can be vulnerable to theft or modification. If you're running any sort of server software, of course, you shouldn't keep anything private on the server machine. Even a machine without server software, however, is vulnerable to viruses, Trojan horses, and other types of skullduggery. It doesn't do much good to encrypt all your communications if someone can pull files off your local disk.

If you're especially paranoid, you should encrypt any sensitive files on your local disk. Keep the key on a removable disk or a smart card, or use a passphrase (but don't write it down anywhere!).

Serialization

JDK 1.1 introduced the technique of *object serialization*, where Java objects can be written to streams and read from streams. By itself, object serialization offers nothing in the way of security. If you write objects out to a file, it's pretty easy for almost anyone to read the file and find out what's in it. Several of the examples in this book, for example, serialize a key to a file for later use. This offers no protection for the key, as it is stored in the clear in the file. To protect sensitive data, you can combine object serialization with an encrypted data stream (that is, wrap an `ObjectOutputStream` around a `CipherOutputStream`). Alternately, you might use a `javax.crypto.SealedObject` (see Chapter 7).

Deleting Files

A more subtle security risk comes from deleted files. Suppose you receive an encrypted message from a fellow freedom fighter. Naturally, you decrypt the message to read it. Then you delete the encrypted and decrypted files.

Next day, the secret police search your house, but you stand tall, arms crossed, confident they won't find anything incriminating, after all, you deleted the files. Unfortunately for you, the secret police have an Undelete program. You are in big trouble.

What happened? It turns out that many operating systems don't actually remove information from the disk when you delete a file. They simply mark the space as unused. When more files are saved, they overwrite this area of disk.

How can you really delete a file? If you're worried about deleted files, you'll need to get some software that overwrites the file's space with random data a few times. Just overwriting the file once won't do it. There are still artifacts on the disk that can be used to reconstruct the file. This kind of software will be very specific to operating systems, not the kind of stuff that you can easily use from Java. If you are worried about undeleted files, you may need a solution that is more closely related to particular hardware than Java.

Virtual Memory

Virtual memory adds another unwelcome wrinkle to the problem of file security. Virtual memory is the technique of using part of a disk as additional computer memory. This allows the computer to run more applications simultaneously, at the cost of the relatively slow operations of swapping sections of memory to and from the disk.

For developers of secure applications, this is just one more reason to start drinking heavily. It means that at any time during your application's execution, its memory space may be partially or fully written to disk. Attack programs could cruise through the virtual memory swap file, looking for private keys, plaintext, or other goodies.

As a developer, there's really nothing you can do about this because virtual memory is a feature of the operating system on which your program runs. Users who are concerned about these attacks should buy more real memory and disable virtual memory on their computers.

Memory Scanning

Even with virtual memory disabled, your application might still be snooped on by another application *as it's running*. Your computer might be running a virus or Trojan horse application that spends its life looking at other running applications, searching for private keys or other secret information.

If you're worried about this kind of attack, you should use an operating system that isolates application memory spaces, preventing snooping.

Network Security

The Internet Protocol, the backbone of the Internet, is not a secure protocol. Although you can use an IP network securely, you need to apply cryptography on top of the IP network—in your application, for example.

You should assume that every piece of data that you send or receive over a network can be observed, recorded, and replayed by an attacker. Likewise, don't trust any network traffic you receive without cryptographic authentication as proof of identity. I get chills down my spine every time I use *ftp* or *telnet*. Those applications still accept a password, in plaintext, as authentication. As we discussed in Chapter 6, *Authentication*, it's a bad idea to send a password over the network.

IPng (IP next generation) is a new protocol that can provide authentication and privacy at the protocol layer. If you'd like to read more, see *http://playground.sun.com/pub/ipng/html/ipng-main.html*.

SafeTalk and CipherMail, presented in Chapter 10 and Chapter 11, *CipherMail*, show how you can use cryptography to provide authentication and confidentiality in networked Java applications. Even these applications, however, have some interesting shortcomings. Consider SafeTalk, for example. Even though it encrypts the contents of a conversation, it can't conceal the existence of the conversation. Even if your enemies can't understand what you and your friends are chatting about, you might not want your enemies to know that you're even talking. CipherMail has the same property: Even though the contents of your email messages are encrypted, anyone snooping on the network will still be able to see the message traveling from you to your recipient. Sometimes merely knowing that

Person A is talking to Person B is enough for a clever spy to figure out what's going on.

Summary

In the end, security is a balancing act; you need to balance cost, risk, and usability. It costs time and money to make a system more secure. A secure system protects something valuable; the more valuable it is, the more you should spend on security. And in general, more secure systems are less usable.

A

BigInteger

Java 1.1 introduced `java.math.BigInteger`, a class that represents arbitrary-precision integers. Many cryptographic algorithms depend on the use of large integers and modular arithmetic. `BigInteger` supplies all of this in a class that has been optimized for speed. In this appendix, I'll briefly describe my usage of `BigInteger` in implementing the ElGamal signature and encryption algorithms (see Chapter 9, *Writing a Provider*).

ElGamal key generation requires three randomly generated numbers. The first, p, is the modulus. The bit length of p is the length of the key. Furthermore, p should be prime. Fortunately, `BigInteger` provides a constructor that does exactly what we want:

public BigInteger(int bitLength, int certainty, Random rnd)
> bitLength is the desired length of the new `BigInteger`. The certainty parameter determines the probability of the number being prime. In particular, for a certainty n, the probability of a prime number is $1 - .5^n$. Finally, this constructor uses the given `Random` object to generate a number. The high-order bit will always be set, ensuring that the bit length of the new number matches the requested bit length.

To begin creating a 2048-bit ElGamal key pair, we might do this:

```
int keyLength = 2048;
int certainty = 16;
SecureRandom sr = new SecureRandom();
BigInteger p = new BigInteger(keyLength, certainty, sr);
```

To continue creating an ElGamal key pair, we need two more random numbers, g and x. Both must be less than p. Another `BigInteger` constructor is appropriate for this task:

public BigInteger(int numBits, Random rndSrc)

> This constructor simply creates a number with the given bit length, using the supplied `Random`. The high-order bit of the number will be set, ensuring that the new `BigInteger` has the correct bit length.

So, the ElGamal key pair generation proceeds like this:

```
BigInteger g = new BigInteger(keyLength - 1, sr);
BigInteger x = new BigInteger(keyLength - 1, sr);
```

To guarantee that g and x are less than p, I've used `keyLength - 1` instead of `keyLength`.

The last step is to calculate $y = g^x \bmod p$. `BigInteger` has methods that implement most mathematical operations. The common ones are `add()`, `subtract()`, `multiply()`, and `divide()`. Many other useful operations are also encapsulated by methods. One method, `modPow()`, precisely suits our needs:

```
BigInteger y = g.modPow(x, p);
```

The `modPow()` call calculates $g^x \bmod p$. That's all there is to it! The public key is p, g, and y; the private key is x.

The math involved in encrypting and decrypting is similar, and it is greatly simplified by the use of `BigInteger`'s methods.

One pitfall that I encountered in implementing the ElGamal cipher has to do with converting a `BigInteger` to a byte array. `Ciphers` deal with byte arrays for input and output, but the ElGamal algorithm operates on large numbers (`BigIntegers`). Thus, the `Cipher`'s input needs to be converted from a byte array to `BigIntegers` before it can be processed, and the results of the encryption or decryption operation must be converted back to byte arrays on the way out of the `Cipher`.

Again, the `BigInteger` class saves our bacon. It has these useful constructors:

```
public BigInteger(byte[] val);
public BigInteger(int signum, byte[] magnitude);
```

The first appears to be the one we want, except that it considers the byte array to be signed, a two's complement representation. In the ElGamal algorithm, we always expect to process positive numbers. Instead, we use the second constructor, which expects an unsigned byte array. The `signum` parameter determines the sign of the resulting `BigInteger`; it may be –1, 0, or 1. In `ElGamalCipher`, I always use the second constructor with `signum` equal to 1. For example, when encrypting, the message value m is constructed from an array of bytes, `messageBytes`, like this:

```
BigInteger m = new BigInteger(1, messageBytes);
```

Converting a `BigInteger` to a byte array is a bit more tricky. There is a useful method that appears exactly right.

```
public byte[] toByteArray();
```

It doesn't do quite the right thing for us, though. It produces a two's complement byte array, whereas we want an unsigned byte array. All of our numbers are positive, which means the sign bit will always be 0, but it is the array length that gets messed up. Consider a 512-bit `BigInteger`. We expect an unsigned byte array representing this number to be 64 bytes long. `toByteArray()`, however, will return a 65-byte array. Why? It represents the number itself in 512 bits and uses an additional bit for sign. The resulting 513-bit quantity must be returned in 65 bytes.

To work around this, `ElGamalCipher` and `ElGamalSignature` use the following helper method. The method simply performs `toByteArray()` if the bit length of the `BigInteger` is not a multiple of 8. In this case, the sign bit will not cause an extra byte to be added to the byte array. If the bit length is a multiple of 8, then the sign bit added by `toByteArray()` will cause an extra byte in the resulting byte array. In this case, `getBytes()` removes the extra byte and returns the result.

```
protected byte[] getBytes(BigInteger big) {
  byte[] bigBytes = big.toByteArray();
  if ((big.bitLength() % 8) != 0) {
    return bigBytes;
  }
  else {
    byte[] smallerBytes = new byte[big.bitLength() / 8];
    System.arraycopy(bigBytes, 1, smallerBytes, 0, smallerBytes.length);
    return smallerBytes;
  }
}
```

B

Base64

Base64 is a system for representing raw byte data as ASCII characters. You could use hexadecimal for the same purpose, but it's not as efficient. One hex digit (eight bits) corresponds to four bits of input. Data represented in hexadecimal will be double the size of the original. As its name implies, base64 improves this ratio by representing six bits with each digit. Thus, 3 input bytes (3 x 8 = 24 bits) translates into 4 base64 digits (4 x 6 = 24 bits). Each base64 digit is represented by an ASCII character. Figure B-1 shows how bytes are converted to base64 digits.

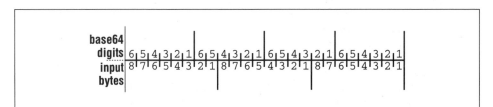

Figure B-1: Byte to base64 conversion

Base64 encoding always extends the input data to a multiple of 24 bits (3 bytes) by padding with zeros. There are three distinct cases:

- The input data is a multiple of 3 bytes. In this case, no padding is needed.

- The input data has one extra byte. This byte is split into two base64 digits, and two special padding digits (the = symbol) are added to the end of the base64 representation.

- The input data has two extra bytes. These bytes are represented by three base64 digits and one padding digit is added to the end of the base64 representation.

The base64 system is fully described in RFC 1521, in section 5.2. You can download this document from *ftp://ds.internic.net/rfc/rfc1521.txt.*

Sun provides base64 conversion classes in the unsupported sun.misc package. If you don't have these classes, you can use the base64 conversion classes presented here instead.

The oreilly.jonathan.util.Base64 class contains static methods that convert from bytes to base64 and vice versa:

```
package oreilly.jonathan.util;

public class Base64 {
```

The first method, encode(), converts a byte array to a String populated with base64 digits. It steps through the byte array, calling a helper method for each block of three input bytes:

```
public static String encode(byte[] raw) {
  StringBuffer encoded = new StringBuffer();
  for (int i = 0; i < raw.length; i += 3) {
    encoded.append(encodeBlock(raw, i));
  }
  return encoded.toString();
}
```

The helper method, encodeBlock(), creates 4 base64 digits from three bytes of input data. We use an integer, block, (a 32-bit quantity) to hold the 24 bits of input data. block's value starts at 0, but we'll build it up from the input data.

```
protected static char[] encodeBlock(byte[] raw, int offset) {
  int block = 0;
```

The slack variable tells how much space is left in the input byte array:

```
int slack = raw.length - offset - 1;
```

It's possible that there are fewer than three bytes in this block, if we've reached the end of the input data. We calculate end to be the upper limit on how many input bytes we can read:

```
int end = (slack >= 2) ? 2 : slack;
```

With this in place, we simply loop through the input data, shift it appropriately, and add it to block. The bytes coming from the input array are signed quantities, so they have to be converted to unsigned quantities before being shifted into block.

```
for (int i = 0; i <= end; i++) {
  byte b = raw[offset + i];
  int neuter = (b < 0) ? b + 256 : b;
```

```
    block += neuter << (8 * (2 - i));
  }
```

Once the block has been built, we just need to extract the base64 digits, which are six-bit quantities, from it. This is a matter of shifting the block correctly, and masking out all but the low six bits (& 0x3f):

```
    char[] base64 = new char[4];
    for (int i = 0; i < 4; i++) {
      int sixbit = (block >>> (6 * (3 - i))) & 0x3f;
      base64[i] = getChar(sixbit);
    }
```

Depending on how much space was left in the input array, the base64 padding character may need to be inserted into the character array:

```
    if (slack < 1)
      base64[2] = '=';
    if (slack < 2)
      base64[3] = '=';
```

encodeBlock() always returns an array of four characters:

```
    return base64;
  }
```

getChar() encapsulates the translation from a six-bit quantity to a base64 digit:

```
    protected static char getChar(int sixBit) {
      if (sixBit >= 0 && sixBit <= 25)
        return (char)('A' + sixBit);
      if (sixBit >= 26 && sixBit <= 51)
        return (char)('a' + (sixBit - 26));
      if (sixBit >= 52 && sixBit <= 61)
        return (char)('0' + (sixBit - 52));
      if (sixBit == 62) return '+';
      if (sixBit == 63) return '/';
      return '?';
    }
```

Decoding a base64 string is the same process in reverse. The decode() method begins by figuring out how many padding digits are on the end of the base64 string:

```
    public static byte[] decode(String base64) {
      int pad = 0;
      for (int i = base64.length() - 1; base64.charAt(i) == '='; i--)
        pad++;
```

It's now possible to calculate the length of the byte array, knowing the relevant bit lengths and compensating for padding:

```
      int length = base64.length() * 6 / 8 - pad;
```

The byte array that holds the results, `raw`, is created with this length:

```
byte[] raw = new byte[length];
```

Now we loop through the base64 value:

```
int rawIndex = 0;
for (int i = 0; i < base64.length(); i += 4) {
```

This time, the block is built from the four base64 digits. A correctly formed base64 string always has some multiple of four characters.

```
int block = (getValue(base64.charAt(i)) << 18)
    + (getValue(base64.charAt(i + 1)) << 12)
    + (getValue(base64.charAt(i + 2)) << 6)
    + (getValue(base64.charAt(i + 3)));
```

Based on the block, the byte array is filled with the appropriate eight-bit values:

```
for (int j = 0; j < 3 && rawIndex + j < raw.length; j++)
  raw[rawIndex + j] = (byte)((block >> (8 * (2 - j))) & 0xff);
rawIndex += 3;
}
return raw;
}
```

The `getValue()` method translates from base64 digits to their six-bit values:

```
protected static int getValue(char c) {
  if (c >= 'A' && c <= 'Z')
    return c - 'A';
  if (c >= 'a' && c <= 'z')
    return c - 'a' + 26;
  if (c >= '0' && c <= '9')
    return c - '0' + 52;
  if (c == '+') return 62;
  if (c == '/') return 63;
  if (c == '=') return 0;
  return -1;
}
}
```

Two additional classes are doppelgängers for classes in the `sun.misc` package. You can use these classes with the examples in Chapter 1, *Introduction*, if you don't have the `sun.misc` package available.

```
package oreilly.jonathan.util;

public class BASE64Encoder {
  public String encode(byte[] raw) {
    return Base64.encode(raw);
  }
}
```

```
package oreilly.jonathan.util;

public class BASE64Decoder {
  public byte[] decodeBuffer(String base64) {
    return Base64.decode(base64);
  }
}
```

C

JAR

The `jar` command-line tool is used to create Java Archives, or JAR files. A JAR contains other files, which may be compressed using the popular ZIP format. The `jar` tool is used to create and modify JARs.

JAR files will someday improve the speed of downloading applets over the network. You can stick all the files an applet needs into a JAR. This offers two speed advantages:

- The client needs to download only one JAR, instead of the many individual files that make up the applet. Applets are typically composed of a number of small class, graphics, and audio files. The cost of setting up a separate network connection for each one is high. Downloading a single, larger file is faster.

- Some of the files in the JAR may be compressed, which makes the download a little faster. Of course, it takes a little time to decompress the files, but bandwidth is clearly the time drain *du jour*.

Currently, only the `appletviewer` tool and HotJava recognize JAR files containing applets. The major browser vendors are expected to follow suit soon.

A JAR file can be signed, using `javakey` in JDK 1.1, or `jarsigner` in JDK 1.2.

Creating

Let's use `jar` to archive the files that make up the `GraphLayout` example applet that comes with the JDK 1.1. First, let's look at the files in that directory:

```
C:\ dir

Volume in drive C is BUENDIA
```

```
Volume Serial Number is 1929-10EE
Directory of C:\jdk1.2beta2\demo\GraphLayout

.              <DIR>       04-16-97  8:28a .
..             <DIR>       04-16-97  8:28a ..
EDGE~1   CLA          316  09-18-96 12:16p Edge.class
GRAPH~1  CLA        3,059  09-18-96 12:16p Graph.class
GRAPH~1  JAV        9,503  12-06-96 10:14a Graph.java
GRAPHP~2 CLA        5,986  09-18-96 12:16p GraphPanel.class
NODE~1   CLA          375  09-18-96 12:16p Node.class
EXAMPL~1 HTM          415  09-18-96 12:16p example1.html
EXAMPL~2 HTM          241  09-18-96 12:16p example2.html
EXAMPL~3 HTM          619  09-18-96 12:16p example3.html
EXAMPL~4 HTM          283  09-18-96 12:16p example4.html
AUDIO          <DIR>       04-16-97  8:28a audio
         9 file(s)        20,797 bytes
         3 dir(s)    222,429,184 bytes free
```

All the applet needs to run are the *.class* files and the sound files contained in the *audio* directory.

You can create a JAR using the -c option. By default, jar sends data to standard output. For most commands, though, you can use the -f option to specify a destination file. In this case, we want to specify the name of the destination JAR as well as the files to put into it, so we combine the -c and -f options:

```
C:\ jar -cf GraphLayout.jar *.class audio
```

This operation is completed in stony silence. If that makes you nervous, you can get some more feedback by adding the -v option (verbose). Like -f, the -v option can be combined with most of jar's other options:

```
C:\ jar -cvf GraphLayout.jar *.class audio
adding: Edge.class (in=316) (out=241) (deflated 23%)
adding: Graph.class (in=3059) (out=1762) (deflated 42%)
adding: GraphPanel.class (in=5986) (out=3492) (deflated 41%)
adding: Node.class (in=375) (out=275) (deflated 26%)
adding: audio/ (in=0) (out=0) (stored 0%)
adding: audio/computer.au (in=21745) (out=20105) (deflated 7%)
adding: audio/drip.au (in=759) (out=764) (deflated 0%)
adding: audio/gong.au (in=42068) (out=37645) (deflated 10%)
```

This shows each entry going into the JAR and how much it got compressed.

Extracting

To examine your handiwork, you can use the -t option to list the contents of a JAR. Again, we use the -f option to specify the JAR name. As before, the -v option is also available.

```
C:\ jar -tvf GraphLayout.jar
   948 Tue Jun 03 15:29:48 EDT 1997 META-INF/MANIFEST.MF
   316 Wed Sep 18 12:16:52 EDT 1996 Edge.class
  3059 Wed Sep 18 12:16:52 EDT 1996 Graph.class
  5986 Wed Sep 18 12:16:54 EDT 1996 GraphPanel.class
   375 Wed Sep 18 12:16:54 EDT 1996 Node.class
     0 Wed Apr 16 08:28:38 EDT 1997 audio/
 21745 Wed Sep 18 12:16:56 EDT 1996 audio/computer.au
   759 Wed Sep 18 12:16:56 EDT 1996 audio/drip.au
 42068 Wed Sep 18 12:16:56 EDT 1996 audio/gong.au
```

But wait a minute! What is *META-INF/MANIFEST.MF*? It's the *manifest file*, a special file that contains information about the rest of the JAR. I'll talk about it soon.

To extract files from a JAR, use the -x option. The -f and -v options are available, as before. You can extract all the files or just specify a few, as we do here:

```
C:\ jar -xvf GraphLayout.jar Edge.class audio
extracted: Edge.class
  created: audio\
extracted: audio\computer.au
extracted: audio\drip.au
extracted: audio\gong.au
```

Conveniently, jar automatically recreates directory structure.

On the Win32 platform, you may have to reverse some of the slashes. For example, to extract just the *computer.au* file in the *audio* subdirectory, you would do this:

```
C:\ jar -xvf GraphLayout.jar audio\computer.au
extracted: audio\computer.au
```

Even though a contents listing (using -t) shows this file as *audio/computer.au* (forward slash), we have to extract it as *audio\computer.au* (backward slash).

The Manifest

The manifest file contains information about the contents of a JAR. It is a human-readable file, consisting of name and value pairs. These are grouped into sections, with each section separated by a blank line. With the exception of the first section, every section corresponds to a file in the JAR. The first section consists of one value, indicating the manifest version used in the rest of the file. Currently, this is 1.0, so the first line of the manifest file looks like this:

```
Manifest-Version: 1.0
```

The section corresponding to the *computer.au* file looks like this:

```
Name: audio/computer.au
Digest-Algorithms: SHA MD5
```

```
SHA-Digest: zJMcY3mfFhSUPj8kdfZxKKJAXUM=
MD5-Digest: 5OWrlZ4NgfWzsXuuiwxrHg==
```

As you can see, the manifest file includes message digests of every file in the JAR. Two different algorithms are used to calculate a message digest, and the value of the digest for each algorithm is listed. Every file has a section like this, with the sections separated by blank lines.

You can specify additional information about an entry. You can specify, for example, that a *.class* file is a Java Bean by adding this entry to its section:

```
Java-Bean: True
```

So how do we add information to the manifest file? When the JAR is created, you can specify additional information that should be included in the manifest. For example, if we wanted to mark *Edge.class* as a Java Bean, we would create a file with the following information:

```
Name: Edge.class
Java-Bean: True
```

Save this file as *add.mf*. Then, we can use `jar`'s -m option to use this file for manifest information, as follows:

```
C:\ jar -cfm GraphLayout.jar add.mf *.class audio
```

In the resulting manifest file, the information we specified is merged with the automatically generated information. The section of the manifest file that corresponds to *Edge.class* now looks like this:

```
Name: Edge.class
Java-Bean: True
Digest-Algorithms: SHA MD5
SHA-Digest: sFKF74y7jL0DJQ3wuuxVgONMmEc=
MD5-Digest: xRwh6TRKszKWp8qMEdiPzw==
```

Signing

When you sign a JAR using `javakey` or `jarsigner`, additional information is placed in the JAR. This happens behind the scenes, but it may be helpful to know exactly what's going on.

Signature information is placed into files in the *META-INF* directory of the JAR, the same directory that contains the manifest file. Each person who signs the file is represented by a signature file, with an extension of *.SF*. The signature file looks a lot like the manifest file. It has a version section (`Signature-Version: 1.0`) and sections for each file in the JAR.

The name of this file is determined from the directive file used when the signature is created. When we used javakey to sign a JAR, earlier in this chapter, the directive file contained this line:

```
signature.file=MARISIGN
```

This would generate the signature file in the JAR as *META-INF/MARISIGN.SF*. Basically, this file just contains message digests for the contents of the JAR. A signed version of this signature file represents the actual JAR signature. The signed version has the same filename but a different extension, determined by the signing algorithm used. Marian used the DSA algorithm to sign the JAR, so the signed file is *META-INF/MARISIGN.DSA*.

We can verify this by examining the contents of the JAR:

```
C:\ jar -tvf signedArchive.jar META-INF
    288 Fri May 30 09:09:00 EDT 1997 META-INF/MANIFEST.MF
    289 Wed Jun 04 15:10:54 EDT 1997 META-INF\MARISIGN.SF
   1289 Wed Jun 04 15:10:54 EDT 1997 META-INF\MARISIGN.DSA
```

D

Javakey

In JDK 1.1, the javakey command-line tool maintains a database of identities and their associated keys and certificates. It's quite a versatile tool.

Creating

The -c option tells javakey to create something. You can create either a normal *identity* or a *signer*. An identity is a person or organization with an associated public key and, perhaps, certificates to verify the public key. A signer is an identity with a private key that can be used for signing files. You should have an identity in your javakey database corresponding to every person that you expect may provide you with signed code. The first step is to create the identity; later on, I'll show you how to associate a public key and certificates with the identity.

When an identity is created, you can tell javakey if the identity should be *trusted* or not. The appletviewer tool recognizes trusted identities. If you use applet-viewer to run an applet that is signed by a trusted identity, then the applet will not be constrained by the usual security restrictions. Although it's a step in the right direction, this is an all-or-nothing policy. You might trust Will Scarlet, but only a little, so it would be nice to specify that applets signed by him be allowed only filesystem access in one directory and not allowed network access at all. Java-Soft promises that more finely tuned access control will be available in future releases. Unless you specify otherwise, identities are not trusted when you first create them with javakey.

For example, the following commands will create Will Scarlet, who is not trusted, Marian, who is a trusted signer, and Sheriff, who is not trusted. The -c option creates an identity, while -cs tells javakey to create a signer.

```
C:\ javakey -c WillScarlet false
Created identity WillScarlet[identitydb.obj][not trusted]

C:\ javakey -cs Marian true
Created identity [Signer]Marian[identitydb.obj][trusted]

C:\ javakey -c Sheriff
Created identity Sheriff[identitydb.obj][not trusted]
```

WARNING   Be careful! When you use javakey to set up a trusted identity, you
allow applets signed by that identity to run with no security restrictions; that is, outside the sandbox. There's good reason for the sandbox to exist; think long and hard before you let a signer's applets get
out.

If you change your mind about an identity's trustworthiness, you can update the
database using the -t option.

```
C:\ javakey -t WillScarlet true
WillScarlet is trusted: true
```

Identities and signers are created without keys and certificates. You'll find out how
to add these later.

Inspecting

You can see the identities in your database by using the -l option:

```
C:\ javakey -l

Scope:sun.security.IdentityDatabase, source file: c:\jdk1.1.1\identitydb.obj

WillScarlet[identitydb.obj][trusted]

 [Signer]Marian[identitydb.obj][trusted]

Sheriff[identitydb.obj][not trusted]
```

The -li option displays detailed information for a particular identity:

```
C:\ javakey -li Marian
Identity: Marian
[Signer]Marian[identitydb.obj][trusted]
        no keys
        no certificates
        No further information available.
```

The -ld option displays detailed information for every identity in the database.

Gimme the Keys...

We can either generate keys for an identity or import them from a file. Generally speaking, you'll generate key pairs for the signers you "own" and import public keys for everyone else. Marian, for example, will generate her own public and private keys. She, however, will import public keys for both Will Scarlet and Sheriff.

Let's begin by generating a public and private key pair for Marian. We'll use the -gk option, which can be abbreviated to -g. To generate the keys, we need to specify which public key cipher algorithm we wish to use. JDK 1.1 ships with support for the DSA algorithm, so that's what we'll use.

Finally, javakey needs to know how long to make the keys. This is the size, in bits, of the keys. Longer keys are more secure, but they take more time to create and use. You need to generate keys only once, though, so you might as well bite the bullet and generate longer keys. You probably won't notice the extra time it takes to use a longer key. The DSA algorithm can generate keys of 512, 768, or 1024 bits.

```
C:\ javakey -gk Marian DSA 1024
Generated DSA keys for Marian (strength: 1024).
```

This is a lengthy process: You should probably kick this off and take a break while it chugs along.

When you generate the keys this way, they are stored in javakey's internal database. If you want to store the keys by themselves in external files, you can specify the filenames at the end of the javakey command, like this:

```
C:\ javakey -gk Marian DSA 1024 public.x509 private.x509
Generated DSA keys for Marian (strength: 1024).
Saved public key to public.x509.
Saved private key to private.x509.
```

The keys are stored in X.509 DER format. (See the sidebar for more information on X.509.)

Importing keys is just as easy. Let's suppose that Marian has a copy of Will Scarlet's public key in a file called *WillScarlet.x509*. She can associate the key with Will Scarlet in the database by using the -ik (import key) option:

```
C:\ javakey -ik WillScarlet WillScarlet.x509
Set public key from WillScarlet.x509 for WillScarlet.
```

Importing keys from files is not very secure. It's more likely that instead of a file representing Will's public key, Marian would have a certificate that contained the value of the key. In the previous example, for instance, let's consider the problem of how Marian obtains the *WillScarlet.x509* file. She might download it from an FTP or HTTP server, but this would allow an attacker to replace the contents of the file with a rogue key. The attacker could then masquerade as Will Scarlet and do considerable damage before Marian discovers she's been duped. Will Scarlet could write the *WillScarlet.x509* file on a disk and hand it to Marian personally, but this kind of delivery is often prohibitively expensive or downright infeasible.

Certificates

A certificate is a statement signed by one entity that associates another entity with a public key. Let's say, for example, that Robin Hood wants to find out Will Scarlet's public key so that he can accept messages signed by Will. Marian has obtained Will's key securely; it now resides in her `javakey` database. She can't just export the key and send a file to Robin Hood, though; the Sheriff might intervene and give Robin Hood a bogus key. So Marian creates a certificate, using information about herself, information about Will, and his public key. Marian is the *issuer* of this certificate, and Will is the *subject*.

Because the information that goes into a certificate can be lengthy, `javakey` uses a *directive file* in addition to command-line options for generating certificates. The directive file contains information about Marian, who is issuing the certificate, and Will, who is the subject of the certificate.

Certificates come in chains. Let's consider the certificate we just talked about. It certifies that Will Scarlet's public key has a certain value, and it is signed by Marian's private key. To verify the certificate, we need to know Marian's public key. How do we verify Marian's public key? We'd have a certificate stating the value of Marian's public key, signed by someone else. We verify that certificate using another certificate, and so on. How does this end? Eventually, we come to a self-signed certificate, issued by a *Certificate Authority* (CA). This is a special certificate whose issuer and subject are the same person or organization. Obviously, this is not very secure; anyone with `javakey` could forge such a certificate. Current thinking suggests that the certificates for CAs will be "widely published," making forgery difficult. It's a goofy system, in some ways, but it's a *de facto* standard.

In this example, Marian will serve as the CA. We'll start by creating the head of the certificate chain, a self-signed certificate for Marian. Let's construct the directive file, line by line. We begin by specifying the identity who is issuing the certificate:

```
issuer.name=Marian
```

This is followed by information about the subject of the certificate. In this case, the subject is also Marian:

```
subject.name=Marian
subject.real.name=Maid Marian
subject.org.unit=Overprotected Daughters
```

```
subject.org=Royal Castle
subject.country=England
```

The certificate has a lifetime, beyond which it is no longer trustworthy. It also has a serial number, which should be unique among certificates from the same issuer.

```
start.date=28 May 1997
end.date=31 December 1997
serial.number=1001
```

We also specify the algorithm to be used for signing the certificate:

```
signature.algorithm=DSA
```

Finally, we can specify a file that will contain the certificate. The certificate is stored in javakey's database as well. This parameter is optional.

```
out.file=Marian.certificate
```

Save this in a file called *Marian.directive*. Then generate the certificate as follows, using the -gc option:

```
C:\ javakey -gc Marian.directive
Generated certificate from directive file Marian.directive.


C:\ javakey -li Marian
Identity: Marian
[Signer]Marian[identitydb.obj][trusted]
        public and private keys initialized
        certificates:
        certificate 1    for  : CN=Maid Marian, OU=Overprotected Daughters,
                                O=Royal Castle, C=England
                        from : CN=Maid Marian, OU=Overprotected Daughters,
                                O=Royal Castle, C=England


        No further information available.
```

As you can see, javakey has generated our certificate and added it as certificate 1 to Marian's identity. There will also be a file version of the certificate in *Marian.certificate*. This file is not human-readable, but it can be transmitted to other people to add to their identity databases. You can get javakey to interpret the file for you by using the -dc (display certificate) option. (In the following code, the p, g, and y lines have been truncated.)

```
C:\ javakey -dc Marian.certificate
[
  X.509v1 certificate,
  Subject is CN=Maid Marian, OU=Overprotected Daughters,
          O=Royal Castle, C=Eng
  Key:  Sun DSA Public Key
parameters:
```

```
    p: fd7f53811d75122952df4a9c2eece4e7f611b7523cef4400c31e3f80b6512669455d40225
    q: 9760508f15230bccb292b982a2eb840bf0581cf5
    g: f7e1a085d69b3ddecbbcab5c36b857b97994afbbfa3aea82f9574c0b3d0782675159578eb

    y: 865437d06f000f2eda235a5cacc34905d51276b9e015bee6f525d601465f52e7b7e3cc52e
       Validity <Tue May 27 19:00:00 EDT 1997> until
               <Tue Dec 30 19:00:00 EST 1997>
       Issuer is CN=Maid Marian, OU=Overprotected Daughters,
               O=Royal Castle, C=Engl
       Issuer signature used [SHA1withDSA]
       Serial number =        03e9
    ]
```

Most of the parameters we specified in the directive file are shown. Also shown are the p, q, and g parameters that the DSA algorithm uses internally.

Note that a self-signed certificate is not trustworthy. Anybody, including the Sheriff of Nottingham, could use javakey to create a self-signed certificate purporting to belong to Marian. When you accept a self-signed certificate, you should be very, very sure that you have the real thing.

Marian, for instance, places this certificate on a floppy disk, which she drops from her tower window to Robin Hood, who happens to be passing by on his horse. Thus, Robin Hood is pretty sure that he has a genuine self-signed certificate of Marian's public key.

A more practical way to be sure you have a genuine copy of a self-signed certificate is to compare the certificate's *fingerprint* with a well-known reference. A certificate fingerprint is a cryptographic message digest of the certificate, represented in hexadecimal. If Robin Hood downloads Marian's certificate from the Internet, it might be a fake. To verify it, he calls Marian on the telephone and reads her the fingerprint of the certificate he downloaded. If it matches the fingerprint on Marian's original certificate, Robin Hood knows he has a good copy. Commercial CAs, like VeriSign, should publish their self-signed (root) certificate fingerprints widely, possibly in newspapers or magazines, for example. The root certificates of CAs are currently distributed as part of browsers. When you download Netscape Navigator or Internet Explorer, they come complete with the root certificates of a dozen or so CAs.

Now that Marian has a self-signed certificate, she can issue a certificate for Will Scarlet. This new certificate will refer to the self-signed certificate as proof of Marian's identity. The directive file looks like this:

```
issuer.name=Marian

subject.name=WillScarlet
subject.real.name=Will Scarlet
```

```
subject.org.unit=Archery
subject.org=Merry Men
subject.country=England

issuer.cert=1

start.date=28 May 1997
end.date=31 December 1997
serial.number=1002

signature.algorithm=DSA

out.file=WillScarlet.certificate
```

Would the Real X.509 Please Stand Up?

X.509 is the de facto standard for certificates. X.509 is actually the name of a document published by the International Telecommunications Union (ITU), formerly known as the CCITT. The document itself is concerned with problems of authentication. The certificate definition is just one part of the document.

The certificate definition is specified in terms of the *Abstract Syntax Notation* language, known as ASN.1. This language is frequently used to specify data structures used in network communications. It specifies data structures, like `struct` in C. A set of encoding rules is needed to convert a `struct`-full of data to a series of bits. Two of the most common encoding rules used with ASN.1 are the Basic Encoding Rules (BER) and Distinguished Encoding Rules (DER).

The file looks a lot like the last one, except that the subject is Will, not Marian. Also, one additional line has mysteriously appeared.

```
issuer.cert=1
```

This line means that the information in Marian's first certificate, the self-signed one we just created, will be used to sign the certificate for Will Scarlet. We know it's numbered 1 from examining Marian's information using `javakey -li Marian`.

To and Fro

Most of the remaining `javakey` options deal with exchanging keys and certificates to and from files. These are summarized, along with the rest of `javakey`'s options, in Table D-1. Parameters in square brackets are optional.

Table D-1: Javakey Options

Option syntax	Description
-c *identity [trust]*	This option creates an identity with the given name. The *trust* parameter should be either "true" or "false." If it is not present, false is the default.
-cs *signer [trust]*	This option is the same as -c, except it creates a signer instead of an identity.
-t *name trust*	You can use this option to change the trust status of the named identity or signer. The *trust* parameter should be "true" or "false."
-ii *name*	You can enter additional information about an identity or signer using this option.
-r *name*	Use this option to remove an identity or signer from the database.
-gk *signer algorithm keysize [pubfile [privfile]]*	This option, which can be abbreviated -g, generates a key pair for the named signer. It generates a key pair for the given algorithm name and strength. The *pubfile* and *privfile* parameters, if specified, are used as filenames to contain the newly generated public and private keys.
-l	Use this option to see the contents of the javakey database.
-ld	This option is the same as -l but shows more detail.
-li *name*	This option displays details about the named identity or signer.
-gc *directivefile*	Use this option to generate a certificate, using the information in the given directive file.
-dc *certfile*	This option displays the certificate contained in the given file.
-gs *directivefile jarfile*	This option signs the given JAR using the information from the given directive file.
-ik *identity pubfile*	Use this option to import a public key from *pubfile* to be associated with the given identity.
-ikp *signer pubfile privfile*	Use this option to import a public and private key pair for the given signer.
-ic *identity certfile*	This option associates the given identity and certificate.
-ek *identity pubfile [privfile]*	This option exports the given identity's public key to the named file. If *privfile* is specified and the identity is a signer, the private key can also be exported.
-ec *identity certnum certfile*	Use this option to export the certificate numbered *certnum* of the given identity to the file *certfile*.

Let's extend the certificate example. If Robin Hood gets a copy of the certificate that Marian issued for Will Scarlet, he can associate it with Will's identity in his javakey database as follows:

```
C:\ javakey -ic WillScarlet WillScarlet.certificate
Imported certificate from WillScarlet.certificate for WillScarlet.
```

Now Robin Hood has a certified copy of Will Scarlet's public key and can verify Will's signature.

A final "import" option, `-ii`, allows you to enter textual information about an identity. The information you type shows up when you look at the detailed identity listing using the `-li` or `-ld` options.

```
C:\ javakey -ii WillScarlet
Please enter the info for this identity.
[End with ctrl-D on Unix and ctrl-Z on Win32]
This is some extraneous,
multi-line babbling about Will Scarlet.
^Z
Set information for WillScarlet
```

Sign of the Times

JDK 1.0 had an inflexible policy with regard to applets. An applet lived in the "sandbox" and was therefore prevented from doing anything really useful, like writing to the hard disk or making arbitrary socket connections. In JDK 1.1, it's possible to create signed applets. This means that a client who has the signer's certificate and trusts it can allow signed applets to run without the usual security restrictions. Two conditions must be met for this to happen:

- The client needs to have installed the signer's certificate using `javakey`.

- The client software that hosts the applet needs to be JDK 1.1 compliant; it must be savvy about JAR files, and it must understand the new security features. As of this writing, only HotJava and `appletviewer` know anything about signed applets. Netscape and Microsoft will follow suit shortly.

You can use `javakey` to sign *Java Archive* (JAR) files. A JAR can contain many files. For example, you could bundle up all of the files needed for a particular applet, classes, graphics, and sound, into a JAR. When you sign an applet JAR, `javakey` adds a signature and one of the signer's certificates to the JAR. See Appendix C, *JAR*, for a description of the `jar` utility, which creates JAR files.

As with certificate generation, applet signing requires a directive file. First, we need to specify who is signing the file:

```
signer=Marian
```

Next, we tell `javakey` which of the signer's certificates we want to include in the JAR. You also need to specify the chain depth, represented by a `chain` entry. This feature is not used yet, so you can just set it to 0. In future versions it will probably specify how many certificates in a chain you would like to include as part of the JAR.

```
cert=1
chain=0
```

Then we specify a filename for the signature. This should be eight characters or fewer:

```
signature.file=MARISIGN
```

An optional parameter is the name of the signed JAR. If we don't specify this, then *.sig* is appended to the original JAR to create the signed JAR name.

```
out.file=signedArchive.jar
```

Save this information in *sign.directive*. We're finally ready to sign the JAR, using the -gs (generate signature) option and specifying both the directive file and the JAR name:

```
C:\ javakey -gs sign.directive Quickie.jar
Adding entry: META-INF/MANIFEST.MF
Creating entry: META-INF\MARISIGN.SF
Creating entry: META-INF\MARISIGN.DSA
Adding entry: Quickie.class
Signed JAR file Quickie.jar using directive file sign.directive.
```

In Appendix C, we talked about the files that get created when you sign a JAR.

The Care and Feeding of Keys

Private keys must be kept secret. This is the whole premise of public key cryptography. Unfortunately, a private key is not something people can memorize. It needs to be stored electronically, whether on fixed media (a hard disk), removable media (a floppy disk), or a hardware device (a smart card). Smart cards are not widely available, so you will most likely store your private key in a disk file of some sort.

Using javakey, there are two possible private key vulnerabilities. If you write your private keys to disk files, those files must be protected. Additionally, private keys are stored in the javakey database file. This file, by default, is *identitydb.obj* and lives in the JDK installation directory. If you wish to change the location of this file, you can specify the identity.database property in the *lib/security/java.security* file found beneath the JDK installation directory. Note that the *java.security* file should also be protected, particularly on a multiuser system.

You can feel safe if these conditions are met:

- You are the only person who uses your computer.
- Your computer is in a physically secure location.
- Your computer is not connected to a network.

This is not a realistic scenario. The last point is the least likely to happen; it's hard to find a computer that isn't on a LAN or connected to the Internet in one way or another. You are actually pretty safe if you are not running any server software. Even if you're not, though, there is always the possibility of operating system bugs that might allow intruders some access to your system. The precautions you take with your private keys should be commensurate with your paranoia. Your paranoia should be commensurate with the amount you can lose if your private key is compromised.

People with multiuser systems need to be especially careful. The safest thing to do is to limit access to javakey, *java.security,* and *identitydb.obj* to the system administrator only. This restriction does not allow users to sign files, however, unless they have their own installation of the JDK and an individual *identitydb.obj.* JavaSoft™ has some recommendations, at *http://www.javasoft.com/security/policy.html.* The functions in javakey do not divide neatly into administrator and user functions.

E

Quick Reference

This appendix contains a summary listing of the cryptography classes I have covered in this book. The classes are organized by package. The following packages are covered:

- `java.security` (partial)
- `java.security.cert`
- `java.security.interfaces`
- `java.security.spec`
- `javax.crypto`
- `javax.crypto.interfaces`
- `javax.crypto.spec`

Package java.security

Class java.security.AlgorithmParameters

Description

This class represents a set of parameters for a specific algorithm. Subclasses of this class can be used with the algorithm-specific initialization methods of `KeyPair-Generator` and `Cipher`.

Class Definition

```
public class java.security.AlgorithmParameters {
```

```
   // Class Methods
   public static final AlgorithmParameters getInstance(String);
   public static final AlgorithmParameters getInstance(String, String);

   // Instance Methods
   protected AlgorithmParameters(AlgorithmParametersSpi, Provider,
      String);
   public final String getAlgorithm();
   public final Provider getProvider();
   public final void init(AlgorithmParameterSpec);
   public final void init(byte[]);
   public final void init(byte[], String);
   public final AlgorithmParameterSpec getParameterSpec(Class);
   public final byte[] getEncoded();
   public final byte[] getEncoded(String);
   public final String toString();
}
```

See Also

KeyPairGenerator

Class java.security.AlgorithmParametersSpi

Description

This is the Security Provider Interface for algorithm parameters. If you want to implement your own algorithm parameters, you do so by subclassing this class and registering your implementation with an appropriate security provider.

Class Definition

```
public abstract class java.security.AlgorithmParametersSpi
   extends java.lang.Object {

   // Constructors
   public AlgorithmParametersSpi();

   // Protected Instance Methods
   protected abstract byte[] engineGetEncoded();
   protected abstract byte[] engineGetEncoded(String);
   protected abstract AlgorithmParameterSpec
      engineGetParameterSpec(Class);
   protected abstract void engineInit(AlgorithmParameterSpec);
   protected abstract void engineInit(byte[]);
   protected abstract void engineInit(byte[], String);
   protected abstract String engineToString();
}
```

See Also

AlgorithmParameters

Class java.security.DigestInputStream

Description

A digest input stream is an input filter stream that is associated with a message digest object. As data is read from the input stream, it is automatically passed to its associated message digest object; once all the data has been read, the message digest object will return the hash of the input data. You must have an existing input stream and an initialized message digest object to construct this class; once the data has passed through the stream, call the methods of the message digest object explicitly to obtain the hash.

Class Definition

```
public class java.security.DigestInputStream
  extends java.io.FilterInputStream {

  // Variables
  protected MessageDigest digest;

  // Constructors
  public DigestInputStream(InputStream, MessageDigest);

  // Instance Methods
  public MessageDigest getMessageDigest();
  public void on(boolean);
  public int read();
  public int read(byte[], int, int);
  public void setMessageDigest(MessageDigest);
  public String toString();
}
```

See Also

DigestOutputStream, MessageDigest

Class java.security.DigestOutputStream

Description

A digest output stream is a filter output stream that is associated with a message digest object. When data is written to the output stream, it is also passed to the message digest object so that when the data has all been written to the output stream, the hash of that data may be obtained from the digest object. You must have an existing output stream and an initialized message digest object to use this class.

Class Definition

```
public classs java.security.DigestOutputStream
    extends java.io.FilterOutputStream {

    // Variables
    protected MessageDigest digest;

    // Constructors
    public DigestOutputStream(OutputStream, MessageDigest);

    // Instance Methods
    public MessageDigest getMessageDigest();
    public void on(boolean);
    public void setMessageDigest(MessageDigest);
    public String toString();
    public void write(int);
    public void write(byte[], int, int);
}
```

See Also

DigestInputStream, MessageDigest

Class java.security.Identity

Description

An identity encapsulates public knowledge about an entity (that is, a person or a corporation, or anything that could hold a public key). Identities have names and may hold a public key, along with a certificate chain to validate the public key. An identity may belong to an identity scope, but this feature is optional and is not typically used.

Class Definition

```
public class java.security.Identity
    extends java.lang.Object
    implements java.security.Principal, java.io.Serializable {

    // Constructors
    protected Identity();
    public Identity(String);
```

```
    public Identity(String, String, Certificate[], PublicKey);
    public Identity(String, IdentityScope);

    // Instance Methods
    public void addCertificate(Certificate);
    public final boolean equals(Object);
    public Certificate[] getCertificates();
    public String getInfo();
    public final String getName();
    public PublicKey getPublicKey();
    public final IdentityScope getScope();
    public int hashCode();
    public void removeCertificate(Certificate);
    public void setInfo(String);
    public void setPublicKey(PublicKey);
    public String toString();
    public String toString(boolean);

    // Protected Instance Methods
    protected boolean identityEquals(Identity);
}
```

See Also

Certificate, IdentityScope, Principal, PublicKey

Class java.security.IdentityScope

Description

An identity scope is a collection of identities; an identity may belong to a single identity scope. The notion is that scope is recursive: An identity scope may itself belong to another identity scope (or it may be unscoped). This class is not often used in Java 1.2.

Class Definition

```
    public abstract class java.security.IdentityScope
        extends java.security.Identity {

    // Constructors
    protected IdentityScope();
    public IdentityScope(String);
    public IdentityScope(String, IdentityScope);

    // Class Methods
    public static IdentityScope getSystemScope();
    protected static void setSystemScope(IdentityScope);
```

```
      // Instance Methods
      public abstract void addIdentity(Identity);
      public abstract Identity getIdentity(String);
      public Identity getIdentity(Principal);
      public abstract Identity getIdentity(PublicKey);
      public abstract Enumeration identities();
      public abstract void removeIdentity(Identity);
      public abstract int size();
      public String toString();
   }
```

See AlsoIdentityScope class

Identity

Interface java.security.Key

Description

A key is essentially a series of bytes that are used by a cryptographic algorithm. Depending on the type of the key, the key may be used only for particular operations and only for particular algorithms, and it may have certain mathematical properties (including a mathematical relationship to other keys). The series of bytes that make up a key is the encoded format of the key.

Interface Definition

```
      public abstract interface java.security.Key
        implements java.io.Serializable {

        // Instance Methods
        public abstract String getAlgorithm();
        public abstract byte[] getEncoded();
        public abstract String getFormat();
   }
```

See Also

PrivateKey, PublicKey, SecretKey

Class java.security.KeyFactory

Description

A key factory is an engine class that is capable of translating between public or private key objects and their external format (and vice versa). Hence, key factories may be used to import or export keys, as well as to translate keys of one class (e.g., com.acme.DSAPublicKey) to another class (e.g., com.xyz.DSAPublicKeyImpl) as long as those classes share the same base class. Key factories operate in terms of key specifications; these specifications are the various external formats in which a key may transmitted. Keys are imported via the generatePublic() and generatePrivate() methods; they are exported via the getKeySpec() method, and they are translated via the translateKey() method.

Class Definition

```
public class java.security.KeyFactory
    extends java.lang.Object {

    // Constructors
    protected KeyFactory(KeyFactorySpi, Provider, String);

    // Class Methods
    public static final KeyFactory getInstance(String);
    public static final KeyFactory getInstance(String, String);

    // Instance Methods
    public final PrivateKey generatePrivate(KeySpec);
    public final PublicKey generatePublic(KeySpec);
    public final String getAlgorithm();
    public final KeySpec getKeySpec(Key, Class);
    public final Provider getProvider();
    public final Key translateKey(Key);
}
```

See Also

AlgorithmParameterSpec, KeyFactorySpi, KeySpec

Class java.security.KeyFactorySpi

Description

This is the Service Provider Interface for a key factory; if you want to implement your own key factory, you do so by extending this class and registering your implementation with an appropriate security provider. Instances of this class are expected to know how to create key objects from external key specifications and vice versa.

Class Definition

```
public abstract class java.security.KeyFactorySpi
    extends java.lang.Object {
```

```
    // Constructors
    public KeyFactorySpi();

    // Protected Instance Methods
    protected abstract PrivateKey engineGeneratePrivate(KeySpec);
    protected abstract PublicKey engineGeneratePublic(KeySpec);
    protected abstract KeySpec engineGetKeySpec(Key, Class);
    protected abstract Key engineTranslateKey(Key);
}
```

See Also

KeyFactory, KeySpec

Class java.security.KeyPair

Description

Public and private keys are mathematically related to each other and hence are generated together; this class provides an encapsulation of both the keys as a convenience to key generation.

Class Definition

```
    public final class java.security.KeyPair
      extends java.lang.Object {

      // Constructors
      public KeyPair(PublicKey, PrivateKey);

      // Instance Methods
      public PrivateKey getPrivate();
      public PublicKey getPublic();
    }
```

See Also

KeyPairGenerator, PrivateKey, PublicKey

Class java.security.KeyPairGenerator

Description

This is an engine class that is capable of generating a public key and its related private key. Instances of this class will generate key pairs that are appropriate for a particular algorithm (DSA, RSA, etc.). A key pair generator may be initialized to return keys of a particular strength (which is usually the number of bits in the key), or it may be initialized in an algorithmic-specific way; the former case is implemented by most key generators. An instance of this class may be used to generate any number of key pairs.

Class Definition

```
public abstract class java.security.KeyPairGenerator
    extends java.security.KeyPairGeneratorSpi {

    // Constructors
    protected KeyPairGenerator(String);

    // Class Methods
    public static KeyPairGenerator getInstance(String);
    public static KeyPairGenerator getInstance(String, String);

    // Instance Methods
    public final KeyPair genKeyPair();
    public String getAlgorithm();
    public final Provider getProvider();
    public void initialize(int);
    public void initialize(AlgorithmParameterSpec);
}
```

See Also

AlgorithmParameterSpec, KeyPair

Class java.security.KeyPairGeneratorSpi

Description

This is the Service Provider Interface class for the key pair generation engine; if you want to implement your own key pair generator, you must extend this class and register your implementation with an appropriate security provider. Instances of this class must be prepared to generate key pairs of a particular strength (or length); they may optionally accept an algorithmic-specific set of initialization values.

Class Definition

```
public abstract class java.security.KeyPairGeneratorSpi
    extends java.lang.Object {

    // Constructors
    public KeyPairGeneratorSpi();
```

```
    // Instance Methods
    public abstract KeyPair generateKeyPair();
    public abstract void initialize(int, SecureRandom);
    public void initialize(AlgorithmParameterSpec, SecureRandom);
}
```

See Also

AlgorithmParameterSpec, KeyPairGenerator, SecureRandom

Class java.security.KeyStore

Description

This class is responsible for maintaining a set of keys and their related owners. In the default implementation, this class maintains the *.keystore* file held in the user's home directory, but you may provide an alternate implementation of this class that holds keys anywhere: in a database, or on a remote filesystem, or on a Java smart card, or any and all of the above. The class that is used to provide the default keystore implementation is specified by the keystore property in the *$JDKHOME/lib/java.security* file. The keystore may optionally require a passphrase for access to the entire keystore (via the load() method); this passphrase is often used only for sanity checking and is often not specified at all. On the other hand, private keys in the keystore should be protected (e.g., encrypted) by using a different passphrase for each private key.

Note that although the keystore associates entities with keys, it does not rely on the Identity class itself.

Class Definition

```
    public abstract class java.security.KeyStore
      extends java.lang.Object {

      // Constructors
      public KeyStore();

      // Class Methods
      public static final KeyStore getInstance();

      // Instance Methods
      public abstract Enumeration aliases();
      public abstract boolean containsAlias(String);
      public abstract void deleteEntry(String);
      public abstract Certificate getCertificate(String);
      public abstract String getCertificateAlias(Certificate);
      public abstract Certificate[] getCertificateChain(String);
```

```
      public abstract Date getCreationDate(String);
      public abstract PrivateKey getPrivateKey(String, String);
      public abstract boolean isCertificateEntry(String);
      public abstract boolean isKeyEntry(String);
      public abstract void load(InputStream, String);
      public abstract void setCertificateEntry(String, Certificate);
      public abstract void setKeyEntry(String, PrivateKey, String,
                  Certificate[]);
      public abstract void setKeyEntry(String, byte[], Certificate[]);
      public abstract int size();
      public abstract void store(OutputStream, String);
  }
```

See Also

Certificate, PublicKey

Class java.security.MessageDigest

Description

The message digest class is an engine class that can produce a one-way hash value for any arbitrary input. Message digests have two properties: They produce a unique hash for each set of input data (subject to the number of bits that are output), and the original input data is indiscernible from the hash output. The hash value is variously called a digital fingerprint or a digest. Message digests are components of digital signatures, but they are useful in their own right to verify that a set of data has not been corrupted. Once a digest object is created, data may be fed to it via the update() methods; the hash itself is returned via the digest() method.

Class Definition

```
  public abstract class java.security.MessageDigest
    extends java.security.MessageDigestSpi {

    // Constructors
    protected MessageDigest(String);

    // Class Methods
    public static MessageDigest getInstance(String);
    public static MessageDigest getInstance(String, String);
    public static boolean isEqual(byte[], byte[]);

    // Instance Methods
    public Object clone();
    public byte[] digest();
```

```
    public byte[] digest(byte[]);
    public int digest(byte[], int, int);
    public final String getAlgorithm();
    public final int getDigestLength();
    public final Provider getProvider();
    public void reset();
    public String toString();
    public void update(byte);
    public void update(byte[]);
    public void update(byte[], int, int);
}
```

Class java.security.MessageDigestSpi

Description

This is the Service Provider Interface for the message digest engine; if you want to implement your own message digest class, you do so by extending this class and registering your implementation with an appropriate security provider. Because the MessageDigest class itself extends this class, you may also extend the MessageDigest class directly. Implementations of this class are expected to accumulate a hash value over data that is fed to it as a series of arbitrary bytes.

Class Definition

```
    public abstract class java.security.MessageDigestSpi
        extends java.lang.Object {

      // Constructors
      public MessageDigestSpi();

      // Instance Methods
      public Object clone();

      // Protected Instance Methods
      protected abstract byte[] engineDigest();
      protected int engineDigest(byte[], int, int);
      protected int engineGetDigestLength();
      protected abstract void engineReset();
      protected abstract void engineUpdate(byte);
      protected abstract void engineUpdate(byte[], int, int);
    }
```

See Also

MessageDigest

Interface java.security.Principal

Description

A principal is anything that has a name, such as an identity. The name in this case is often an X.500 distinguished name, but that is not a requirement.

Interface Definition

```
public abstract interface java.security.Principal {

    // Instance Methods
    public abstract boolean equals(Object);
    public abstract String getName();
    public abstract int hashCode();
    public abstract String toString();
}
```

See Also

Identity

Interface java.security.PrivateKey

Description

A private key is a key with certain mathematical properties that allow it to perform inverse cryptographic operations with its matching public key. Classes implement this interface only for type identification.

Interface Definition

```
public abstract interface java.security.PrivateKey
    implements java.security.Key {
}
```

See Also

Key, PublicKey

Class java.security.Provider

Description

An instance of the Provider class is responsible for mapping particular implementations to desired algorithm/engine pairs; instances of this class are consulted (indirectly) by the getInstance() methods of the engine classes to find a class that implements the desired operation. Instances of this class must be registered either with the Security class or by listing them in the *$JDKHOME/lib/security/java.security* file as a security.provider property.

Class Definition

```
public abstract class java.security.Provider
  extends java.util.Properties {

  // Constructors
  protected Provider(String, double, String);

  // Instance Methods
  public synchronized void clear();
  public String getInfo();
  public String getName();
  public double getVersion();
  public synchronized Object put(Object, Object);
  public synchronized Object remove(Object);
  public String toString();
}
```

See Also

Security

Interface java.security.PublicKey

Description

A public key is a key with certain mathematical properties that allow it to perform inverse cryptographic operations with its matching private key. Classes implement this interface only for type identification.

Interface Definition

```
public abstract interface java.security.PublicKey
  implements java.security.Key {
}
```

See Also

Key, PrivateKey

Class java.security.SecureRandom

Description

This class generates random numbers. Unlike the standard random-number generator, numbers generated by this class are cryptographically secure, that is, they are less subject to pattern guessing and other attacks that can be made on a traditional random-number generator.

Class Definition

```
public class java.security.SecureRandom
    extends java.util.Random {

    // Constructors
    public SecureRandom();
    public SecureRandom(byte[]);

    // Class Methods
    public static byte[] getSeed(int);

    // Instance Methods
    public synchronized void nextBytes(byte[]);
    public void setSeed(long);
    public synchronized void setSeed(byte[]);

    // Protected Instance Methods
    protected final int next(int);
}
```

Class java.security.Security

Description

This class manages the list of providers that have been installed into the virtual machine; this list of providers is consulted to find an appropriate class to provide the implementation of a particular operation when the getInstance() method of an engine class is called. The list of providers initially comes from the *$JDKHOME/lib/security/java.security* file, and applications may use methods of this class to add and remove providers from that list.

Class Definition

```
public final class java.security.Security
    extends java.lang.Object {
```

```
    // Class Methods
    public static int addProvider(Provider);
    public static String getAlgorithmProperty(String, String);
    public static String getProperty(String);
    public static Provider getProvider(String);
    public static Provider[] getProviders();
    public static int insertProviderAt(Provider, int);
    public static void removeProvider(String);
    public static void setProperty(String, String);
}
```

See Also

Provider

Class java.security.Signature

Description

This engine class provides the ability to create or verify digital signatures by employing different algorithms that have been registered with the Security class. As with all engine classes, instances of this class are obtained via the getInstance() method. The signature object must be initialized with the appropriate private key (to sign) or public key (to verify), then data must be fed to the object via the update() methods, and then the signature can be obtained (via the sign() method) or verified (via the verify() method). Signature objects may support algorithm-specific parameters, though this is not a common implementation.

Class Definition

```
    public abstract class java.security.Signature
      extends java.security.SignatureSpi {

    // Constants
    protected static final int SIGN;
    protected static final int UNINITIALIZED;
    protected static final int VERIFY;

    // Variables
    protected int state;

    // Constructors
    protected Signature(String);

    // Class Methods
    public static Signature getInstance(String);
```

```
    public static Signature getInstance(String, String);

    // Instance Methods
    public Object clone();
    public final String getAlgorithm();
    public final Object getParameter(String);
    public final Provider getProvider();
    public final void initSign(PrivateKey);
    public final void initSign(PrivateKey, SecureRandom);
    public final void initVerify(PublicKey);
    public final void setParameter(String, Object);
    public final void setParameter(AlgorithmParameterSpec);
    public final byte[] sign();
    public String toString();
    public final void update(byte);
    public final void update(byte[]);
    public final void update(byte[], int, int);
    public final boolean verify(byte[]);
}
```

See Also

```
Provider
```

Class java.security.SignatureSpi

Description

This is the Security Provider Interface for the signature engine. If you want to implement your own signature engine, you must extend this class and register your implementation with an appropriate security provider. Because the Signature class already extends this class, your implementation may extend the Signature class directly. Implementations of this class must be prepared both to sign and to verify data that is passed to the engineUpdate() method. Initialization of the engine may optionally support a set of algorithm-specific parameters.

Class Definition

```
    public abstract class java.security.SignatureSpi
      extends java.lang.Object {

    // Variables
    protected SecureRandom appRandom;

    // Constructors
    public SignatureSpi();
```

```
    // Instance Methods
    public Object clone();

    // Protected Instance Methods
    protected abstract Object engineGetParameter(String);
    protected abstract void engineInitSign(PrivateKey);
    protected void engineInitSign(PrivateKey, SecureRandom);
    protected abstract void engineInitVerify(PublicKey);
    protected abstract void engineSetParameter(String, Object);
    protected void engineSetParameter(AlgorithmParameterSpec);
    protected abstract byte[] engineSign();
    protected abstract void engineUpdate(byte);
    protected abstract void engineUpdate(byte[], int, int);
    protected abstract boolean engineVerify(byte[]);
}
```

See Also

Provider, Signature

Class java.security.SignedObject

Description

A signed object is a container class for another (target) object; the signed object contains a serialized version of the target along with a digital signature of the data contained in the target object. You must provide a serializable object and a private key to create a signed object, after which you can remove the embedded object and verify the signature of the signed object by providing the appropriate public key.

Class Definition

```
    public final class java.security.SignedObject
      extends java.lang.Object
      implements java.io.Serializable {

    // Constructors
    public SignedObject(Serializable, PrivateKey, Signature);

    // Instance Methods
    public String getAlgorithm();
    public Object getObject();
    public byte[] getSignature();
    public boolean verify(PublicKey, Signature);
}
```

See Also

Signature

Class java.security.Signer

Description

A signer abstracts the notion of a principal (that is, an individual or a corporation) that has a private key and a corresponding public key. Signers may optionally belong to an identity scope, but that usage is now rare.

Class Definition

```
public abstract class java.security.Signer
    extends java.security.Identity {

    // Constructors
    protected Signer();
    public Signer(String);
    public Signer(String, IdentityScope);

    // Instance Methods
    public PrivateKey getPrivateKey();
    public final void setKeyPair(KeyPair);
    public String toString();
}
```

See Also

Identity, Principal

Package java.security.cert

Class java.security.cert.Certificate

Description

The Certificate class represents any type of cryptographic certificate. A certificate contains a public key (see getPublicKey()) and other associated information. The certificate contains an internal signature that protects its integrity. You can verify the integrity of the certificate by calling one of the verify() methods with the public key of the certificate's issuer. (Note: don't confuse this class with the java.security.Certificate interface, which is deprecated.)

Class Definition

```
public abstract class java.security.cert.Certificate
    extends java.lang.Object {
```

```
    // Constructors
    public Certificate();

    // Instance Methods
    public boolean equals(Object);
    public abstract byte[] getEncoded();
    public abstract PublicKey getPublicKey();
    public int hashCode();
    public abstract String toString();
    public abstract void verify(PublicKey);
    public abstract void verify(PublicKey, String);
}
```

See Also

PublicKey, X509Certificate

Class java.security.cert.RevokedCertificate

Description

A RevokedCertificate represents a certificate whose contained key is no longer safe to use. Instances of this class are returned by X509CRL's getRevokedCertificate() method. You can examine the certificate's revocation date and X.509 extensions.

Class Definition

```
    public abstract class java.security.cert.RevokedCertificate
      extends java.lang.Object
      implements java.security.cert.X509Extension {

    // Constructors
    public RevokedCertificate();

    // Instance Methods
    public abstract Set getCriticalExtensionOIDs();
    public abstract byte[] getExtensionValue(String);
    public abstract Set getNonCriticalExtensionOIDs();
    public abstract Date getRevocationDate();
    public abstract BigInteger getSerialNumber();
    public abstract boolean hasExtensions();
    public abstract String toString();
}
```

See Also

Certificate, X509CRL, X509Extension

Class java.security.cert.X509Certificate

Description

This subclass of Certificate represents certificates as defined in the X.509 standard. Such certificates associate a public key with a *subject*, which is usually a person or organization. You can find out the certificate's subject by calling getSubjectDN(). You can retrieve the subject's public key using getPublicKey(), which is inherited from Certificate. The certificate's *issuer* is the person or organization that generated and signed the certificate (see getIssuerDN()).

If you have a certificate file in the format described by RFC 1421, you can create an X509Certificate from it using one of the getInstance() methods.

Class Definition

```
public abstract class java.security.cert.X509Certificate
    extends java.security.cert.Certificate
    implements java.security.cert.X509Extension {

    // Constructors
    public X509Certificate();

    // Class Methods
    public static final X509Certificate getInstance(InputStream);
    public static final X509Certificate getInstance(byte[]);

    // Instance Methods
    public abstract void checkValidity();
    public abstract void checkValidity(Date);
    public abstract int getBasicConstraints();
    public abstract Set getCriticalExtensionOIDs();
    public abstract byte[] getExtensionValue(String);
    public abstract Principal getIssuerDN();
    public abstract boolean[] getIssuerUniqueID();
    public abstract boolean[] getKeyUsage();
    public abstract Set getNonCriticalExtensionOIDs();
    public abstract Date getNotAfter();
    public abstract Date getNotBefore();
    public abstract BigInteger getSerialNumber();
    public abstract String getSigAlgName();
    public abstract String getSigAlgOID();
    public abstract byte[] getSigAlgParams();
    public abstract byte[] getSignature();
    public abstract Principal getSubjectDN();
    public abstract boolean[] getSubjectUniqueID();
    public abstract byte[] getTBSCertificate();
    public abstract int getVersion();
}
```

See Also

Principal, PublicKey, X509Extension

Class java.security.cert.X509CRL

Description

A Certificate Revocation List (CRL) is a list of certificates whose keys are no longer valid. This class represents CRLs as defined in the X.509 standard. If you have a CRL file you would like to examine, you can construct an X509CRL object from the file using one of the getInstance() factory methods. A CRL, just like a certificate, has an internal signature that protects its integrity. To verify the integrity of the CRL itself, call one of the verify() methods with the issuer's public key. To find out if a particular certificate is revoked, call isRevoked() with the certificate's serial number.

Class Definition

```
public abstract class java.security.cert.X509CRL
    extends java.lang.Object
    implements java.security.cert.X509Extension {

    // Constructors
    public X509CRL();

    // Class Methods
    public static final X509CRL getInstance(InputStream);
    public static final X509CRL getInstance(byte[]);

    // Instance Methods
    public boolean equals(Object);
    public abstract Set getCriticalExtensionOIDs();
    public abstract byte[] getEncoded();
    public abstract byte[] getExtensionValue(String);
    public abstract Principal getIssuerDN();
    public abstract Date getNextUpdate();
    public abstract Set getNonCriticalExtensionOIDs();
    public abstract RevokedCertificate getRevokedCertificate(BigInteger);
    public abstract Set getRevokedCertificates();
    public abstract String getSigAlgName();
    public abstract String getSigAlgOID();
    public abstract byte[] getSigAlgParams();
    public abstract byte[] getSignature();
    public abstract byte[] getTBSCertList();
    public abstract Date getThisUpdate();
    public abstract int getVersion();
```

```
    public int hashCode();
    public abstract boolean isRevoked(BigInteger);
    public abstract String toString();
    public abstract void verify(PublicKey);
    public abstract void verify(PublicKey, String);
}
```

See Also

Certificate, PublicKey, RevokedCertificate, X509Extension

Interface java.security.cert.X509Extension

Description

The X509Extension interface represents the certificate extensions defined by the X.509v3 standard. Extensions are additional bits of information contained in a certificate. Each extension is designated as critical or noncritical. An application that handles a certificate should either correctly interpret the critical extensions or produce some kind of error if they cannot be recognized.

Interface Definition

```
    public abstract interface java.security.cert.X509Extension {

    // Instance Methods
    public abstract Set getCriticalExtensionOIDs();
    public abstract byte[] getExtensionValue(String);
    public abstract Set getNonCriticalExtensionOIDs();
}
```

See Also

RevokedCertificate, X509Certificate, X509CRL

Package java.security.interfaces

Interface java.security.interfaces.DSAKey

Description

This interface represents public and private keys that are suitable for use in DSA signature algorithms. This interface allows you to retrieve DSA-specific information from a suitable DSA key.

Interface Definition

```
public interface java.security.interfaces.DSAKey {

    // Instance Methods
    public DSAParams getParams();
}
```

See Also

PrivateKey, PublicKey

Interface java.security.interfaces.DSAKeyPairGenerator

Description

This interface represents key generators that can be used to generate pairs of DSA keys. Key pair generators that implement this interface can be initialized with information specific to DSA key generation.

Interface Definition

```
public interface java.security.interfaces.DSAKeyPairGenerator {

    // Instance Methods
    public void initialize(DSAParams, SecureRandom);
    public void initialize(int, boolean, SecureRandom);
}
```

See Also

KeyPairGenerator

Interface java.security.interfaces.DSAParams

Description

Classes that implement this interface allow you to obtain the three variables that are common to both DSA public and private keys.

Interface Definition

```
public interface java.security.interfaces.DSAParams {

    // Instance Methods
    public BigInteger getP();
```

```
    public BigInteger getQ();
    public BigInteger getG();
}
```

See Also

DSAPrivateKey, DSAPublicKey

Interface java.security.interfaces.DSAPrivateKey

Description

Classes that implement this interface allow you to retrieve the private key parameter used to calculate a DSA private key.

Interface Definition

```
public interface java.security.interfaces.DSAPrivateKey {

    // Instance Methods
    public BigInteger getX();
}
```

See Also

DSAParams, DSAPublicKey

Interface java.security.interfaces.DSAPublicKey

Description

Classes that implement this interface allow you to retrieve the public key parameter used to calculate a DSA public key.

Interface Definition

```
public interface java.security.interfaces.DSAPublicKey {

    // Instance Methods
    public BigInteger getY();
}
```

See Also

DSAParams, DSAPrivateKey

Package java.security.spec

Interface java.security.spec.AlgorithmParameterSpec

Description

Algorithm parameter specifications are used to import and export keys via a key factory. This interface is used strictly for type identification; the specifics of the parameters are left to the implementing class.

Interface Definition

```
public interface java.security.spec.AlgorithmParameterSpec {
}
```

See Also

DSAParameterSpec, KeyFactory

Class java.security.spec.DSAParameterSpec

Description

This class provides the basis for DSA key generation via parameters; it encapsulates the three parameters that are common to DSA algorithms.

Class Definition

```
public class java.security.spec.DSAParameterSpec
    extends java.lang.Object
    implements java.security.spec.AlgorithmParameterSpec,
        java.security.interfaces.DSAParams {

    // Constructors
    public DSAParameterSpec(BigInteger, BigInteger, BigInteger);

    // Instance Methods
    public BigInteger getG();
    public BigInteger getP();
    public BigInteger getQ();
}
```

See Also

AlgorithmParameterSpec, DSAParams, DSAPrivateKeySpec, DSAPublicKey-Spec

Class java.security.spec.DSAPrivateKeySpec

Description

This class provides the ability to calculate a DSA private key based on the four parameters that constitute the key.

Class Definition

```
public class java.security.spec.DSAPrivateKeySpec
    extends java.lang.Object
    implements java.security.spec.KeySpec {

    // Constructors
    public DSAPrivateKeySpec(BigInteger, BigInteger,
                BigInteger, BigInteger);

    // Instance Methods
    public BigInteger getG();
    public BigInteger getP();
    public BigInteger getQ();
    public BigInteger getX();
}
```

See Also

DSAPublicKeySpec, KeyFactory

Class java.security.spec.DSAPublicKeySpec

Description

This class provides the ability to calculate a DSA public key based on the four parameters that constitute the key.

Class Definition

```
public class java.security.spec.DSAPublicKeySpec
    extends java.lang.Object
    implements java.security.spec.KeySpec {

    // Constructors
    public DSAPublicKeySpec(BigInteger, BigInteger,
                BigInteger, BigInteger);

    // Instance Methods
    public BigInteger getG();
```

```
    public BigInteger getP();
    public BigInteger getQ();
    public BigInteger getY();
}
```

See Also

DSAPrivateKeySpec, KeyFactory

Class java.security.spec.EncodedKeySpec

Description

This class is used to translate between keys and their external encoded format. The encoded format is always simply a series of bytes, but the format of the encoding of the key information into those bytes may vary depending on the algorithm used to generate the key.

Class Definition

```
public abstract class java.security.spec.EncodedKeySpec
    extends java.lang.Object
    implements java.security.spec.KeySpec {

    // Constructors
    public EncodedKeySpec();

    // Instance Methods
    public abstract byte[] getEncoded();
    public abstract String getFormat();
}
```

See Also

KeyFactory, KeySpec, PKCS8EncodedKeySpec, X509EncodedKeySpec

Interface java.security.spec.KeySpec

Description

A key specification is used to import and export keys via a key factory. This may be done either based on the algorithm parameters used to generate the key or via an encoded series of bytes that represent the key. Classes that deal with the latter case implement this interface, which is used strictly for type identification.

Interface Definition

```
public abstract interface java.security.spec.KeySpec {
}
```

See Also

AlgorithmParameterSpec, EncodedKeySpec, KeyFactory

Class java.security.spec.PKCS8EncodedKeySpec

Description

This class represents the PKCS#8 encoding of a private key; the key is encoded in DER format. This is the class that is typically used when dealing with DSA private keys in a key factory.

Class Definition

```
public class java.security.spec.PKCS8EncodedKeySpec
  extends java.security.spec.EncodedKeySpec {

  // Constructors
  public PKCS8EncodedKeySpec(byte[]);

  // Instance Methods
  public byte[] getEncoded();
  public final String getFormat();
}
```

See Also

EncodedKeySpec, X509EncodedKeySpec

Class java.security.spec.X509EncodedKeySpec

Description

This class represents the X509 encoding of a public key. It may also be used for private keys although the PKCS#8 encoding is typically used for those keys.

Class Definition

```
public class java.security.spec.X509EncodedKeySpec
  extends java.security.spec.EncodedKeySpec {
```

```
    // Constructors
    public X509EncodedKeySpec(byte[]);

    // Instance Methods
    public byte[] getEncoded();
    public final String getFormat();
}
```

See Also

EncodedKeySpec, PKCS8EncodedKeySpec

Package javax.crypto

Class javax.crypto.Cipher

Description

This class represents a cryptographic cipher, either symmetric or asymmetric. To get a cipher for a particular algorithm, call one of the getInstance() methods. You should specify an algorithm name, a cipher mode, and a padding scheme. The cipher should be initialized for encryption or decryption using the init() method and an appropriate key. To actually perform the encryption or decryption, use update() and doFinal(). The following example shows how to encrypt plaintext using a DES cipher in ECB mode with PKCS#5 padding:

```
public byte[] simpleEncrypt(byte[] plaintext, Key key) throws Exception
{
    Cipher cipher = Cipher.getInstance("DES/ECB/PKCS5Padding");
    cipher.init(Cipher.ENCRYPT_MODE, key);
    byte[] ciphertext = cipher.doFinal(stringBytes);
    return ciphertext;
}
```

Class Definition

```
public class javax.crypto.Cipher
    extends java.lang.Object {

    // Constants
    public static final int DECRYPT_MODE;
    public static final int ENCRYPT_MODE;

    // Constructors
    protected Cipher(CipherSpi, Provider, String);

    // Class Methods
```

```
    public static final Cipher getInstance(String);
    public static final Cipher getInstance(String, String);

    // Instance Methods
    public final byte[] doFinal();
    public final byte[] doFinal(byte[]);
    public final int doFinal(byte[], int);
    public final byte[] doFinal(byte[], int, int);
    public final int doFinal(byte[], int, int, byte[]);
    public final int doFinal(byte[], int, int, byte[], int);
    public final int getBlockSize();
    public final byte[] getIV();
    public final int getOutputSize(int);
    public final Provider getProvider();
    public final void init(int, Key);
    public final void init(int, Key, SecureRandom);
    public final void init(int, Key, AlgorithmParameterSpec);
    public final void init(int, Key, AlgorithmParameterSpec,
        SecureRandom);
    public final byte[] update(byte[]);
    public final byte[] update(byte[], int, int);
    public final int update(byte[], int, int, byte[]);
    public final int update(byte[], int, int, byte[], int);
}
```

See Also

AlgorithmParameterSpec, CipherSpi, Key, Provider, SecureRandom

Class javax.crypto.CipherInputStream

Description

A CipherInputStream is a subclass of java.io.FilterInputStream that passes
its data through a Cipher. You can construct a CipherInputStream by specifying
an underlying stream and supplying an initialized Cipher.

Class Definition

```
    public class javax.crypto.CipherInputStream
      extends java.io.FilterInputStream {

      // Constructors
      protected CipherInputStream(InputStream);
      public CipherInputStream(InputStream, Cipher);

      // Instance Methods
      public int available();
      public void close();
```

```
        public boolean markSupported();
        public int read();
        public int read(byte[]);
        public int read(byte[], int, int);
        public long skip(long);
    }
```

See Also

Cipher

Class javax.crypto.CipherOutputStream

Description

This class is a subclass of `java.io.FilterOutputStream` that passes all its data through a `Cipher`. You can construct a `CipherOutputStream` by specifying an underlying stream and an initialized `Cipher`.

Class Definition

```
    public class javax.crypto.CipherOutputStream
        extends java.io.FilterOutputStream {

        // Constructors
        protected CipherOutputStream(OutputStream);
        public CipherOutputStream(OutputStream, Cipher);

        // Instance Methods
        public void close();
        public void flush();
        public void write(int);
        public void write(byte[]);
        public void write(byte[], int, int);
    }
```

See Also

Cipher

Class javax.crypto.CipherSpi

Description

The `CipherSpi` class is the parent class of all cipher implementations. To implement a particular cipher algorithm, create a subclass of `CipherSpi` and define all its methods. Most of the methods correspond to methods in `Cipher`'s API; for example, a call to `Cipher`'s `getBlockSize()` method results in a call to the implementation's `engineGetBlockSize()`.

Class Definition

```
public abstract class javax.crypto.CipherSpi
  extends java.lang.Object {

  // Constructors
  public CipherSpi();

  // Protected Instance Methods
  protected abstract byte[] engineDoFinal(byte[], int, int);
  protected abstract int engineDoFinal(byte[], int, int, byte[], int);
  protected abstract int engineGetBlockSize();
  protected abstract byte[] engineGetIV();
  protected abstract int engineGetOutputSize(int);
  protected abstract void engineInit(int, Key, SecureRandom);
  protected abstract void engineInit(int, Key, AlgorithmParameterSpec,
    SecureRandom);
  protected abstract void engineSetMode(String);
  protected abstract void engineSetPadding(String);
  protected abstract byte[] engineUpdate(byte[], int, int);
  protected abstract int engineUpdate(byte[], int, int, byte[], int);
}
```

See Also

AlgorithmParameterSpec, Cipher, Key, SecureRandom

Class javax.crypto.KeyAgreement

Description

This class represents a *key agreement protocol*, which is an arrangement by which two parties can agree on a secret value. You can obtain an instance of this class by calling `getInstance()`. Once the `KeyAgreement` is initialized (see `init()`), you can step through the phases of the key agreement protocol using `doPhase()`. Once the phases are complete, the secret value is returned from `generateSecret()`.

Class Definition

```
public class javax.crypto.KeyAgreement
  extends java.lang.Object {

  // Constructors
```

```
    protected KeyAgreement(KeyAgreementSpi, Provider, String);

    // Class Methods
    public static final KeyAgreement getInstance(String);
    public static final KeyAgreement getInstance(String, String);

    // Instance Methods
    public final Key doPhase(Key, boolean);
    public final byte[] generateSecret();
    public final int generateSecret(byte[], int);
    public final SecretKey generateSecret(String);
    public final String getAlgorithm();
    public final Provider getProvider();
    public final void init(Key);
    public final void init(Key, SecureRandom);
    public final void init(Key, AlgorithmParameterSpec);
    public final void init(Key, AlgorithmParameterSpec, SecureRandom);
}
```

See Also

AlgorithmParameterSpec, Key, KeyAgreementSpi, Provider, SecureRandom

Class javax.crypto.KeyAgreementSpi

Description

KeyAgreementSpi is the superclass of all key agreement protocol implementations. If you want to implement a key agreement algorithm, create a subclass of KeyAgreementSpi and define all of its methods.

Class Definition

```
    public abstract class javax.crypto.KeyAgreementSpi
      extends java.lang.Object {

    // Constructors
    public KeyAgreementSpi();

    // Protected Instance Methods
    protected abstract Key engineDoPhase(Key, boolean);
    protected abstract byte[] engineGenerateSecret();
    protected abstract int engineGenerateSecret(byte[], int);
    protected abstract SecretKey engineGenerateSecret(String);
    protected abstract void engineInit(Key, SecureRandom);
    protected abstract void engineInit(Key, AlgorithmParameterSpec,
        SecureRandom);
}
```

See Also

AlgorithmParameterSpec, Key, KeyAgreement, SecureRandom

Class javax.crypto.KeyGenerator

Description

A KeyGenerator creates random keys for use with symmetric ciphers. To obtain a KeyGenerator, call getInstance() with an algorithm name. Then initialize the KeyGenerator by calling one of the init() methods. To create a new random key, call generateKey(). The following example shows how to create a random key for a DES cipher:

```
KeyGenerator kg = KeyGenerator.getInstance("DES");
kg.init(new SecureRandom());
SecretKey key = kg.generateKey();
```

Class Definition

```
public class javax.crypto.KeyGenerator
  extends java.lang.Object {

  // Constructors
  protected KeyGenerator(KeyGeneratorSpi, Provider, String);

  // Class Methods
  public static final KeyGenerator getInstance(String);
  public static final KeyGenerator getInstance(String, String);

  // Instance Methods
  public final SecretKey generateKey();
  public final String getAlgorithm();
  public final Provider getProvider();
  public final void init(int);
  public final void init(int, SecureRandom);
  public final void init(SecureRandom);
  public final void init(AlgorithmParameterSpec);
  public final void init(AlgorithmParameterSpec, SecureRandom);
}
```

See Also

AlgorithmParameterSpec, KeyGeneratorSpi, Provider, SecretKey, Secure-Random

Class javax.crypto.KeyGeneratorSpi

Description

KeyGenerator implementations descend from KeyGeneratorSpi. To create an implementation of a key generation algorithm, make a subclass of KeyGeneratorSpi and define each of its methods.

Class Definition

```
public abstract class javax.crypto.KeyGeneratorSpi
  extends java.lang.Object {

  // Constructors
  public KeyGeneratorSpi();

  // Protected Instance Methods
  protected abstract SecretKey engineGenerateKey();
  protected abstract void engineInit(int, SecureRandom);
  protected abstract void engineInit(SecureRandom);
  protected abstract void engineInit(AlgorithmParameterSpec,
      SecureRandom);
}
```

See Also

AlgorithmParameterSpec, KeyGenerator, SecretKey, SecureRandom

Class javax.crypto.NullCipher

Description

As its name implies, NullCipher is a Cipher that does nothing. You can use it to test cryptographic programs. Because NullCipher performs no transformations, its ciphertext will be exactly the same as its plaintext.

Class Definition

```
public class javax.crypto.NullCipher
  extends javax.crypto.Cipher {

  // Constructors
  public NullCipher();
}
```

See Also

Cipher

Class javax.crypto.SealedObject

Description

A SealedObject is a container for another object. The contained object is encrypted using a Cipher. You can construct a SealedObject using any Serializable object and a Cipher that is initialized for encryption. To decrypt the contained object, call getObject() with a Cipher that is initialized for decryption.

Class Definition

```
public class javax.crypto.SealedObject
    extends java.lang.Object
    implements java.io.Serializable {

    // Constructors
    public SealedObject(Serializable, Cipher);

    // Instance Methods
    public final Object getObject(Cipher);
}
```

See Also

PublicKey, PrivateKey

Interface javax.crypto.SecretKey

Description

SecretKey is a semantic extension to the java.security.Key interface. It represents a key that is used with a symmetric cipher.

Interface Definition

```
public abstract interface javax.crypto.SecretKey
    implements java.security.Key {
}
```

See Also

Key

Class javax.crypto.SecretKeyFactory

Description

A `SecretKeyFactory` is used to convert between secret key data formats. For example, you might use a `SecretKeyFactory` to convert a DES `SecretKey` into an array of bytes, or to some other representation (a `KeySpec`). Similarly, a `Secret-KeyFactory` can translate from a `KeySpec` to a `SecretKey`. As usual, you can obtain a `SecretKeyFactory` for a particular algorithm by calling `getInstance()`. You can translate from a `SecretKey` to a `KeySpec` using `translateKey()`. If you want to create a `SecretKey` from a corresponding `KeySpec`, use `generateSecret()`.

Class Definition

```
public class javax.crypto.SecretKeyFactory
    extends java.lang.Object {

    // Constructors
    protected SecretKeyFactory(SecretKeyFactorySpi, Provider, String);

    // Class Methods
    public static final SecretKeyFactory getInstance(String);
    public static final SecretKeyFactory getInstance(String, String);

    // Instance Methods
    public final SecretKey generateSecret(KeySpec);
    public final String getAlgorithm();
    public final KeySpec getKeySpec(SecretKey, Class);
    public final Provider getProvider();
    public final SecretKey translateKey(SecretKey);
}
```

See Also

KeySpec, Provider, SecretKey, SecretKeyFactorySpi

Class javax.crypto.SecretKeyFactorySpi

Description

This class represents the implementation of a `SecretKeyFactory`. To create such an implementation, make a subclass of `SecretKeyFactorySpi` and define each of its methods.

Class Definition

```
public abstract class javax.crypto.SecretKeyFactorySpi
  extends java.lang.Object {

  // Constructors
  public SecretKeyFactorySpi();

  // Protected Instance Methods
  protected abstract SecretKey engineGenerateSecret(KeySpec);
  protected abstract KeySpec engineGetKeySpec(SecretKey, Class);
  protected abstract SecretKey engineTranslateKey(SecretKey);
}
```

See Also

KeySpec, SecretKey, SecretKeyFactory

Package javax.crypto.interfaces

Interface javax.crypto.interfaces.DHKey

Description

This interface represents a key used in the Diffie-Hellman KeyAgreement implementation.

Interface Definition

```
public abstract interface javax.crypto.interfaces.DHKey {

  // Instance Methods
  public abstract DHParameterSpec getParams();
}
```

See Also

DHPrivateKey, DHPublicKey

Interface javax.crypto.interfaces.DHPrivateKey

Description

This interface represents a private key in a Diffie-Hellman key agreement protocol.

Interface Definition

```
public abstract interface javax.crypto.interfaces.DHPrivateKey
    implements javax.crypto.interfaces.DHKey, java.security.PrivateKey {

    // Instance Methods
    public abstract BigInteger getX();
}
```

See Also

DHKey, DHPublicKey, PrivateKey

Interface javax.crypto.interfaces.DHPublicKey

Description

This interface represents a public key in a Diffie-Hellman key agreement protocol. The public key value, y, is calculated from the private key value, x.

Interface Definition

```
public abstract interface javax.crypto.interfaces.DHPublicKey
    implements javax.crypto.interfaces.DHKey, java.security.PublicKey {

    // Instance Methods
    public abstract BigInteger getY();
}
```

See Also

DHKey, DHPrivateKey, PublicKey

Interface javax.crypto.interfaces.RSAPrivateKey

Description

RSAPrivateKey represents a private key, suitable for use with an RSA asymmetric cipher. Although the JCE does not support RSA, you can buy third-party implementations of RSA that plug in to the provider architecture. This interface is the traditional representation of an RSA private key, which consists of a modulus and a private exponent.

Interface Definition

```
public abstract interface javax.crypto.interfaces.RSAPrivateKey
    implements java.security.PrivateKey {
```

```
    // Instance Methods
    public abstract BigInteger getModulus();
    public abstract BigInteger getPrivateExponent();
}
```

See Also

PrivateKey, RSAPublicKey

Interface javax.crypto.interfaces.RSAPrivateKeyCrt

Description

This interface is an alternate representation of an RSA private key. It uses the Chinese Remainder Theorem (CRT) to represent the values of the private key.

Interface Definition

```
public abstract interface javax.crypto.interfaces.RSAPrivateKeyCrt
    implements javax.crypto.interfaces.RSAPrivateKey {

    // Instance Methods
    public abstract BigInteger getCrtCoefficient();
    public abstract BigInteger getPrimeExponentP();
    public abstract BigInteger getPrimeExponentQ();
    public abstract BigInteger getPrimeP();
    public abstract BigInteger getPrimeQ();
    public abstract BigInteger getPublicExponent();
}
```

See Also

PrivateKey, RSAPrivateKey, RSAPublicKey

Interface javax.crypto.interfaces.RSAPublicKey

Description

RSAPublicKey represents a public key, suitable for use with an RSA asymmetric cipher. This interface is the traditional representation of an RSA public key, which consists of a modulus and a public exponent.

Interface Definition

```
public abstract interface javax.crypto.interfaces.RSAPublicKey
    implements java.security.PublicKey {
```

```
// Instance Methods
public abstract BigInteger getModulus();
public abstract BigInteger getPublicExponent();
}
```

See Also

PublicKey, RSAPrivateKey

Package javax.crypto.spec

Class javax.crypto.spec.DESKeySpec

Description

This class represents a key that is used with a DES symmetric cipher. This class is useful for converting between byte arrays and DES SecretKeys:

- To convert from a byte array to a SecretKey, construct a DESKeySpec from the byte array. Then use SecretKeyFactory's generateSecret() to create the SecretKey.

- To convert from a DES SecretKey to a DESKeySpec, give the SecretKey to SecretKeyFactory's translateKey().

Class Definition

```
public class javax.crypto.spec.DESKeySpec
   extends java.lang.Object
   implements java.security.spec.KeySpec {

   // Constructors
   public DESKeySpec(byte[]);
   public DESKeySpec(byte[], int);

   // Class Methods
   public static boolean isParityAdjusted(byte[], int);
   public static boolean isWeak(byte[], int);

   // Instance Methods
   public byte[] getKey();
}
```

See Also

SecretKeyFactory

Class javax.crypto.spec.DESedeKeySpec

Description

This class represents a DESede key. It can be used with a `SecretKeyFactory` to translate between DESede `SecretKeys` and byte arrays.

Class Definition

```
public class javax.crypto.spec.DESedeKeySpec
    extends java.lang.Object
    implements java.security.spec.KeySpec {

    // Constructors
    public DESedeKeySpec(byte[]);
    public DESedeKeySpec(byte[], int);

    // Class Methods
    public static boolean isParityAdjusted(byte[], int);

    // Instance Methods
    public byte[] getKey();
}
```

See Also

`SecretKeyFactory`

Class javax.crypto.spec.DHGenParameterSpec

Description

Instances of this class may be passed to the algorithm-specific initialization methods of `AlgorithmParameterGenerator`.

Class Definition

```
public class javax.crypto.spec.DHGenParameterSpec
    extends java.lang.Object
    implements java.security.spec.AlgorithmParameterSpec {

    // Constructors
    public DHGenParameterSpec(int, int);

    // Instance Methods
    public int getExponentSize();
```

```
    public int getPrimeSize();
}
```

See Also

AlgorithmParameterGenerator, AlgorithmParameterSpec

Class javax.crypto.spec.DHParameterSpec

Description

This class encapsulates the public parameters used in the Diffie-Hellman key agreement protocol. Typically, an application uses a standard modulus and base to generate Diffie-Hellman keys. This class encapsulates the modulus (getP()) and the base (getG()). Instances of this class can be passed to the algorithm-specific initialization methods of KeyPairGenerator.

Class Definition

```
public class javax.crypto.spec.DHParameterSpec
    extends java.lang.Object
    implements java.security.spec.AlgorithmParameterSpec {

    // Constructors
    public DHParameterSpec(BigInteger, BigInteger);
    public DHParameterSpec(BigInteger, BigInteger, int);

    // Instance Methods
    public BigInteger getG();
    public int getL();
    public BigInteger getP();
}
```

See Also

AlgorithmParameterSpec, KeyPairGenerator

Class javax.crypto.spec.DHPrivateKeySpec

Description

This class represents a private key for the Diffie-Hellman key agreement protocol. It can be used with a KeyFactory to convert between Diffie-Hellman parameters and PrivateKeys.

Class Definition

```
public class javax.crypto.spec.DHPrivateKeySpec
   extends java.lang.Object
   implements java.security.spec.KeySpec {

   // Constructors
   public DHPrivateKeySpec(BigInteger, BigInteger, BigInteger);
   public DHPrivateKeySpec(BigInteger, BigInteger, BigInteger, int);

   // Instance Methods
   public BigInteger getG();
   public int getL();
   public BigInteger getP();
   public BigInteger getX();
}
```

See Also

DHParameterSpec, DHPublicKeySpec, KeySpec

Class javax.crypto.spec.DHPublicKeySpec

Description

This class represents a public key for the Diffie-Hellman key agreement protocol. It can be used with a KeyFactory to convert between Diffie-Hellman parameters and PublicKeys.

Class Definition

```
public class javax.crypto.spec.DHPublicKeySpec
   extends java.lang.Object
   implements java.security.spec.KeySpec {

   // Constructors
   public DHPublicKeySpec(BigInteger, BigInteger, BigInteger);
   public DHPublicKeySpec(BigInteger, BigInteger, BigInteger, int);

   // Instance Methods
   public BigInteger getG();
   public int getL();
   public BigInteger getP();
   public BigInteger getY();
}
```

See Also

DHParameterSpec, DHPrivateKeySpec, KeySpec

Class javax.crypto.spec.IvParameterSpec

Description

This class represents an IV for a cipher that uses a feedback mode. Ciphers in CBC, PCBC, CFB, and OFB modes need to be initialized with an IV. This object can be passed to Cipher's algorithm-specific initialization methods.

Class Definition

```
public class javax.crypto.spec.IvParameterSpec
   extends java.lang.Object
   implements java.security.spec.AlgorithmParameterSpec {

   // Constructors
   public IvParameterSpec(byte[]);
   public IvParameterSpec(byte[], int, int);

   // Instance Methods
   public byte[] getIV();
}
```

See Also

AlgorithmParameterSpec, Cipher

Class javax.crypto.spec.PBEKeySpec

Description

This class represents a key that is used with passphrase encryption. The JCE includes an implementation of this technique whose name is PBEWithMD5AndDES. To create a secret key from a passphrase, do something like this:

```
KeySpec ks = new PBEKeySpec(passphrase);
SecretKeyFactory skf =
SecretKeyFactory.getInstance("PBEWithMD5AndDES");
SecretKey key = skf.generateSecret(ks);
```

Class Definition

```
public class javax.crypto.spec.PBEKeySpec
   extends java.lang.Object
   implements java.security.spec.KeySpec {
```

```
    // Constructors
    public PBEKeySpec(String);

    // Instance Methods
    public final String getPassword();
}
```

See Also

PBEParameterSpec, SecretKey, SecretKeyFactory

Class javax.crypto.spec.PBEParameterSpec

Description

This class encapsulates the salt and iteration count that are used in passphrase-based encryption. Instances of this class should be used to initialize a PBEWithMD5AndDES Cipher.

Class Definition

```
    public class javax.crypto.spec.PBEParameterSpec
      extends java.lang.Object
      implements java.security.spec.AlgorithmParameterSpec {

      // Constructors
      public PBEParameterSpec(byte[], int);

      // Instance Methods
      public int getIterationCount();
      public byte[] getSalt();
    }
```

See Also

AlgorithmParameterSpec, Cipher, PBEKeySpec

Class javax.crypto.spec.RSAPrivateKeyCrtSpec

Description

This class represents a private key for the RSA cipher algorithm, specified using the Chinese Remainder Theorem (CRT). Instances of this class may be used with an appropriate KeyFactory to generate PrivateKeys. Because the JCE does not support RSA, you'll have to buy a third-party implementation.

Class Definition

```
public class javax.crypto.spec.RSAPrivateKeyCrtSpec
  extends javax.crypto.spec.RSAPrivateKeySpec {

  // Constructors
  public RSAPrivateKeyCrtSpec(BigInteger, BigInteger, BigInteger,
    BigInteger, BigInteger, BigInteger, BigInteger, BigInteger);

  // Instance Methods
  public BigInteger getCrtCoefficient();
  public BigInteger getPrimeExponentP();
  public BigInteger getPrimeExponentQ();
  public BigInteger getPrimeP();
  public BigInteger getPrimeQ();
  public BigInteger getPublicExponent();
}
```

See Also

KeyFactory, KeySpec, PrivateKey, RSAPrivateKeySpec

Class javax.crypto.spec.RSAPrivateKeySpec

Description

This class represents a private key for the RSA cipher algorithm, specified as a modulus and a private exponent. Instances of this class may be used with an appropriate KeyFactory to generate PrivateKeys.

Class Definition

```
public class javax.crypto.spec.RSAPrivateKeySpec
  extends java.lang.Object
  implements java.security.spec.KeySpec {

  // Constructors
  public RSAPrivateKeySpec(BigInteger, BigInteger);

  // Instance Methods
  public BigInteger getModulus();
  public BigInteger getPrivateExponent();
}
```

See Also

KeyFactory, KeySpec, PrivateKey, RSAPrivateKeyCrtSpec

Class javax.crypto.spec.RSAPublicKeySpec

Description

This class represents a public key for the RSA cipher algorithm, specified as a modulus and a public exponent. Instances of this class may be used with an appropriate KeyFactory to generate PublicKeys.

Class Definition

```
public class javax.crypto.spec.RSAPublicKeySpec
  extends java.lang.Object
  implements java.security.spec.KeySpec {

  // Constructors
  public RSAPublicKeySpec(BigInteger, BigInteger);

  // Instance Methods
  public BigInteger getModulus();
  public BigInteger getPublicExponent();
}
```

See Also

KeyFactory, KeySpec, PublicKey

Index

About the Author

Jonathan Knudsen is a staff writer for O'Reilly & Associates, a job that allows him to exercise the right and left sides of his brain but little of his body. In 1977, when Jonathan was knee-high to a grasshopper, he began his computer career by programming in BASIC on a TRS-80. In 1993 he graduated cum laude from Princeton with a degree in mechanical engineering. Jonathan is still unsure what mechanical engineers do for a living. His current interests include embedded system MIDI programming, Java Sound, and user interface design. He is coauthor of the *Java Fundamental Classes Reference* and writes a column for *Sun Server*.

Jonathan lives in New Jersey with his wife and technical advisor, Kristen, his children, Daphne and Luke, and two black and white cats. In his spare time he enjoys playing the piano and bicycling.

Colophon

Our look is the result of reader comments, our own experimentation, and feedback from distribution channels. Distinctive covers complement our distinctive approach to technical topics, breathing personality and life into potentially dry subjects.

Hanna Dyer designed the cover of this book, based on a series design by Edie Freedman. The image was photographed by Kevin Thomas and manipulated by Michael Snow using Adobe Photoshop 3.0 and Adobe Gallery Effects filters. The cover layout was produced with Quark XPress 3.3 using the Bodoni Black font from URW Software and bt bodoni Bold Italic from Bitstream. The inside layout was designed by Nancy Priest and implemented by Mike Sierra in FrameMaker 5.0. The heading font is Bodoni BT; the text font is New Baskerville. The screen shots that appear in the book were created in Adobe Photoshop 4, and the illustrations were created in Macromedia Freehand 7.0 by Robert Romano.

Whenever possible, our books use RepKover™, a durable and flexible lay-flat binding. If the page count exceeds RepKover's limit, perfect binding is used.

More Titles from O'Reilly

Java

Java Message Service

By Richard Monson-Haefel & David Chappell
1st Edition December 2000
240 pages, ISBN 0-596-00068-5

This book is a thorough introduction to Java Message Service (JMS) from Sun Microsystems. It shows how to build applications using the point-to-point and publish-and-subscribe models; use features like transactions and durable subscriptions to make applications reliable; and use messaging within Enterprise JavaBeans. It also introduces a new EJB type, the MessageDrivenBean, that is part of EJB 2.0, and discusses integration of messaging into J2EE.

Java Distributed Computing

By Jim Farley
1st Edition January 1998
384 pages, ISBN 1-56592-206-9

Java Distributed Computing offers a general introduction to distributed computing, meaning programs that run on two or more systems. It focuses primarily on how to structure and write distributed applications and discusses issues like designing protocols, security, working with databases, and dealing with low bandwidth situations.

Java Network Programming, 2nd Edition

By Elliotte Rusty Harold
2nd Edition August 2000
760 pages, ISBN 1-56592-870-9

Java Network Programming, 2nd Edition, is a complete introduction to developing network programs (both applets and applications) using Java, covering everything from networking fundamentals to remote method invocation (RMI). It includes chapters on TCP and UDP sockets, multicasting protocol and content handlers, and servlets. This second edition also includes coverage of Java 1.1, 1.2 and 1.3. New chapters cover multithreaded network programming, I/O, HTML parsing and display, the Java Mail API, the Java Secure Sockets Extension, and more.

Java Security

By Scott Oaks
1st Edition May 1998
474 pages, ISBN 1-56592-403-7

This essential Java 2 book covers Java's security mechanisms and teaches you how to work with them. It discusses class loaders, security managers, access lists, digital signatures, and authentication and shows how to use these to create and enforce your own security policy.

Java Threads, 2nd Edition

By Scott Oaks & Henry Wong
2nd Edition January 1999
336 pages, ISBN 1-56592-418-5

Revised and expanded to cover Java 2, Java Threads, 2nd Edition shows you how to take full advantage of Java's thread facilities: where to use threads to increase efficiency, how to use them effectively, and how to avoid common mistakes. It thoroughly covers the Thread and ThreadGroup classes, the Runnable interface, and the language's synchronized operator. The book pays special attention to threading issues with Swing, as well as problems like deadlock, race condition, and starvation to help you write code without hidden bugs.

Database Programming with JDBC and Java, 2nd Edition

By George Reese
2nd Edition August 2000
352 pages, ISBN 1-56592-616-1

This book describes the standard Java interfaces that make portable object-oriented access to relational databases possible, and offers a robust model for writing applications that are easy to maintain. The second edition has been completely updated for JDBC 2.0, and includes reference listings for JDBC and the most important RMI classes. The book begins with a quick overview of SQL for developers who may be asked to handle a database for the first time, and goes on to explain how to issue database queries and updates through SQL and JDBC.

O'REILLY®

TO ORDER: **800-998-9938** • *order@oreilly.com* • *http://www.oreilly.com/*
OUR PRODUCTS ARE AVAILABLE AT A BOOKSTORE OR SOFTWARE STORE NEAR YOU.
FOR INFORMATION: **800-998-9938** • **707-829-0515** • *info@oreilly.com*

Java

Creating Effective JavaHelp

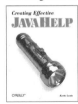

By Kevin Lewis
1st Edition June 2000
188 pages, ISBN 1-56592-719-2

JavaHelp is an online help system developed in the Java™ programming language. *Creating Effective JavaHelp* covers the main features and options of JavaHelp and shows how to create a basic JavaHelp system, prepare help topics, and deploy the help system in an application. Written for all levels of Java developers and technical writers, the book takes a chapter-by-chapter approach to building concepts, to impart a complete understanding of how to create usable JavaHelp systems and integrate them into Java applications and applets.

Developing Java Beans

By Robert Englander
1st Edition June 1997
316 pages, ISBN 1-56592-289-1

Developing Java Beans is a complete introduction to Java's component architecture. It describes how to write Beans, which are software components that can be used in visual programming environments. This book discusses event adapters, serialization, introspection, property editors, and customizers, and shows how to use Beans within ActiveX controls.

Java Internationalization

By Andy Deitsch & David Czarnecki
1st Edition March 2001 (est.)
350 pages (est.), ISBN 0-596-00019-7

Java Internationalization shows how to write software that is truly multi-lingual, using Java's very sophisticated Unicode internationalization facilities. *Java Internationalization* brings Java developers up to speed for the new generation of software development: writing software that is no longer limited by language boundaries.

Java Performance Tuning

By Jack Shirazi
1st Edition September 2000
440 pages, ISBN 0-596-00015-4

Java Performance Tuning contains step-by-step instructions on all aspects of the performance tuning process, right from such early considerations as setting goals, measuring performance, and choosing a compiler. Extensive examples for tuning many parts of an application are described in detail, and any pitfalls are identified. The book also provides performance tuning checklists that enable developers to make their tuning as comprehensive as possible.

Learning Java

By Pat Niemeyer & Jonathan Knudsen
1st Edition, May 2000
726 pages, Includes CD-ROM
ISBN 1-56592-718-4

For programmers either just migrating to Java or already working steadily in the forefront of Java development, *Learning Java* gives a clear, systematic overview of the Java 2 Standard Edition. It covers the essentials of hot topics like Swing and JFC; describes new tools for signing applets; and shows how to write networked clients and servers, servlets, JavaBeans, and state-of-the-art user interfaces. Includes a CD-ROM containing the Java 2 SDK, version 1.3.

Enterprise JavaBeans, 2nd Edition

By Richard Monson-Haefel
2nd Edition March 2000
492 pages, ISBN 1-56592-869-5

Enterprise JavaBeans, 2nd Edition provides a thorough introduction to EJB 1.1 and 1.0 for the enterprise software developer. It shows you how to develop enterprise Beans to model your business objects and processes. The EJB architecture provides a highly flexible system in which components can easily be reused, and which can be changed to suit your needs without upsetting other parts of the system. *Enterprise JavaBeans* teaches you how to take advantage of the flexibility and simplicity that this powerful new architecture provides.

Java

Java Servlet Programming

By Jason Hunter with William Crawford
1st Edition November 1998
528 pages, ISBN 1-56592-391-X

Java servlets offer a fast, powerful, portable replacement for CGI scripts. *Java Servlet Programming* covers everything you need to know to write effective servlets. Topics include: serving dynamic Web content, maintaining state information, session tracking, database connectivity using JDBC, and applet-servlet communication.

JavaServer Pages

By Hans Bergsten
1st Edition December 2000
572 pages, ISBN 1-56592-746-X

JavaServer Pages shows how to develop Java-based web applications without having to be a hardcore programmer. The author provides an overview of JSP concepts and illuminates how JSP fits into the larger picture of web applications. There are chapters for web authors on generating dynamic content, handling session information, and accessing databases, as well as material for Java programmers on creating Java components and custom JSP tags for web authors to use in JSP pages.

Java and XML

By Brett McLaughlin
1st Edition June 2000
498 pages, ISBN 0-596-00016-2

Java revolutionized the programming world by providing a platform-independent programming language. XML takes the revolution a step further with platform-independent language for interchanging data. *Java and XML* shows how to put the two together, building real-world applications in which both the code and the data are truly portable.

The Java Enterprise CD Bookshelf

By O'Reilly & Associates, Inc.
1st Edition December 2000
622 pages, Features CD-ROM
ISBN 1-56592-850-4

The Java Enterprise CD Bookshelf contains a powerhouse of books from O'Reilly: both electronic and print versions of *Java Enterprise in a Nutshell*, plus electronic versions of *Java in a Nutshell, 3rd Edition*; *Java Foundation Classes in a Nutshell*; *Enterprise JavaBeans, 2nd Edition*; *Java Servlet Programming*; *Java Security*; and *Java Distributed Computing*.

How to stay in touch with O'Reilly

1. Visit Our Award-Winning Web Site

http://www.oreilly.com/

★ "Top 100 Sites on the Web" —*PC Magazine*
★ "Top 5% Web sites" —*Point Communications*
★ "3-Star site" —*The McKinley Group*

Our web site contains a library of comprehensive product information (including book excerpts and tables of contents), downloadable software, background articles, interviews with technology leaders, links to relevant sites, book cover art, and more. File us in your Bookmarks or Hotlist!

2. Join Our Email Mailing Lists

New Product Releases

To receive automatic email with brief descriptions of all new O'Reilly products as they are released, send email to:
ora-news-subscribe@lists.oreilly.com
Put the following information in the first line of your message (*not* in the Subject field):
subscribe ora-news

O'Reilly Events

If you'd also like us to send information about trade show events, special promotions, and other O'Reilly events, send email to:
ora-news-subscribe@lists.oreilly.com
Put the following information in the first line of your message (*not* in the Subject field):
subscribe ora-events

3. Get Examples from Our Books via FTP

There are two ways to access an archive of example files from our books:

Regular FTP

- ftp to:
  ftp.oreilly.com
  (login: anonymous
  password: your email address)
- Point your web browser to:
  ftp://ftp.oreilly.com/

FTPMAIL

- Send an email message to:
  ftpmail@online.oreilly.com
  (Write "help" in the message body)

4. Contact Us via Email

order@oreilly.com
To place a book or software order online. Good for North American and international customers.

subscriptions@oreilly.com
To place an order for any of our newsletters or periodicals.

books@oreilly.com
General questions about any of our books.

software@oreilly.com
For general questions and product information about our software. Check out O'Reilly Software Online at **http://software.oreilly.com/** for software and technical support information. Registered O'Reilly software users send your questions to: **website-support@oreilly.com**

cs@oreilly.com
For answers to problems regarding your order or our products.

booktech@oreilly.com
For book content technical questions or corrections.

proposals@oreilly.com
To submit new book or software proposals to our editors and product managers.

international@oreilly.com
For information about our international distributors or translation queries. For a list of our distributors outside of North America check out:
http://www.oreilly.com/distributors.html

5. Work with Us

Check out our website for current employment opportunites:
http://jobs.oreilly.com/

O'Reilly & Associates, Inc.
101 Morris Street, Sebastopol, CA 95472 USA
TEL   707-829-0515 or 800-998-9938
          (6am to 5pm PST)
FAX   707-829-0104

Titles from O'Reilly

International Distributors

http://international.oreilly.com/distributors.html

UK, EUROPE, MIDDLE EAST AND AFRICA (EXCEPT FRANCE, GERMANY, AUSTRIA, SWITZERLAND, LUXEMBOURG, AND LIECHTENSTEIN)

INQUIRIES
O'Reilly UK Limited
4 Castle Street
Farnham
Surrey, GU9 7HS
United Kingdom
Telephone: 44-1252-711776
Fax: 44-1252-734211
Email: information@oreilly.co.uk

ORDERS
Wiley Distribution Services Ltd.
1 Oldlands Way
Bognor Regis
West Sussex PO22 9SA
United Kingdom
Telephone: 44-1243-843294
UK Freephone: 0800-243207
Fax: 44-1243-843302 (Europe/EU orders)
or 44-1243-843274 (Middle East/Africa)
Email: cs-books@wiley.co.uk

FRANCE

INQUIRIES & ORDERS
Éditions O'Reilly
18 rue Séguier
75006 Paris, France
Tel: 1-40-51-71-89
Fax: 1-40-51-72-26
Email: france@oreilly.fr

GERMANY, SWITZERLAND, AUSTRIA, LUXEMBOURG, AND LIECHTENSTEIN

INQUIRIES & ORDERS
O'Reilly Verlag
Balthasarstr. 81
D-50670 Köln, Germany
Telephone: 49-221-973160-91
Fax: 49-221-973160-8
Email: anfragen@oreilly.de (inquiries)
Email: order@oreilly.de (orders)

CANADA (FRENCH LANGUAGE BOOKS)
Les Éditions Flammarion ltée
375, Avenue Laurier Ouest
Montréal (Québec) H2V 2K3
Tel: 00-1-514-277-8807
Fax: 00-1-514-278-2085
Email: info@flammarion.qc.ca

HONG KONG
City Discount Subscription Service, Ltd.
Unit A, 6th Floor, Yan's Tower
27 Wong Chuk Hang Road
Aberdeen, Hong Kong
Tel: 852-2580-3539
Fax: 852-2580-6463
Email: citydis@ppn.com.hk

KOREA
Hanbit Media, Inc.
Chungmu Bldg. 210
Yonnam-dong 568-33
Mapo-gu
Seoul, Korea
Tel: 822-325-0397
Fax: 822-325-9697
Email: hant93@chollian.dacom.co.kr

PHILIPPINES
Global Publishing
G/F Benavides Garden
1186 Benavides Street
Manila, Philippines
Tel: 632-254-8949/632-252-2582
Fax: 632-734-5060/632-252-2733
Email: globalp@pacific.net.ph

TAIWAN
O'Reilly Taiwan
1st Floor, No. 21, Lane 295
Section 1, Fu-Shing South Road
Taipei, 106 Taiwan
Tel: 886-2-27099669
Fax: 886-2-27038802
Email: mori@oreilly.com

INDIA
Shroff Publishers & Distributors Pvt. Ltd.
12, "Roseland", 2nd Floor
180, Waterfield Road, Bandra (West)
Mumbai 400 050
Tel: 91-22-641-1800/643-9910
Fax: 91-22-643-2422
Email: spd@vsnl.com

CHINA
O'Reilly Beijing
SIGMA Building, Suite B809
No. 49 Zhichun Road
Haidian District
Beijing, China PR 100080
Tel: 86-10-8809-7475
Fax: 86-10-8809-7463
Email: beijing@oreilly.com

JAPAN
O'Reilly Japan, Inc.
Yotsuya Y's Building
7 Banch 6, Honshio-cho
Shinjuku-ku
Tokyo 160-0003 Japan
Tel: 81-3-3356-5227
Fax: 81-3-3356-5261
Email: japan@oreilly.com

SINGAPORE, INDONESIA, MALAYSIA AND THAILAND
TransQuest Publishers Pte Ltd
30 Old Toh Tuck Road #05-02
Sembawang Kimtrans Logistics Centre
Singapore 597654
Tel: 65-4623112
Fax: 65-4625761
Email: wendiw@transquest.com.sg

ALL OTHER ASIAN COUNTRIES
O'Reilly & Associates, Inc.
101 Morris Street
Sebastopol, CA 95472 USA
Tel: 707-829-0515
Fax: 707-829-0104
Email: order@oreilly.com

AUSTRALIA
Woodslane Pty., Ltd.
7/5 Vuko Place
Warriewood NSW 2102
Australia
Tel: 61-2-9970-5111
Fax: 61-2-9970-5002
Email: info@woodslane.com.au

NEW ZEALAND
Woodslane New Zealand, Ltd.
21 Cooks Street (P.O. Box 575)
Waganui, New Zealand
Tel: 64-6-347-6543
Fax: 64-6-345-4840
Email: info@woodslane.com.au

ARGENTINA
Distribuidora Cuspide
Suipacha 764
1008 Buenos Aires
Argentina
Phone: 5411-4322-8868
Fax: 5411-4322-3456
Email: libros@cuspide.com

O'REILLY®

TO ORDER: **800-998-9938** • **order@oreilly.com** • **http://www.oreilly.com/**
OUR PRODUCTS ARE AVAILABLE AT A BOOKSTORE OR SOFTWARE STORE NEAR YOU.
FOR INFORMATION: **800-998-9938** • **707-829-0515** • **info@oreilly.com**